Family Tree Maker® Version 8

fast&easy®

The Official Guide

Family Tree Maker® Version 8

fast&easy®

The Official Guide

Rhonda R. McClure

PRIMA TECH

A DIVISION OF PRIMA PUBLISHING

A Division of Prima Publishing

Prima Publishing and colophon and Fast & Easy are registered trademarks of Prima Communications, Inc. PRIMA TECH is a trademark of Prima Communications, Inc., Roseville, California 95661.

Publisher: Stacy L. Hiquet
Marketing Manager: Judi Taylor Wade
Associate Marketing Manager: Heather Buzzingham
Managing Editor: Sandy Doell
Acquisitions Editor: Emi Nakamura
Project Editor: Cathleen D. Snyder
Technical Reviewer: Bryan Hiquet
Copy Editor: Tom Dinse
Interior Layout: Shawn Morningstar
Cover Design: Prima Design Team
Indexer: Christine Ryan

Family Tree Maker is a registered trademark and Broderbund is a trademark of Mattel Interactive. World Family Tree, FamilyFinder, Family Archives, and InterneTree are all trademarks and/or registered trademarks of Genealogy.com. All other trademarks are the property of their respective owners.

Important: Prima Publishing cannot provide software support. Please contact the appropriate software manufacturer's technical support line or Web site for assistance.

Prima Publishing and the author have attempted throughout this book to distinguish proprietary trademarks from descriptive terms by following the capitalization style used by the manufacturer.

Information contained in this book has been obtained by Prima Publishing from sources believed to be reliable. However, because of the possibility of human or mechanical error by our sources, Prima Publishing, or others, the Publisher does not guarantee the accuracy, adequacy, or completeness of any information and is not responsible for any errors or omissions or the results obtained from use of such information. Readers should be particularly aware of the fact that the Internet is an ever-changing entity. Some facts may have changed since this book went to press.

ISBN: 0-7615-2998-5

Library of Congress Catalog Card Number: 00-106649

Printed in the United States of America

00 01 02 03 04 DD 10 9 8 7 6 5 4 3 2 1

To families and petunias

Acknowledgments

No book is the result of a single person. There are so many who work hard to make sure that the final product is nothing but the best. It is these people that I wish to thank now. To Emi Nakamura for asking me to do this in the first place. Thanks to Cathleen Snyder, who has looked at each chapter and helped to make it better. Thanks to Tom Dinse for his copy editing and Bryan Hiquet for his tech editing. Special thanks to Bryan Jennings; when I called with questions about the program, he was always right there with the answers.

About the Author

RHONDA R. MCCLURE has managed to combine the best of both worlds—computers and genealogy. She has been using a computer to aid in her genealogical research since 1985, and has been teaching genealogists the benefits of getting the most from their genealogy software for over ten years. She can be found at national conferences, guiding genealogists to an understanding of Family Tree Maker. This is her first *Fast & Easy* book for Prima Tech, although she worked with Myra Vanderpool Gormley, Certified Genealogist, on *Prima's Official Companion to Family Tree Maker Version 7* in 1999.

Contents at a Glance

Introduction xix

PART I
GETTING FAMILIAR WITH FAMILY TREE MAKER . . 1

Chapter 1   Getting Started with Family Tree Maker. 3
Chapter 2   Entering Information into Family Tree Maker 25

PART II
THE FEATURES IN FAMILY TREE MAKER 43

Chapter 3   Enhancing the Family 45
Chapter 4   Documenting Sources 63
Chapter 5   Using More About Options. 81
Chapter 6   Understanding More About Notes 97
Chapter 7   Working with the More About Marriage Window 117

PART III
WORKING IN FAMILY TREE MAKER 127

Chapter 8   Searching Your Family Tree File. 129
Chapter 9   Correcting Information 151
Chapter 10   Fixing Relationships and Duplicates 169

PART IV
VISUALIZING YOUR FAMILY
IN FAMILY TREE MAKER 191

Chapter 11	Managing Tree Reports in Family Tree Maker 193
Chapter 12	Working with Reports 211
Chapter 13	Viewing and Printing Reports and Trees. 227
Chapter 14	Creating Genealogy Style and Genealogical Reports 239

PART V
PUBLISHING YOUR FAMILY HISTORY 255

Chapter 15	Creating a Scrapbook 257
Chapter 16	Creating a Family History Book 277
Chapter 17	Creating Your Personal Family Tree Maker Home Page. 293

PART VI
APPENDIXES 307

| Appendix A | Installing Family Tree Maker . . . . 309 |
| Appendix B | Using Keyboard Shortcuts. . . . . 315 |

| | Glossary. . . . . 319 |
| | Index . . . . 323 |

Contents

Introduction xix

PART I
GETTING FAMILIAR WITH FAMILY TREE MAKER . . 1

Chapter 1   **Getting Started with Family Tree Maker** 3

Launching Family Tree Maker 4

    Starting Your Family Tree 5

Exploring Family Tree Maker's Features 10

    Using Menus 10

    Using Toolbars 12

    Understanding Dialog Boxes 13

    Moving around with Scroll Bars 13

Navigating the Fields 15

Understanding the Different Views 17

    Exploring the Family Page 17

    Working with the Ancestor Tree 20

    Using the Descendant Tree 21

    Working with the Hourglass Tree 22

Moving Information 23

Exiting Family Tree Maker 24

Chapter 2   **Entering Information into Family Tree Maker** **25**

Entering a Primary Individual 26

Entering an Event 27

Changing the Date Format 29

Adding Individuals 32

Adding a Spouse 32

Adding Children 34

Adding an Additional Spouse 35

Designating a Preferred Spouse 37

Switching to another Spouse 38

Moving a Child to the Primary Individual Position 39

Part I Review Questions 41

PART II
THE FEATURES IN FAMILY TREE MAKER **43**

Chapter 3   **Enhancing the Family**. **45**

Adding Parents 46

Working with Children 48

Adding Siblings 48

Adding another Set of Parents 49

Lining up Children 53

Adding a Child 53

Moving a Child 55

Sorting Children 58

Using the More About Lineage Window 59

Chapter 4   **Documenting Sources** **63**

Where Can You Cite Sources? 64

Citing a Source 65

Creating a Master Source 65

Citing a Master Source 70

Changing a Master Source 75

Searching for a Master Source 78

Chapter 5   **Using More About Options** **81**

     Working with the More About Facts Window 82

         Adding Additional Facts 83

         Adding Additional Names 85

         Selecting a Preferred Name 86

         Creating a New Fact Name 87

     Using the Address Window 89

     Working with Medical Information 91

     Using the More About Lineage Window 93

         Entering AKA Names 94

         Working with Special Relationships 95

         Excluding Relationships 96

Chapter 6   **Understanding More About Notes** **97**

     Working with Notes and Stories 98

         Entering Notes and Stories 98

         Copying Notes and Stories 100

         Moving Notes and Stories 101

     Finding Text in Notes 105

     Formatting Notes for Printing 109

     Importing Text to Notes 111

         Copying Text 111

         Importing Text 114

     Exporting Notes 116

Chapter 7   **Working with the More About Marriage Window** . . 117

     Accessing the More About Marriage Window 118

     Using the More About Marriage Facts Window 119

         Entering a Reference Number 119

         Adding a Marriage Fact 120

         Using the Preferred Check Box 122

     Working with Marriage Notes 124

     Part II Review Questions 126

PART III
WORKING IN FAMILY TREE MAKER 127

Chapter 8 **Searching Your Family Tree File 129**

Using Quick Search by Name 130

Working with the Find Feature 132

Rearranging the Index 134

Using the Find Individual Feature 138

Searching by Name 139

Searching by Date 140

Searching by Location 142

Searching by Source 143

Searching by Comment 144

Working with the FamilyFinder Center 145

Chapter 9 **Correcting Information 151**

Working with the Family Tree Maker Spell Checker 152

Checking Spelling in the Entry Screens 152

Checking Spelling in the Notes Windows 154

Untying the Marriage Knot 155

Removing People from Your Files 157

Deleting One Person 158

Deleting a Group of People 159

Checking the Family File for Errors 161

Data Entry Checking 161

Using the Find Error Command 163

Working with the Data Errors Report 166

Chapter 10 **Fixing Relationships and Duplicates 169**

Fixing Relationships 170

Linking Children to Their Parents 170

Detaching a Child from the Wrong Parents 173

Linking Individuals by Marriage 175

Fixing Duplicates 182

    Fixing Duplicate Files 182

    Merging Specific Individuals 186

Using Global Search and Replace 188

Part III Review Questions 190

PART IV
VISUALIZING YOUR FAMILY
IN FAMILY TREE MAKER 191

Chapter 11 Managing Tree Reports in Family Tree Maker 193

Displaying Ancestor Trees 194

    Creating Fan Charts 194

    Creating a Pedigree Chart 195

    Creating a Vertical Ancestor Tree 197

Displaying Hourglass Trees 199

    Working with Fan Format 199

    Working with Standard Format 201

Displaying Descendant Trees 202

    Creating a Standard Tree 202

    Creating an Outline Tree 203

Displaying All-in-One Trees 204

    Creating an All-in-One Tree 204

    Setting Display Size 205

    Pruning the Display 206

Enhancing Tree Views 207

    Emphasizing Relationships 207

    Adding a Background Image 209

Chapter 12 Working with Reports 211

Creating a Custom Report 212

    Adding Items to Include in Your Report 213

    Choosing Individuals to Include in Your Report 214

    Creating a Title and Footnote 216

    Adjusting Column Widths 217

    Sorting Reports 218

Creating a Kinship Report 219

Working with Address and Birthday Reports 221

   Creating an Address Report 221

   Creating the Birthday Report 222

Using the Research Journal 224

   Working with the Genealogy How-To Guide 226

Chapter 13 **Viewing and Printing Reports and Trees 227**

Viewing the Tree You Want to Print 228

Customizing the View 228

   Changing the Text Font 229

   Working with Text Style 230

   Working with Text Size 231

   Text Color 232

Changing the Print Setup 233

   Changing the Paper Orientation 233

   Adjusting Margins 234

   Changing Other Settings 235

Printing the Tree 237

Chapter 14 **Creating Genealogy Style and**
Genealogical Reports. 239

Using Genealogy Style Reports 240

   Working with Register Format 240

   Working with NGSQ Format 242

   Using Ahnentafel Style 243

Using Endnotes 245

Formatting the Report 246

   Adjusting Page Numbering and Title 246

   Changing the Number of Generations 247

   Including Notes and Other Options 248

Locating Conflicting Facts 249

Creating a Bibliography Report 251

Creating a Documented Events Report 253

Part IV Review Questions 254

PART V
PUBLISHING YOUR FAMILY HISTORY 255

Chapter 15 **Creating a Scrapbook** 257

Using the Scrapbook 258

Inserting Scrapbook Images 259

    Using Images 259

    Using Sound Clips 261

    Using OLE Objects 263

Entering Information about Scrapbook Objects 265

Rearranging Scrapbook Objects 267

    Moving Objects 267

    Copying Objects 268

Editing Pictures and Objects 270

Searching for Objects 271

Sharing Your Scrapbook 272

    Playing a Scrapbook 273

    Printing a Scrapbook 274

Chapter 16 **Creating a Family History Book** 277

Selecting Available Items 278

    Selecting Front Matter 279

    Adding Trees and Reports 281

    Including Text with Pictures 282

Working with Outline Items 285

    Organizing the Items 285

    Working with Item Properties 286

Finalizing the Book 288

    Adding Page Breaks 288

    Creating a Customized Index 289

Chapter 17 **Creating Your Personal**
Family Tree Maker Home Page **293**
Creating Your First Home Page 294
Working with the Wizard 294
Registering Your Home Page 296
Working with Your Home Page 297
Adding Reports 297
Adding an InterneTree 299
Adding a Book 301
Removing Items from Your Home Page 303
Removing a Family Tree Maker Report or Book 303
Deleting Your Home Page 304
Part V Review Questions 306

PART VI
APPENDIXES **307**
Appendix A **Installing Family Tree Maker** **309**
Installing Family Tree Maker Version 8 310
Choosing Components 312
Uninstalling Family Tree Maker 314
Appendix B **Using Keyboard Shortcuts** **315**
Learning the Keyboard Shortcuts 316
Getting Help 316
Working in Family Tree Maker 316
Working with Text 317
Selecting Text 317
Copying and Pasting Text 317

Glossary **319**

Index **323**

Introduction

This *Fast & Easy* book from Prima Tech will help you learn Family Tree Maker®
Version 8, so you can spend more of your time researching your family history and
less time entering it into a program. Family Tree Maker is a multifaceted program
that can track your ancestry and also produce beautiful reports so you can share
your findings. Even if you have never used a genealogy program before, you will find
that Family Tree Maker's interface and options make it possible to track even the
most tangled of family trees. With the ability to include digitized images as well as
audio and visual clips, Family Tree Maker gives you the opportunity to share more
than just names, dates, and places. This book introduces you to many of the features
available in Family Tree Maker, so you can enjoy this hobby you've discovered.

Who Should Read This Book

This book is written with the novice computer user in mind. In it, you are taken on a
hands-on trip through the Family Tree Maker program. The many illustrations let you
check your progress as you master each new feature or process. Even if you are
familiar with computers, you may have been introduced to Family Tree Maker only
recently. In either case, this book offers you an easy-to-follow tour of the program
and all that you can accomplish.

This book is organized by tasks. Some tasks may require many steps and others may
branch off into enhancements or additional features. A quick perusal of the Table of
Contents should lead you right to the process you want to accomplish—then it is just
a matter of reading through the steps!

Special Features of This Book

As you work with this book, you will discover that the emphasis is on tasks. This is by design, so that you can master skills in an easy-to-follow format. There are a couple of features, though, that will supply you with additional information as you work with the Family Tree Maker program.

- **Tips** offer you useful hints about features in Family Tree Maker that can speed up the task at hand or enhance your report output.

- **Notes** offer additional information about Family Tree Maker or about genealogy and sharing your family tree.

In the appendixes you will find instructions for installing the Family Tree Maker software, and useful tables of keyboard shortcuts to speed up your data entry.

Happy family tree climbing!

PART I

Getting Familiar with Family Tree Maker

Chapter 1
**Getting Started
with Family Tree Maker** **3**

Chapter 2
**Entering Information
into Family Tree Maker** **25**

1

Getting Started with Family Tree Maker

Learning any new program requires an introduction to the program's interface. There are usually some new menu items, buttons, and choices that are specific to the program. This is true of Family Tree Maker, and this chapter introduces you to those items. In this chapter, you'll learn how to:

- Start Family Tree Maker
- Execute commands with menus and toolbars
- Understand dialog boxes and scroll bars
- Navigate the various Family Page fields
- Select different views
- Move information
- Exit Family Tree Maker

Launching Family Tree Maker

Before you can enter your family history data into Family Tree Maker, you must launch the program. You accomplish this in Windows with a couple simple mouse clicks.

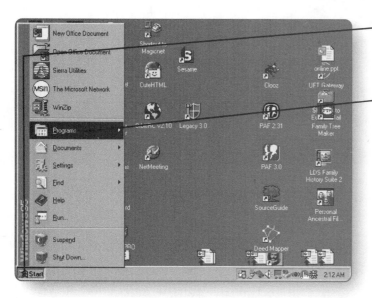

1. Click on the **Start button** on the Windows Taskbar. The Start menu will appear.

2. Move the **mouse pointer** to Programs. The Programs menu will appear.

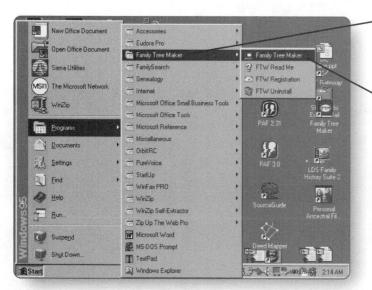

3. Move the **mouse pointer** to Family Tree Maker. The Family Tree Maker menu will appear.

4. Click on **Family Tree Maker**. Family Tree Maker will start.

Starting Your Family Tree

Family Tree Maker offers an easy introduction to help you enter data about yourself and your family. As soon as Family Tree Maker opens, a wizard appears to help you enter information.

1. Type your **name** in the Your name field.

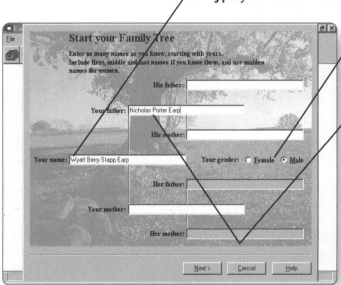

2. Click on the appropriate **gender radio button**. The radio button will be selected.

3. Click in the **Your father field** and **enter** your **father's name**.

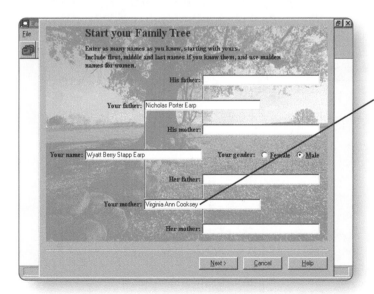

4. Press the **Tab key**. The cursor will move to the Your mother field.

5. Type your **mother's name** in the Your mother field.

6. Press the **Tab key**. The cursor will move to the His father field.

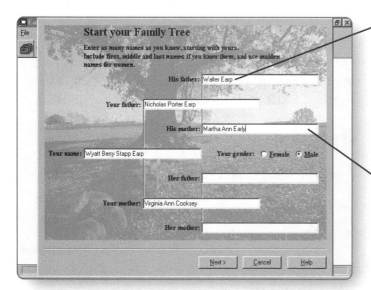

7. Type the **name** of your father's father in the His father field.

8. Press the **Tab key.** The cursor will move to the His mother field.

9. Type the **name** of your father's mother in the His mother field.

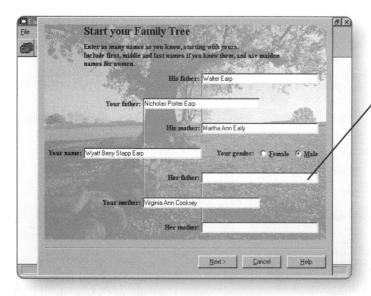

10. Press the **Tab key**. The cursor will move to the Her father field.

11. Type the **name** of your mother's father in the Her father field.

12. Press the **Tab key.** The cursor will move to the Her mother field.

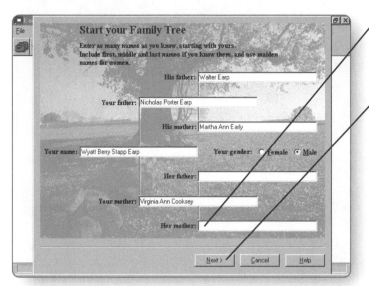

13. Type the **name** of your mother's mother in the Her mother field.

14. **Click** on the **Next button**. The Births screen will appear.

NOTE

Don't worry if you don't know all this information now. Fill in as much as you can so you'll have some working data.

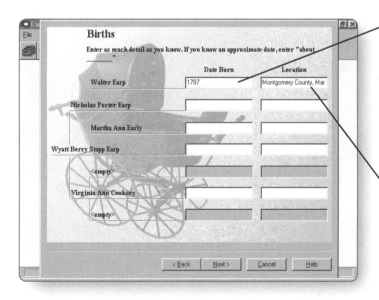

15. In the Date Born field, **enter** the **date of birth** for the first person in the Births screen.

16. **Press** the **Tab key**. The cursor will move to the Location field.

17. In the Location field, **type** the **place of birth** for that person.

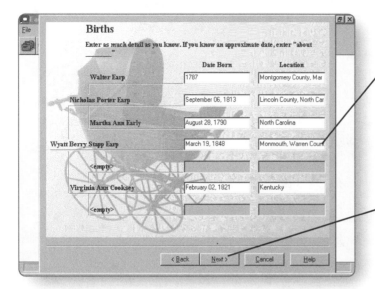

NOTE

Press the Tab key to work through the remaining individuals in the Births screen. Enter any known birthplaces and dates of birth.

18. Click on the **Next button**. The Deaths screen will appear.

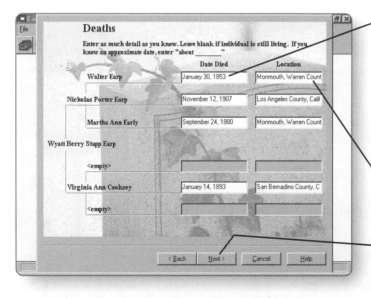

19. In the Date Died field, **type** the **date of death** for the first person in the Deaths screen.

20. Press the **Tab key**. The cursor will move to the Location field.

21. In the Location field, **enter** the **place of death** for that person.

22. When you have finished entering death information for each person, **click** on the **Next button**. The FamilyFinder Search screen will appear.

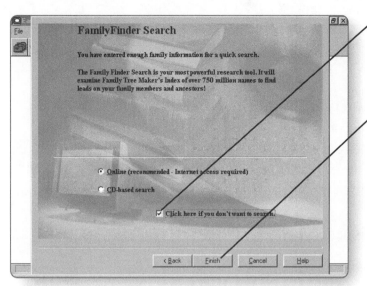

23. Click on the **Click here if you don't want to search check box**. A check mark will appear in the check box.

24. Click on the **Finish button**. A Family Tree Maker message box will appear, telling you that you can run a search any time by clicking on the FamilyFinder icon.

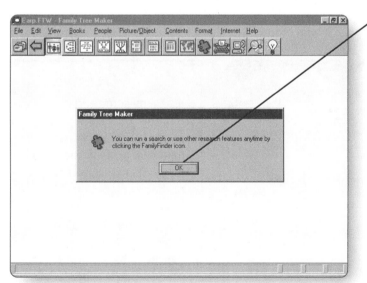

25. Click on **OK**. The message box will disappear.

NOTE

You will be introduced to FamilyFinder Search and Report in Chapter 8, "Searching Your Family Tree File."

Exploring Family Tree Maker's Features

There are a number of buttons, menus, and tabs in the Family Tree Maker window. The buttons allow you to perform the different tasks in the program, while the tabs allow you to maneuver through your family history database. With the menus, you can print, save, and customize your family history data. This section introduces you to many of these features.

Using Menus

Menus are lists of the functions built into Family Tree Maker and other software programs. They are activated by clicking on the words that appear along the top bar in Family Tree Maker. Each menu contains a list of related commands.

1. **Click** on a **menu**. The menu you chose will appear.

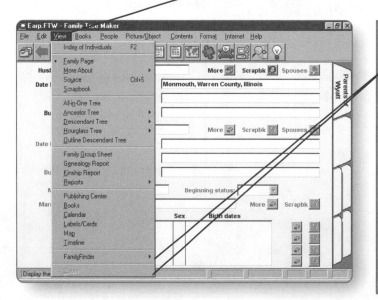

NOTE

If a menu command is followed by a right-pointing arrow, another menu will appear when you move the mouse pointer to that menu option. If a menu command is grayed out, the command is not currently available. You may need to perform some other action in order to activate the grayed-out command.

TIP

Some menu commands have keyboard shortcuts. You will find the keyboard shortcuts to the right of the applicable menu commands. You can use these shortcuts to execute commands, rather than using the menus. To learn about some of the most popular keyboard shortcuts, see Appendix B, "Using Keyboard Shortcuts."

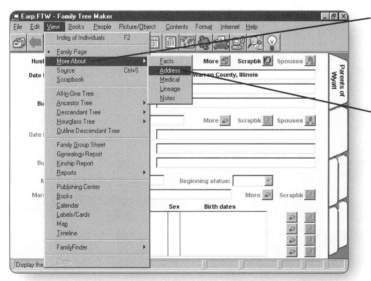

2. **Place** the **mouse pointer** over a menu item with a right-pointing arrow. A second menu will appear.

3. **Move** the **mouse pointer** so that it is over an option on the second menu. The menu item will be highlighted.

NOTE

Click on a menu option to execute that command. This might change the view of the screen, open a dialog box requesting additional information or choices, or open another window.

Using Toolbars

Family Tree Maker has one toolbar. It offers some of the more popular views, as well as a few shortcut buttons to some of the unique commands.

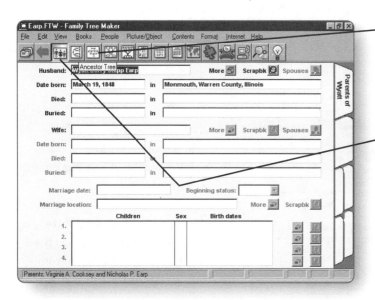

1. **Place** the **mouse pointer** over each of the toolbar buttons. A tip describing the function of that toolbar button will appear.

2. **Click** on the **Family Page button**. The Family Page will appear.

NOTE

When you click on the various toolbar buttons or make certain menu choices, Family Tree Maker will open a cue card. The cue card offers some tips for working with that option.

TIP

If you do not wish to see the cue cards, you can turn them off. Click on the Click here if you don't want to see this Help Window again check box.

Understanding Dialog Boxes

In Family Tree Maker, dialog boxes allow you to make choices and select additional options, items, or preferences. Before you work with the example in this section, be sure you are in the Family Page, which is the default screen in Family Tree Maker.

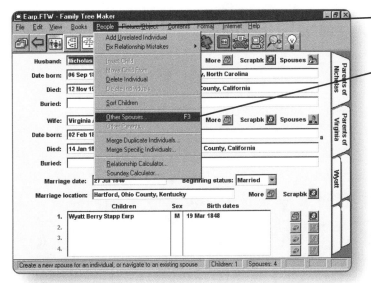

1. **Click** on **People**. The People menu will appear.

2. **Click** on **Other Spouses**. The Other Spouses dialog box will open.

TIP

You can also access the Other Spouses dialog box by pressing the F3 key.

Moving around with Scroll Bars

In Family Tree Maker, scroll bars are found to the right of and at the bottom of windows, where the text or report extends beyond the limits of the window. There are three different ways to move up and down or sideways using the scroll bars.

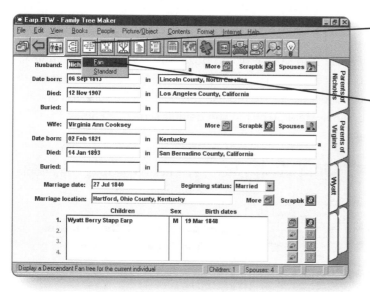

1. Click on the **Descendant Tree button**. The Descendant Tree menu will appear.

2. Click on **Fan**. The Descendant Fan Tree will appear.

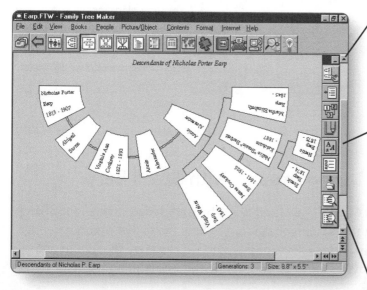

3a. Click on the **arrow** at either end of the scroll bar. This will scroll the page up or down (or side to side) one line at a time.

OR

3b. Press and hold the **mouse button** on the scroll box and drag the **scroll box** up or down within the scroll bar. This will move you through more of the page at a time.

OR

3c. Click inside the scroll bar. This will move the page up or down (or side to side) one screen at a time.

Navigating the Fields

When you work in Family Tree Maker's main entry screens, you will need to jump from field to field. Keyboard commands are the easiest way to do this.

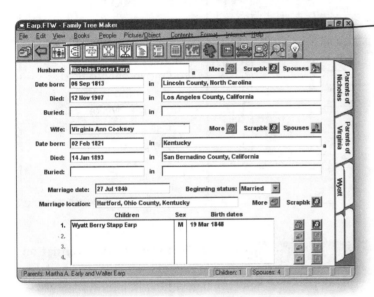

1. Click on the **Family Page button**. The Family Page will appear.

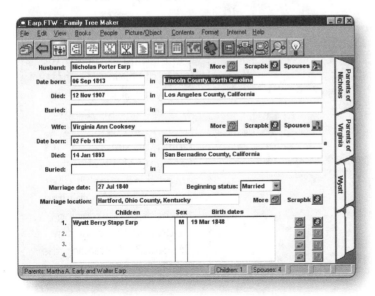

2. Navigate through the **fields** using one of the following methods:

- **Press** the **Tab key** to move from one field to another within the Family Page.

- **Press** the **Enter key** to move from one field to another within the Family Page.

- **Press** the **Up Arrow or Down Arrow** to move from one field to another within the Family Page.

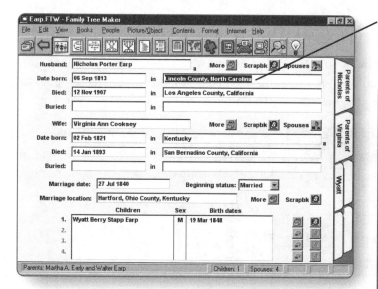

As you move through the fields, each field that the cursor arrives at will be highlighted.

NOTE

When you navigate in the Family Page using any of the keyboard commands, you move only to fields where typing is allowed. Family Tree Maker will bypass any other options on the page.

3. Type some new **information** in one of the fields. The highlighted field's information will change.

TIP

You do not want to use this method to change the order of children. Do not simply highlight the child in question and type the name of the new child. Doing this simply changes the name of the already entered individual; it does not rearrange the children. Methods of rearranging children are examined in Chapter 3, "Enhancing the Family."

Understanding the Different Views

Family Tree Maker offers different views to display the family data. Some of these views are limited to a single-family unit, while others display multi-generational charts of ancestors, descendants, or both.

Exploring the Family Page

The Family Page is where you will spend the most time. This is where you'll access and enter much of the data.

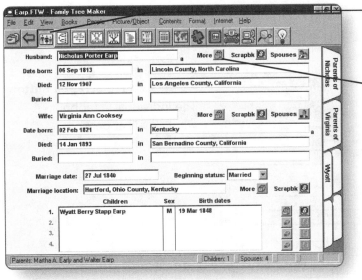

1. Click on the **Family Page button**. The Family Page will appear.

2. Click on the **More button**. The More About window will appear.

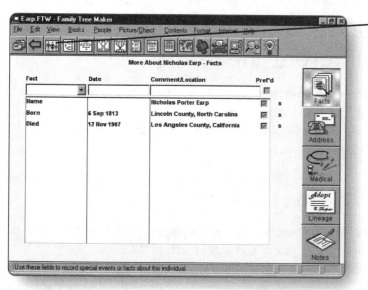

3. Click on the **Family Page button.** The Family Page will appear.

4. Click on the **Scrapbk button.** The Individual Scrapbook window will appear.

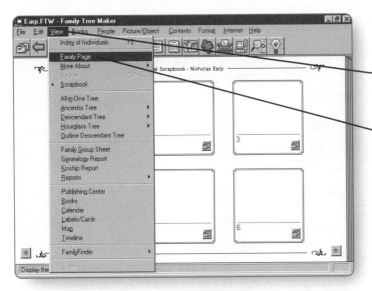

To get back to the Family Page, you can use the View menu.

5. **Click** on **View**. The View menu will appear.

6. **Click** on **Family Page**. The Family Page will appear.

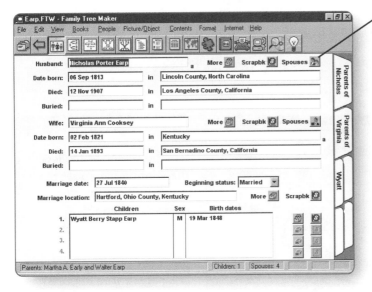

7. **Click** on the **Spouses button**. The Spouses of dialog box will open.

NOTE

You will work more closely with the Spouses of dialog box in Chapter 3, "Enhancing the Family."

Working with the Ancestor Tree

The Ancestor Tree offers a chart of the ancestors of a selected individual. There are three different formats to display this information.

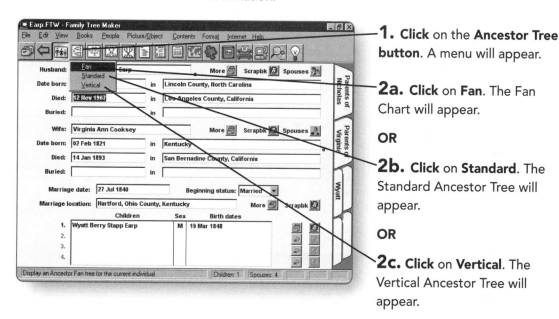

1. Click on the **Ancestor Tree button**. A menu will appear.

2a. Click on **Fan**. The Fan Chart will appear.

OR

2b. Click on **Standard**. The Standard Ancestor Tree will appear.

OR

2c. Click on **Vertical**. The Vertical Ancestor Tree will appear.

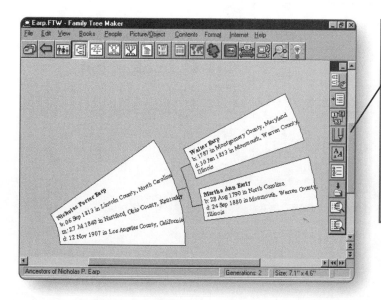

NOTE

Use the scroll bar to view the information about the individuals of the selected person's lineage. Additional information on ancestor trees is discussed in Chapter 11, "Managing Tree Reports in Family Tree Maker."

Using the Descendant Tree

The Descendant Tree offers a chart of the descendants of a selected individual. There are two different formats in which you can display this information.

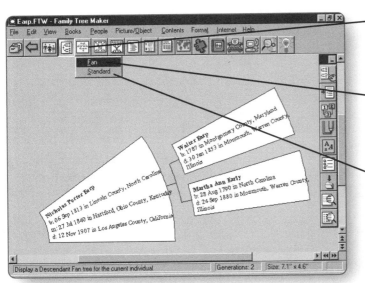

1. Click on the **Descendant Tree button**. A menu will appear.

2a. Click on **Fan**. The Fan Chart will appear.

OR

2b. Click on **Standard**. The Standard Descendant Tree will appear.

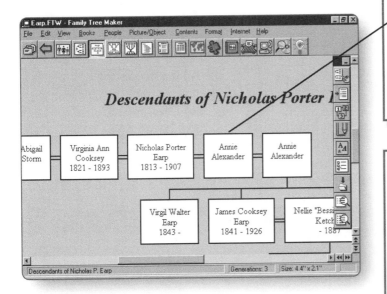

NOTE

The Standard Descendant Tree is commonly referred to as a box chart because the information about each individual appears inside a box.

TIP

Double lines between boxes indicate a marriage or parental relationship. Single lines between boxes indicate a child or sibling relationship.

Working with the Hourglass Tree

The Hourglass Tree offers a chart of both the descendants and ancestors of a selected individual. There are two different formats in which you can display this information.

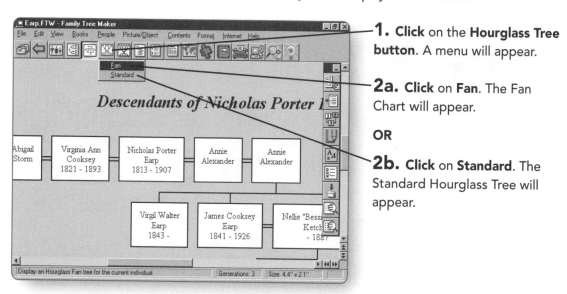

1. Click on the **Hourglass Tree button**. A menu will appear.

2a. Click on **Fan**. The Fan Chart will appear.

OR

2b. Click on **Standard**. The Standard Hourglass Tree will appear.

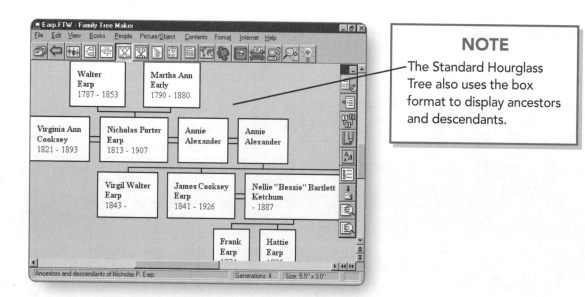

NOTE

The Standard Hourglass Tree also uses the box format to display ancestors and descendants.

Moving Information

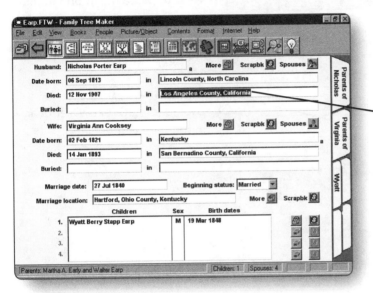

Family Tree Maker allows you to use Windows' copy and paste functions to move information from field to field.

1. Place the **mouse pointer** in front of the first character you want to select and **click and drag** the **pointer** until you reach the last character you wish to cut or copy. The selected text will be highlighted.

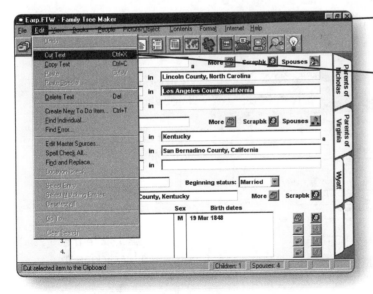

2. Click on **Edit**. The Edit menu will appear.

3. Click on either **Cut Text or Copy Text**. The selected text will be placed on the clipboard.

NOTE

The Cut Text command removes the text from the highlighted field and places it on the clipboard. The Copy Text command leaves the text in the highlighted field and creates a copy on the clipboard.

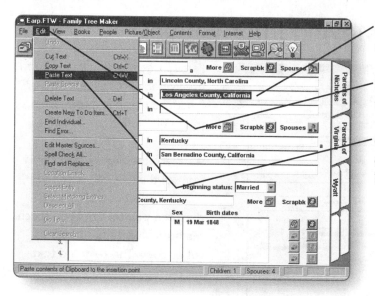

4. Click in the **field** where you want to paste the information.

5. Click on **Edit**. The Edit menu will appear.

6. Click on **Paste Text**. The copied (or cut) text will appear in the field you selected.

Exiting Family Tree Maker

You now have seen the basics of Family Tree Maker. When you are finished working in the program, you can close it.

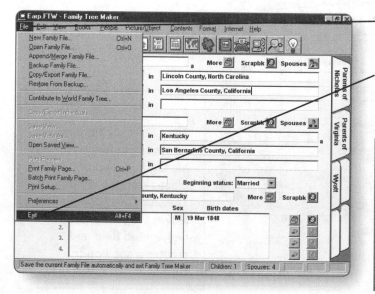

1. Click on **File**. The File menu will appear.

2. Click on **Exit**. Family Tree Maker will close.

TIP

You can also close the program by clicking the close button (☒) in the upper right corner of the Family Tree Maker window.

2

Entering Information into Family Tree Maker

Most of your time with Family Tree Maker will be spent entering the data you have uncovered about your family. At first, this information will be about yourself, your parents, and perhaps your grandparents. However, eventually you will find yourself with ancestral lines that go back many generations. Family Tree Maker helps you organize this information.

In this chapter, you'll learn how to:

- Enter a primary individual
- Enter an event
- Change the date format
- Add a spouse
- Add children
- Add an additional spouse
- Move a child to the primary individual position

Entering a Primary Individual

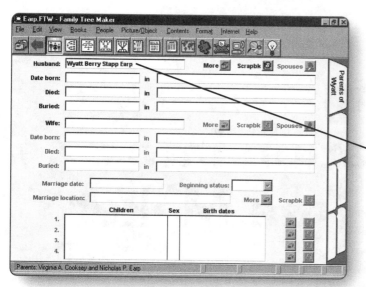

Family Tree Maker allows you to record the information for each individual in your family history. The Family Page lets you enter specific information for the husband, wife, and children.

1. Type the **husband's name** in the Husband field.

NOTE

The primary individual can be entered in either the Husband field or the Wife field, depending on his or her gender.

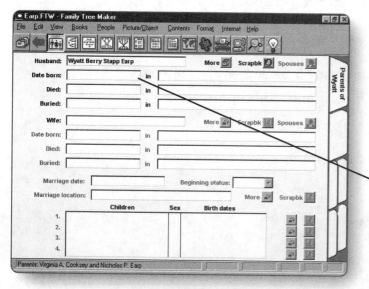

TIP

An individual's name is made up of given names (first and middle names) and the surname (last name), typed in that order.

2. Press the **Tab key**. The cursor will move to the Date born field.

> **NOTE**
>
> Notice that when the Tab key is pressed, it bypasses the options to the right of the husband's name. These features are accessed by clicking on them or by selecting the appropriate menu item.

Entering an Event

When you record your family history, you first must concentrate on names, dates, and places. Therefore, Family Tree Maker includes these basic fields in the Family Page.

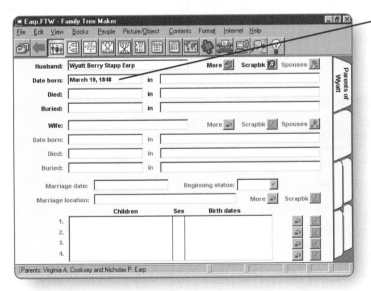

1. **Type** a **date** in the Date born field.

2. **Press** the **Tab key**. The cursor will move to the next field.

> **TIP**
>
> The traditional method for recording dates is to enter the numerals of the day, followed by the first three letters of the month, followed by the full four numerals of the year. Family Tree Maker defaults to a different setting. You'll learn how to change this setting later in this chapter, in the "Changing the Date Format" section.

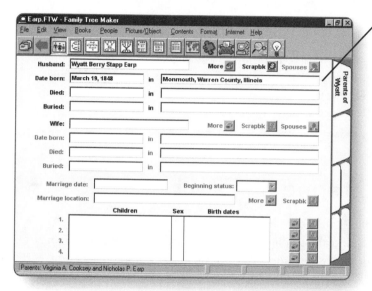

3. **Type** a **location** in the in field, if known.

4. **Press** the **Tab key**. The cursor will move to the next field.

NOTE

When you enter the place name, use a comma to separate the different divisions. Places should always be entered from smallest division, such as a town, to largest division, such as a state or country.

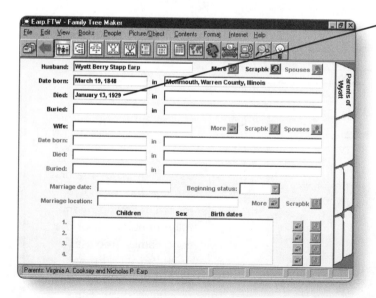

5. **Type** a **date** in the Died field, if known.

6. **Press** the **Tab key**. The cursor will move to the next field.

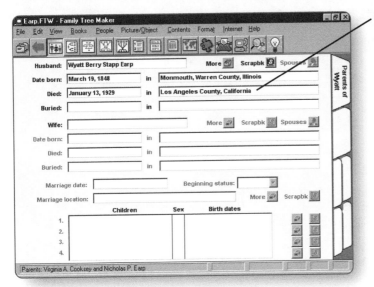

7. Type a **location** in the in field, if known.

Changing the Date Format

As mentioned earlier, Family Tree Maker's default for dates does not coincide with the standard followed in the genealogical community. However, this is easy enough to change.

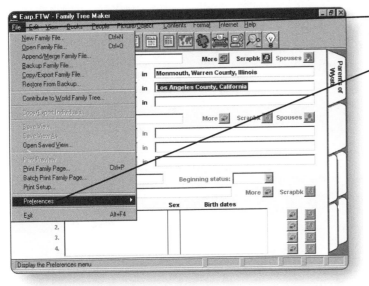

1. Click on **File**. The File menu will appear.

2. Click on **Preferences**. The Preferences submenu will appear.

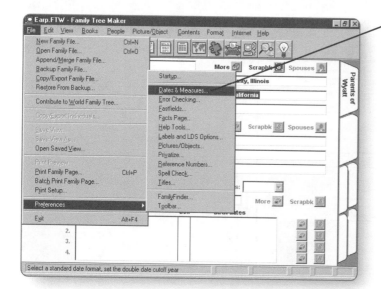

3. Click on **Dates & Measures**. The Dates & Measures dialog box will open.

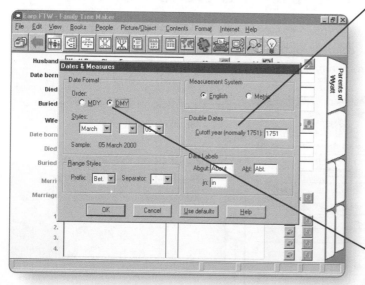

NOTE

In the Dates & Measures dialog box, you can set the cutoff date for double dating. Double dating was the result of the change from the Julian to the Gregorian calendar. The Gregorian calendar determined that January would be the first month of the year. This took place for England and its colonies in 1751.

4. Choose the **DMY option** to conform to standard genealogical dating. The option will be selected.

5. Select the **month style** from the Styles drop-down list. The standard method is to use the first three letters of the month.

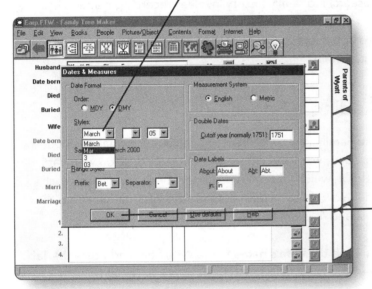

TIP

Similar drop-down lists are available for changing the separator between the day, month, and year, and also for the format of the words for each day.

6. Click on **OK**. The Dates & Measures dialog box will close.

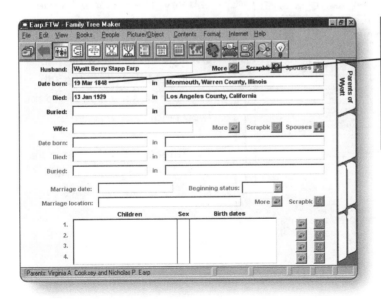

NOTE

The selections made in the Dates & Measures dialog box will automatically take effect in the Family Page.

Adding Individuals

Researching family history involves recording names, dates, and places. Programs like Family Tree Maker help make that easier by keeping track of the familial connections as you enter them.

Adding a Spouse

The Family Page is designed to include information about the husband, wife, and children, and it provides you with data fields in which you can type certain basic facts about each one. Now that you have entered the information about the husband, it is time to add the wife.

1. Type the **wife's name** in the Wife field and **press** the **Tab key**. The cursor will move to the Date born field.

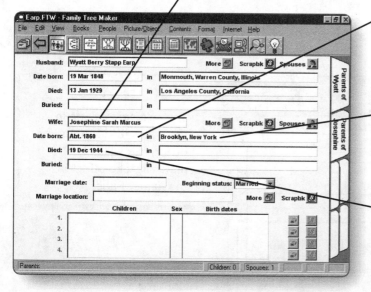

2. Enter the **birth date** in the Date born field and **press** the **Tab key**. The cursor will move to the in field.

3. Type the **place of birth** in the in field and **press** the **Tab key**. The cursor will move to the Died field.

4. Enter the **death date** in the Died field and **press** the **Tab key**. The cursor will move to the in field.

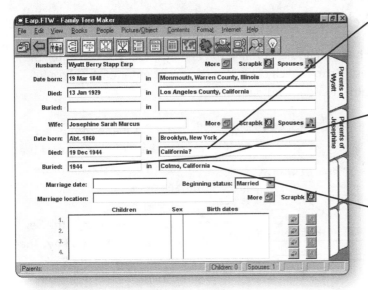

5. Type the **place of death** in the in field and **press** the **Tab key**. The cursor will move to the Buried field.

6. Enter the **burial date** in the Buried field and **press** the **Tab key**. The cursor will move to the in field.

7. Type the **place of burial** in the in field and **press** the **Tab key**. The cursor will move to the Marriage date field.

8. Enter the **marriage date** in the Marriage date field and **press** the **Tab key**. The cursor will move to the Marriage location field.

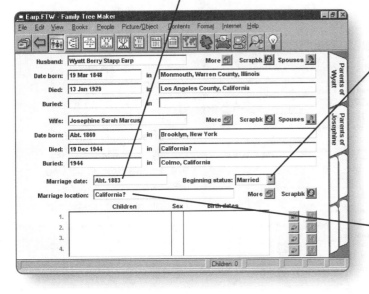

TIP

The Beginning status drop-down list allows you to select the type of relationship between the two individuals. For most of them you will select the Married option.

9. Type the **place of marriage** in the Marriage location field.

Adding Children

When you add children in the Family Page, you can enter the basics about each child. You can easily enter each child's full name, gender, and date of birth.

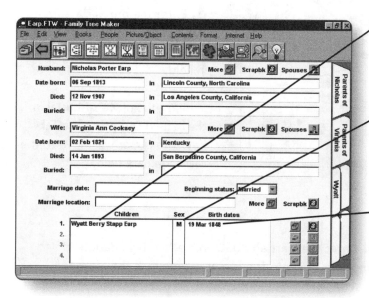

1. Type the **name** of the first child in the 1 field and **press** the **Tab key**. The cursor will move to the Sex field.

2. Enter the **gender** in the Sex field and **press** the **Tab key**. The cursor will move to the Birth dates field.

3. Type the **date of birth** in the Birth dates field and **press** the **Tab key**. The cursor will move to the 2 field for the name of the next child.

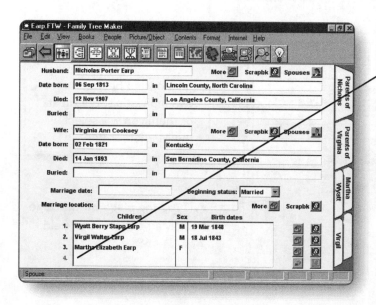

NOTE

You can add as many children as necessary. When you press the Tab key after each birth date, Family Tree Maker takes you to the next child line, where you can enter information for the next child.

Adding an Additional Spouse

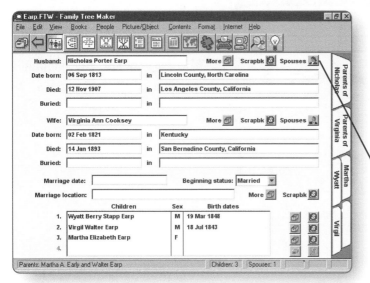

The Family Page only allows one spouse to be displayed at a time. However, there are times when a researcher needs to enter more than one spouse for an individual. Family Tree Maker can support multiple spouses.

1. In the Family Page, **click** on the **Spouses button**. The Spouses of dialog box will open.

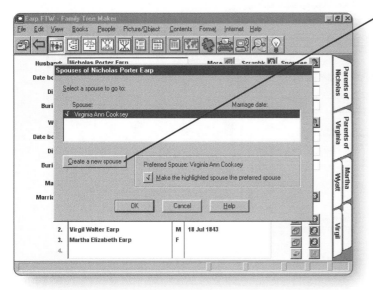

2. Click on the **Create a new spouse button**. A message box will appear, asking whether you want the new spouse to be associated with the children previously entered for an individual.

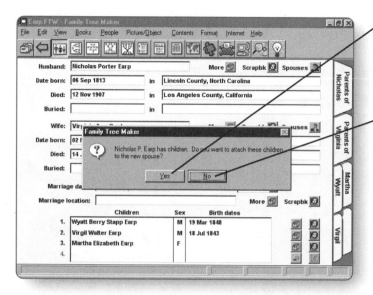

3a. **Click** on **Yes**. The children will have the new spouse as one of their parents.

OR

3b. **Click** on **No**. The children will not have the new spouse added as their parent.

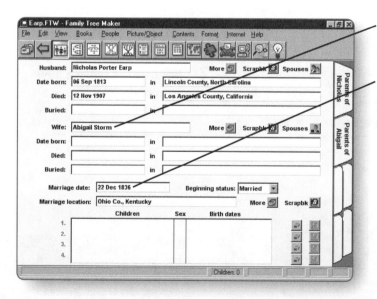

4. Type the **name** of the new spouse in the Wife field.

5. Enter the **information** that you know about the marriage event.

Designating a Preferred Spouse

Family Tree Maker requires that one spouse be selected as the preferred spouse when working with reports and displaying the family in the Family Page.

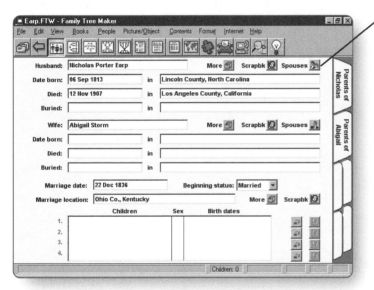

1. In the Family Page, **click** on the **Spouses button**. The Spouses of dialog box will open.

NOTE

Notice that the Spouses button now displays two small people. This lets you know that the individual has more than one spouse.

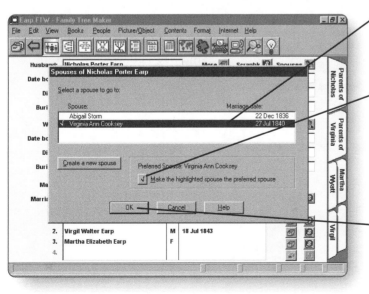

2. Click on the **spouse** you want as the preferred spouse. The spouse will be highlighted.

3. Click on the **Make the high-lighted spouse the preferred spouse button.** The preferred spouse character will show at the left of the selected individual.

4. Click on **OK**. The Spouses of dialog box will close.

Switching to another Spouse

Because you can only view the information and children of one spouse, it is necessary to switch spouses when you want to work on a specific family. You also need to change spouses if you want to add additional information about a particular marriage.

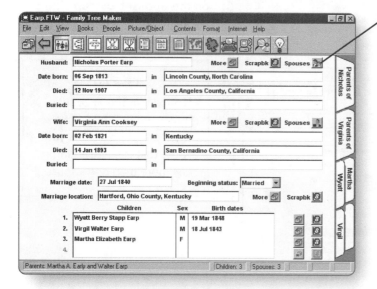

1. Click on the **Spouses button**. The Spouses of dialog box will open.

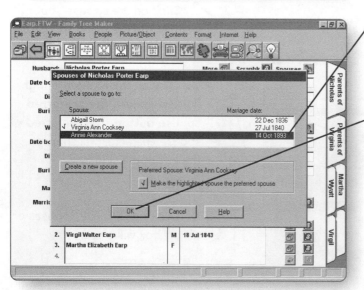

2. Select the **spouse** for the marriage on which you want to work. The spouse will be highlighted.

3. Click on **OK**. The Spouses of dialog box will close.

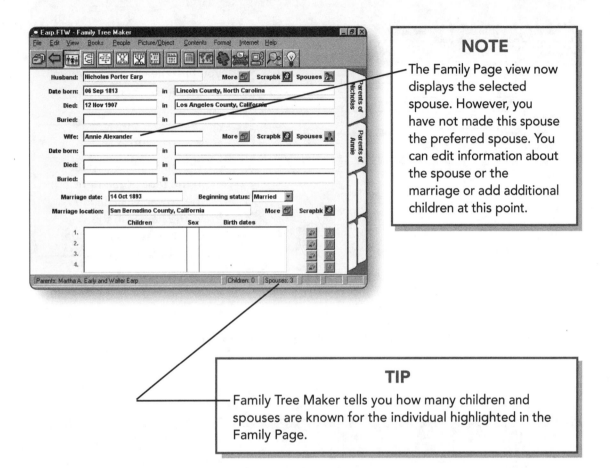

NOTE

The Family Page view now displays the selected spouse. However, you have not made this spouse the preferred spouse. You can edit information about the spouse or the marriage or add additional children at this point.

TIP

Family Tree Maker tells you how many children and spouses are known for the individual highlighted in the Family Page.

Moving a Child to the Primary Individual Position

After you have entered the children, you might want to concentrate on a specific child. To do this, you move that child to the primary husband or wife position.

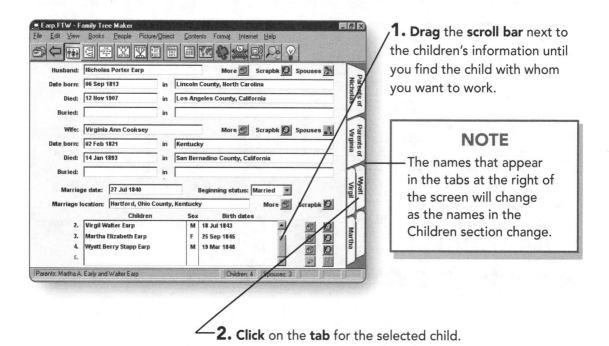

1. Drag the **scroll bar** next to the children's information until you find the child with whom you want to work.

> ### NOTE
> The names that appear in the tabs at the right of the screen will change as the names in the Children section change.

2. Click on the **tab** for the selected child.

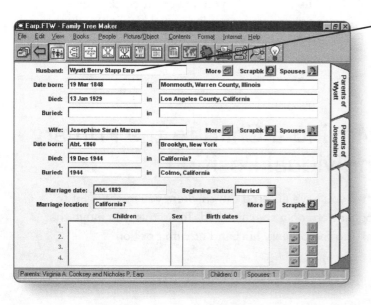

The child will replace the parent in the Husband or Wife field, and all the other fields on the Family Page will change in accordance with the information currently known about that child.

Part I Review Questions

1. How do you open Family Tree Maker?
   See "Launching Family Tree Maker" in Chapter 1

2. How do you discover the keyboard shortcuts available in Family Tree Maker? *See "Using Menus" in Chapter 1*

3. How are dialog boxes used in Family Tree Maker?
   See "Understanding Dialog Boxes" in Chapter 1

4. What are the three ways to move from one field to another in Family Tree Maker? *See "Navigating the Fields" in Chapter 1*

5. What are the four main views found on the toolbar?
   See "Understanding the Different Views" in Chapter 1

6. In what view do you enter the name of an ancestor?
   See "Entering a Primary Individual" in Chapter 2

7. How can you change the way dates are displayed in Family Tree Maker? *See "Changing the Date Format" in Chapter 2*

8. Can you enter more than four children for a family?
   See "Adding Children" in Chapter 2

9. How do you make the child the primary individual? *See "Moving a Child to the Primary Individual Position" in Chapter 2*

10. Can you have more than one spouse for an individual?
    See "Adding an Additional Spouse" in Chapter 2

PART II

The Features in Family Tree Maker

Chapter 3
Enhancing the Family **45**

Chapter 4
Documenting Sources **63**

Chapter 5
Using More About Options. **81**

Chapter 6
Understanding More About Notes **97**

Chapter 7
**Working with the More
About Marriage Window**. **117**

3

Enhancing the Family

The family structure in a genealogical search is constantly changing. You are always finding new individuals that need to be connected in your database. In this chapter, you'll learn how to:

- Add parents and siblings
- Line up children
- Add additional parental links
- Add facts in the More About Lineage window

Adding Parents

It is likely that when you were working through Chapter 2, "Entering Information into Family Tree Maker," you entered information about your immediate family. Now you want to add the parents of the first person you entered.

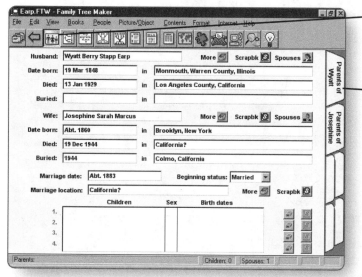

1. **Click** on the **Family Page button**. The Family Page will appear.

2. **Click** on the **Parents tab** for either the husband or the wife. The new Family Page with the basic information for one child will be displayed. The child whose basic information is displayed is the individual who was the husband or wife in the previous screen.

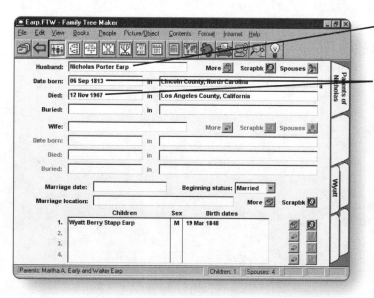

3. **Enter** the **father's name** in the Husband field.

4. **Enter** the **father's birth and death information** in the appropriate fields.

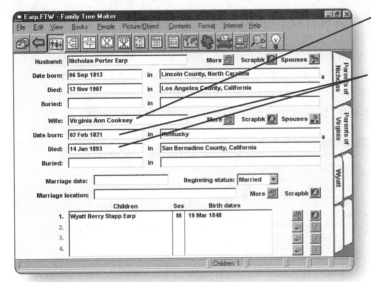

5. Type the **mother's name** in the Wife field.

6. Enter the **mother's birth and death information** in the appropriate fields.

TIP

When typing the names of females, always enter them with their maiden name. That is the surname they had at birth.

NOTE

There will be times when you do not know the maiden name of the woman. The proper way to enter an unknown surname is to use the following set of characters: [—?—]. However, be aware that Family Tree Maker will question such a surname.

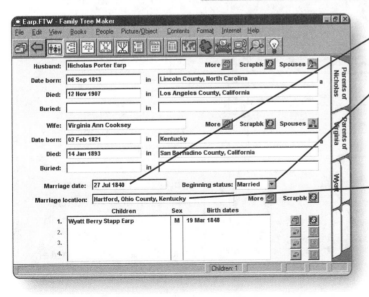

7. Type the **parents' marriage date** in the Marriage date field.

8. Select a **beginning status** from the Beginning status drop-down list. You will probably choose Married for this option.

9. Enter a **marriage location** in the Marriage location field.

Working with Children

When working in the Family Page, you will find that there are times when you need to add additional siblings. Through the Children fields, you can also add another set of parents in addition to the child's natural or biological parents.

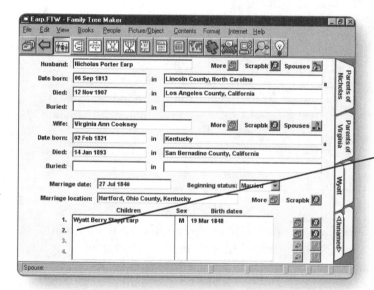

Adding Siblings

Usually, after you have added the information for the parents, you will want to work on your ancestor's siblings.

1. Click in the **2 field**.

2. Type the **name** of the next known child, as well as the rest of the information known about that child.

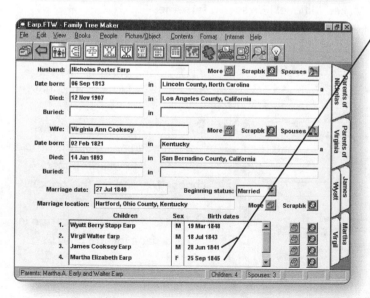

3. Enter the **next child's information** and **add information** for the rest of the children in the family.

NOTE

There will be times when the children you have entered are not in their correct birth order. You will learn how to adjust their order in the "Lining up Children" section, found later in this chapter.

Adding another Set of Parents

There will be times when you will have two sets of parents for an individual, such as in cases of adoption. Or, in other cases, an individual might have a stepparent. Naturally, you want to record all the information for this person.

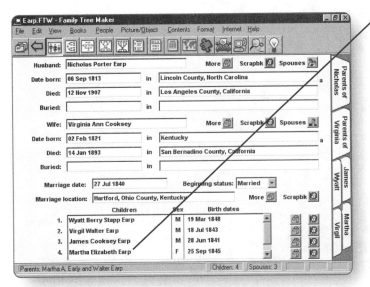

1. Click on the **child** you wish to select. The child will be selected.

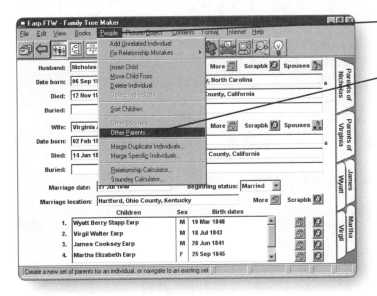

2. Click on **People**. The People menu will appear.

3. Click on **Other Parents**. The Parents of dialog box will open.

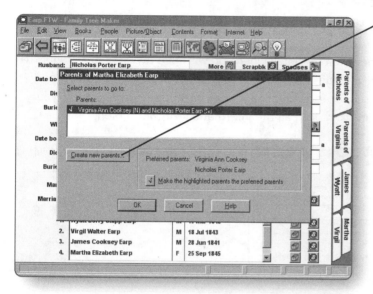

4. Click on the **Create new parents button**. The Create New Parents dialog box will open.

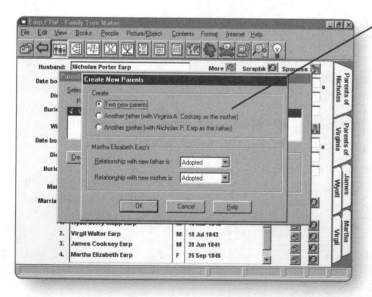

5. Choose between **Two new parents**, **Another father**, or **Another mother**. The option you choose will be selected.

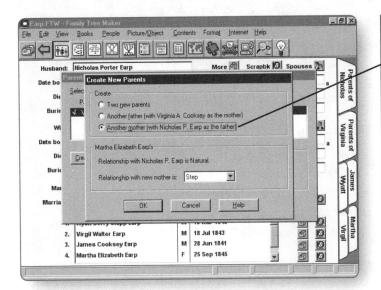

NOTE

When you select Another father or Another mother, the relationship options reflect the selection. You can only change the relationship for the appropriate chosen parent.

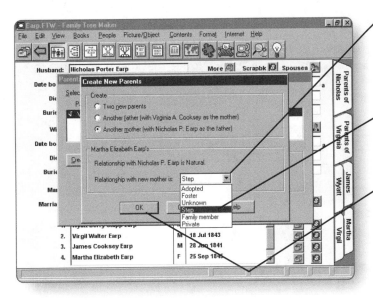

6. **Click** on the **down arrow** in the Relationship with field. The Relationship with drop-down list will appear.

7. **Click** on the **appropriate relationship** from the list. The relationship will be selected.

8. **Click** on **OK** to accept the selection.

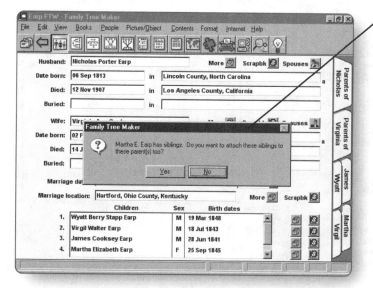

The Create New Parents dialog box will close and a message box will appear, asking you whether the child's siblings should be attached to the new parent(s).

9. Type the **new parent's name** in the appropriate name field. Notice that the information for the remaining parent has carried over, and that the child's information has been brought to the new screen.

Lining up Children

In a perfect world, you would already know everything about all the children in a particular family. However, this is not usually the case. Sometimes you will need to add a child or change the order of the children previously entered.

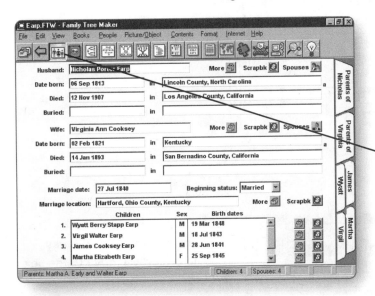

Adding a Child

The best way to add an additional child to the list of children is to select the Insert Child option.

1. Click on the **Family Page button**. The Family Page will appear.

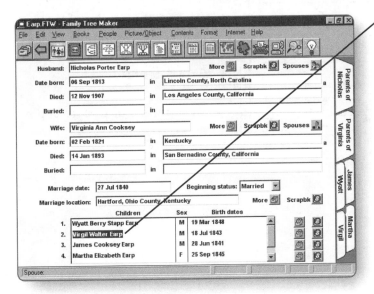

2. In the Children section, **click** on the **row** where you want to insert the new child.

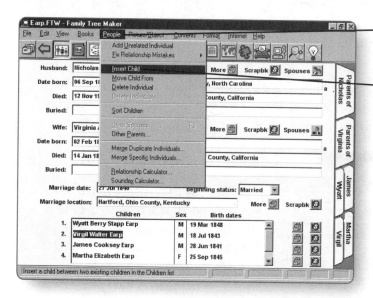

3. Click on **People**. The People menu will appear.

4. Click on **Insert Child**. Family Tree Maker will insert a blank child row.

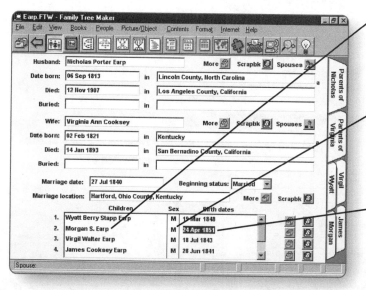

5. Enter the **name** of the new child and **press** the **Tab key**. The cursor will move to the Sex field.

6. Type the **gender** of the new child and **press** the **Tab key**. The cursor will move to the Birth dates field.

7. Enter the **birth date** of the new child.

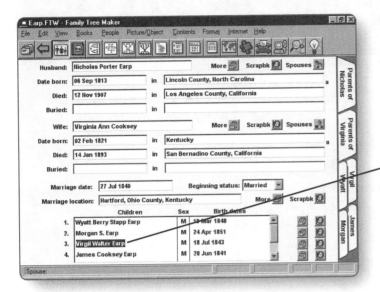

Moving a Child

After you have entered or updated a child's information, you might need to move the child so that he or she appears in the proper birth order.

1. Click on the **child** you want to move. The child will be selected.

2. Click on **People**. The People menu will appear.

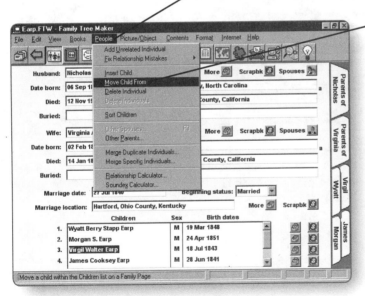

3. Click on **Move Child From**. A message box will appear, telling you how to move the child into a new position in the Children list.

TIP

To move a child, you cannot just type over the previously entered child's name. Family Tree Maker uses internal tracking that is not altered when you do this. If there are spouses or descendants associated with the original child, such a manual change can ruin the links previously created.

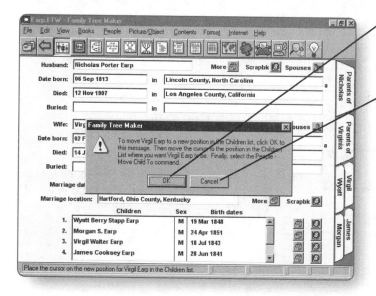

4a. **Click** on **OK** to continue with the move.

OR

4b. **Click** on **Cancel** to stop the move.

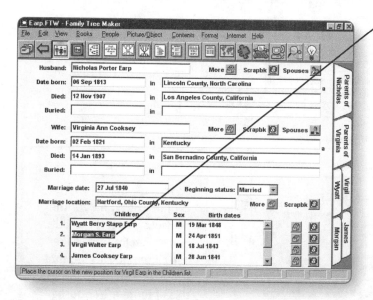

5. In the Children section, **click** on the **position** where you want to move the child.

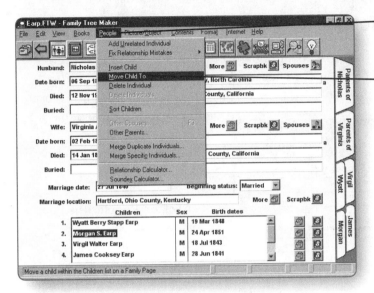

6. Click on **People**. The People menu will appear.

7. Click on **Move Child To**. The child will move to the new position.

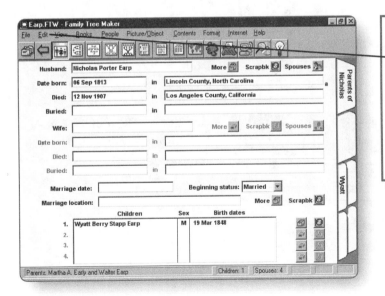

TIP

If you discover that you have not moved the correct child or you want to undo what you have done, use the Undo command, found in the Edit menu.

Sorting Children

If you are working with records that do not list the children in order, it is not necessary to figure out the correct order before entering them on the Family Page. Family Tree Maker offers a sort command that will rearrange the children chronologically after you have entered them.

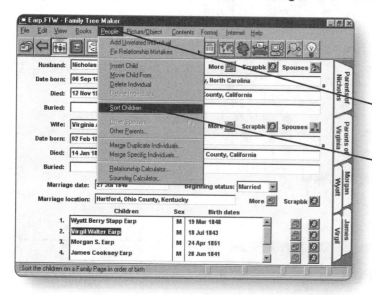

1. Click on **People**. The People menu will appear.

2. Click on **Sort Children**. A dialog box will open, confirming that you want to sort the children by birth order (oldest first).

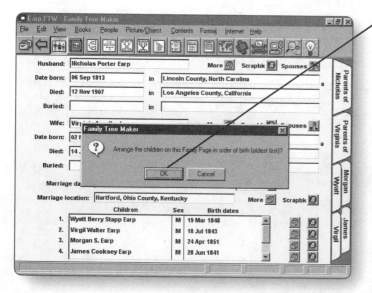

3. Click on **OK** to have Family Tree Maker arrange the children in this order.

Using the More About Lineage Window

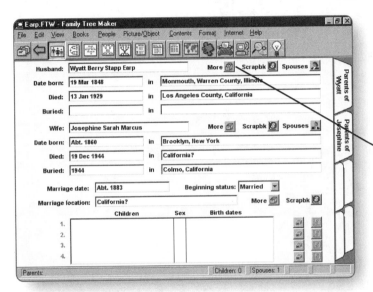

There are many additional facts and tidbits that you may want to record for an ancestor, such as titles and nicknames. This is done using the More About Lineage window.

1. Click the **More button** to the right of the person for whom you want to add information. The More About window will appear.

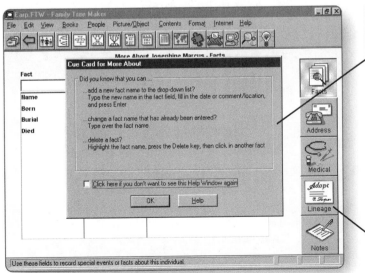

NOTE

Depending on which More About window was last open, Family Tree Maker might open a help dialog box. You can bypass this dialog box by pressing the Escape key or by clicking on OK.

2. Click on the **More About Lineage button**. The More About Lineage window will appear.

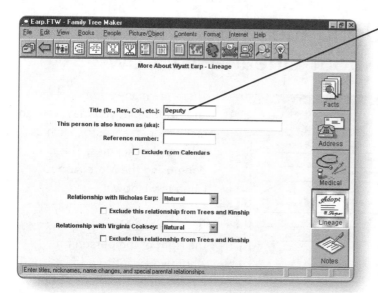

3. Enter the appropriate **additional information** about the individual.

4. Click on a **relationship** from the Relationship with drop-down list for the individual's father. The relationship will be selected.

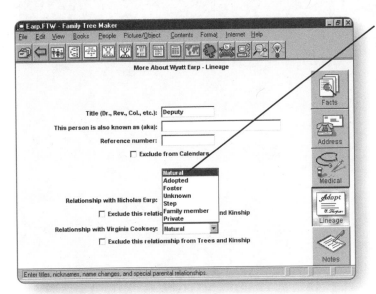

5. Click on a **relationship** from the Relationship with drop-down list for the individual's mother. The relationship will be selected.

6. Click on the **Family Page button**. The Family Page will reappear so that you can continue working on the family.

TIP

You can exclude certain individuals from reports by clicking on the Exclude this relationship from Trees and Kinship check box under the relationship you do not want included in the report.

4

Documenting Sources

Citing the sources you are relying on is one of the most important aspects of your research. Citing sources helps you keep track of the records you have used, which helps you avoid wasting time revisiting sources. In this chapter, you'll learn how to:

- Determine where you can cite a source
- Cite a source
- Create and change a master source
- Search for a master source

Where Can You Cite Sources?

Family Tree Maker makes it possible for you to cite sources for the names of individuals and each of their specific events. This allows you to document your research so that others with whom you share information will know what you used to draw your conclusions.

1. **Click** on the **Family Page button**. The Family Page will appear.

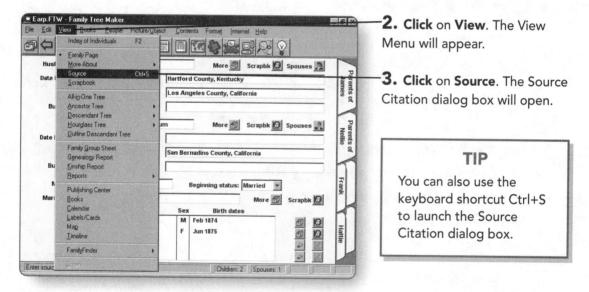

2. **Click** on **View**. The View Menu will appear.

3. **Click** on **Source**. The Source Citation dialog box will open.

> **TIP**
>
> You can also use the keyboard shortcut Ctrl+S to launch the Source Citation dialog box.

You can cite sources in several fields, including these:

- Name
- Birth date and location
- Death date and location
- Burial date and location
- Marriage date and location
- Marriage ending date and location
- Each of the Fact fields
- Cause of death
- Medical information

Citing a Source

There are a few steps you need to take to create a source and cite it as proof of an individual event (or of a person's life as a whole). You must first create a master source listing, and then refer to that listing when you want to cite the source.

Creating a Master Source

The master source is information about a source that doesn't change. For example, the author, title, and publication information don't change for a book. However, items like the page number from which a citation comes will change depending on the person about whom you are entering information.

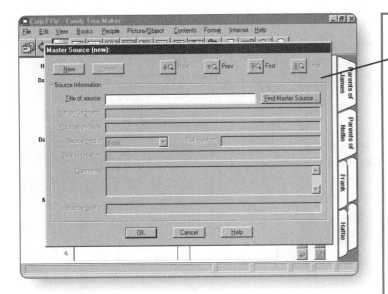

NOTE

You only need to enter a source one time. You can then recall it from the list the next time you want to cite it as proof of an individual's specific event. This is especially useful when a lot of information comes out of a single source, such as a book. Remember that for every event or conclusion you include in your family file, you should have a source cited.

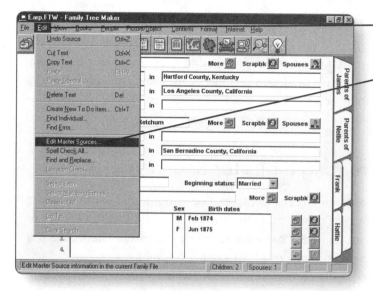

1. Click on **Edit**. The Edit menu will appear.

2. Click on **Edit Master Sources**. The Master Source dialog box will open.

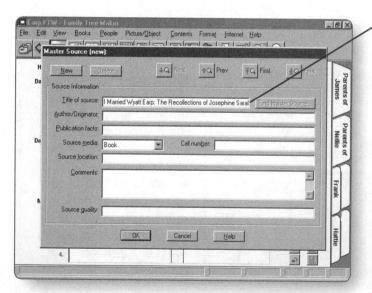

3. Type the **book title** in the Title of source field and **press** the **Tab key**. The rest of the fields will be activated and the cursor will move to the Author/Originator field.

NOTE

The Title of source field has been programmed so that the title will print out in italics when source citations are included on reports.

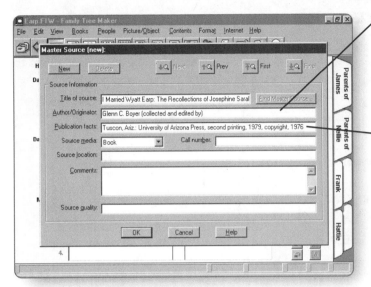

4. Enter the **author's name** and **press** the **Tab key**. The cursor will move to the Publication facts field.

5. Type the **publication information**.

> **NOTE**
>
> Publication information includes the place of publication, the name of the publishing company, and the copyright date. The format is Anytown, Florida: Anywhere Publishing Company, 2000.

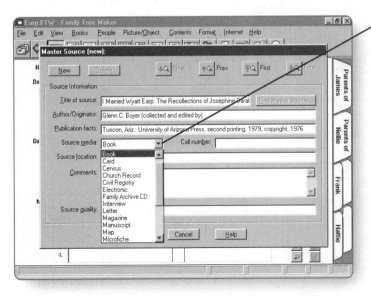

6. Select the **type of media** from the Source media drop-down list.

> **TIP**
>
> The Source media type provides a way for you to quickly see the format of original source. This will help you later, when you need to evaluate the proof you used to draw your conclusions.

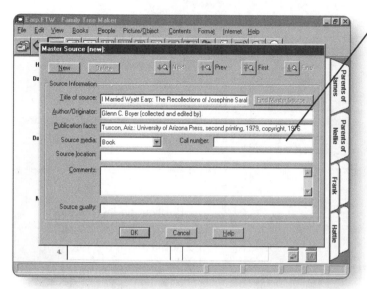

7. **Type** the **call number** in the Call number field and **press** the **Tab key**. The cursor will move to the Source location field.

NOTE

The Call number is the number assigned to the source in the repository where it was found. This could be a microfilm number, a Dewey Decimal system number, or some other numbering system unique to that particular library or archive.

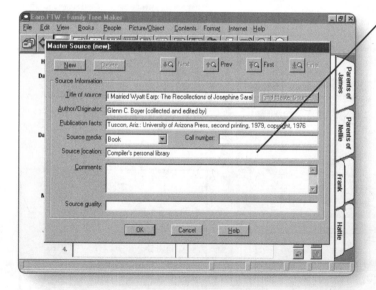

8. **Enter** the **source location** and **press** the **Tab key**. The cursor will move to the Comments field.

NOTE

The source location may be a library, archive, county courthouse, or a cousin's residence. The source location is where the original source used exists. You want to know this so that if you need to refer back to it, you know exactly where to return.

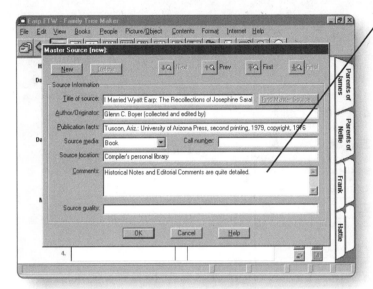

9. Type your **comments** and **press** the **Tab key**. The cursor will move to the Source quality field.

NOTE

The Comments section offers you a place to put your thoughts about the source and the information it includes. This information is not included when the source is printed on reports; it is only for your personal reference.

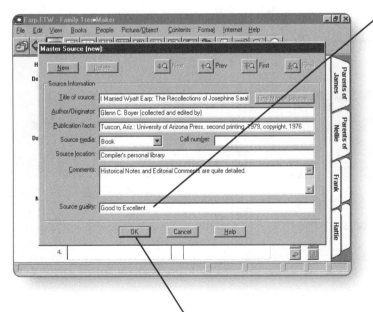

10. Type the **quality** of the source.

NOTE

The quality of the source is your reference to how reliable the source is. If the source is difficult to read because of unclear handwriting or faded ink, then it is possible that the information found could be questioned.

11. Click on **OK**. The Master Source dialog box will close.

Citing a Master Source

The Source Citation dialog box is where you will select the appropriate master source for the information you are citing. You can enter source information as you are entering the data and details for each ancestor.

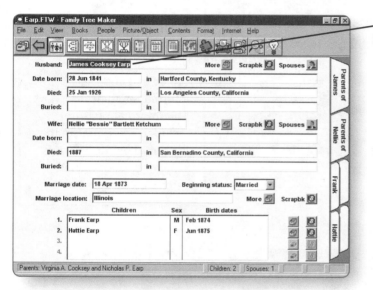

1. Click in the **field** where you want to add a source citation.

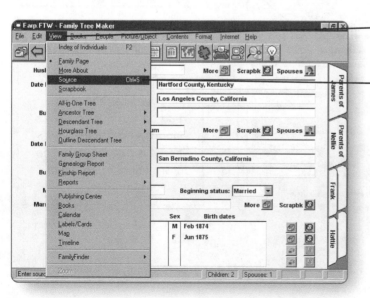

2. Click on **View**. The View menu will appear.

3. Click on **Source**. The Source Citation dialog box will open.

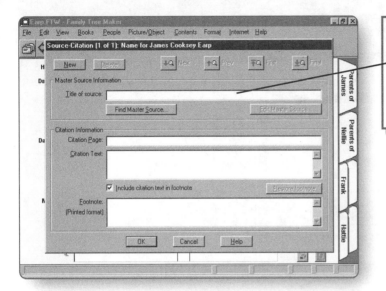

NOTE

The Source Citation dialog box will be empty because you have not yet selected a source.

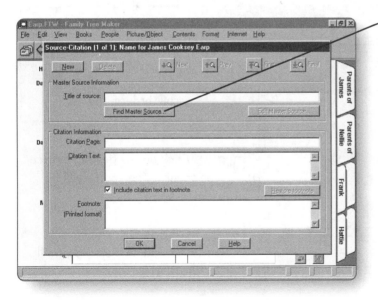

4. **Click** on the **Find Master Source button**. The Find Master Source dialog box will open.

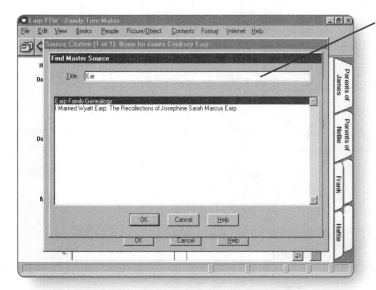

5. Type part of the **title** in the Title field. Family Tree Maker will highlight the first title that matches the word you've typed.

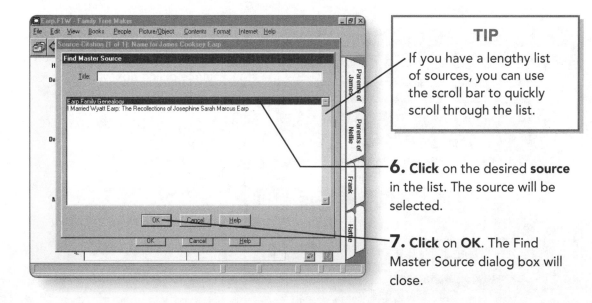

TIP

If you have a lengthy list of sources, you can use the scroll bar to quickly scroll through the list.

6. Click on the desired **source** in the list. The source will be selected.

7. Click on **OK**. The Find Master Source dialog box will close.

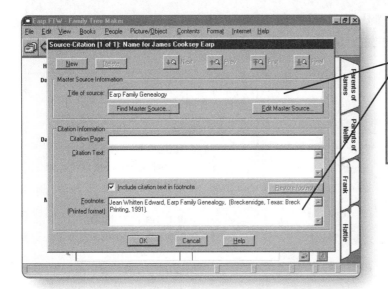

NOTE

Notice that the title of the source is now displayed in the Source Citation dialog box, and that the printed format of the footnote is also displayed.

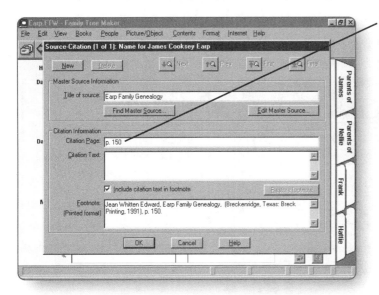

8. Type the **page number** of the citation in the Citation Page field.

TIP

Not all source citations will have a page number included on this screen. For more information about source citations, read Elizabeth Shown Mills' *Evidence! Citation and Analysis for the Family Historian* (Genealogical Publication Co., 1997).

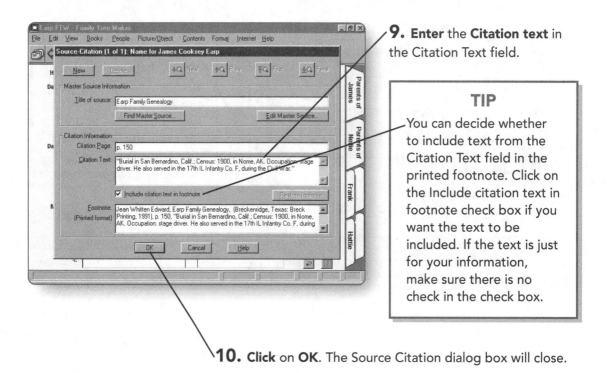

9. Enter the **Citation text** in the Citation Text field.

TIP

You can decide whether to include text from the Citation Text field in the printed footnote. Click on the Include citation text in footnote check box if you want the text to be included. If the text is just for your information, make sure there is no check in the check box.

10. Click on **OK**. The Source Citation dialog box will close.

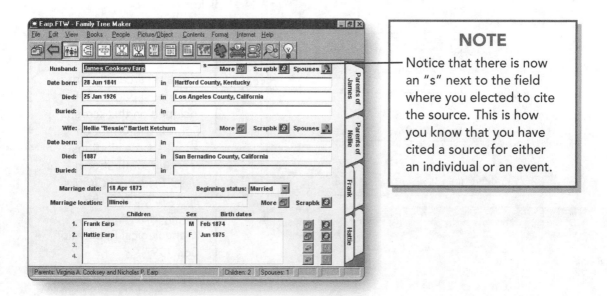

NOTE

Notice that there is now an "s" next to the field where you elected to cite the source. This is how you know that you have cited a source for either an individual or an event.

Changing a Master Source

While we would like to think we are perfect, there will be times when you discover that you've made an error. In a source, that should be fixed as soon as it is noticed. Usually you will notice such an error when you're working with that source in the Source Citation dialog box.

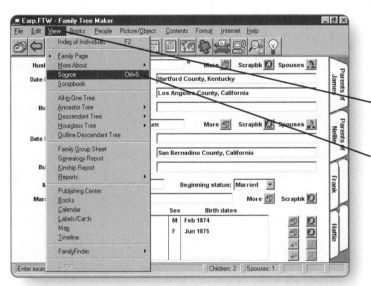

1. Click on **View**. The View menu will appear.

2. Click on **Source**. The Source Citation dialog box will open.

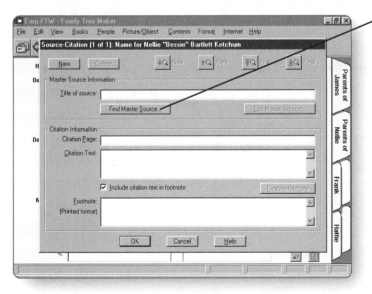

3. Click on the **Find Master Source button**. The Find Master Source dialog box will open.

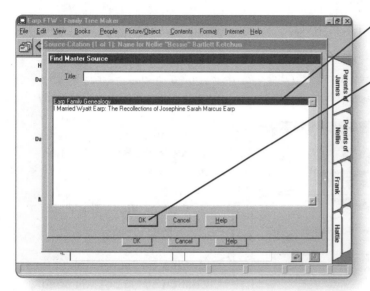

4. Select a **master source** from the list of available sources.

5. Click on **OK**. The Find Master Source dialog box will close. You will notice that the Edit Master Source button has now been activated in the Source Citation dialog box.

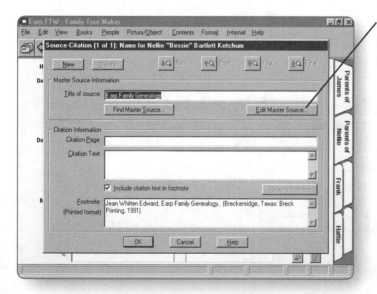

6. Click on the **Edit Master Source button**. The Master Source dialog box will open.

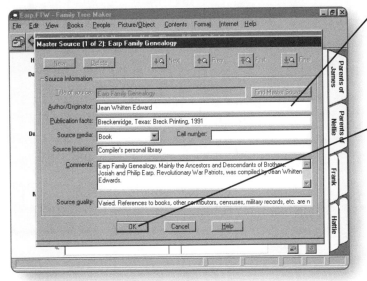

7. Make the appropriate **changes** to the Master Source fields. Usually you'll be changing a typo or fixing the publication date.

8. Click on **OK**. The Master Source dialog box will close.

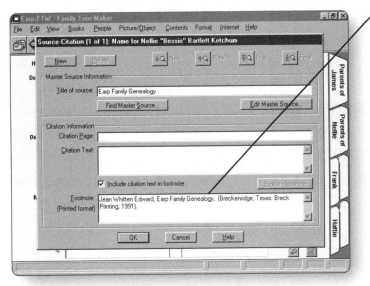

The changes you made to the source will take effect in the printed format of the footnote.

TIP

You can also go directly to the Master Source dialog box to make your changes.

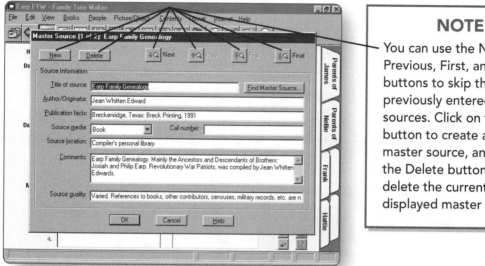

NOTE

You can use the Next, Previous, First, and Final buttons to skip through previously entered master sources. Click on the New button to create a new master source, and use the Delete button to delete the currently displayed master source.

Searching for a Master Source

At some point, you might want to look at a specific master source. The easiest way to do this is through the Master Source dialog box.

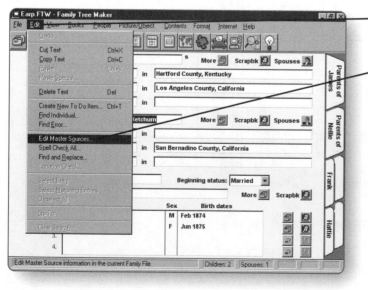

1. Click on **Edit**. The Edit menu will appear.

2. Click on **Edit Master Sources**. The Master Source dialog box will open.

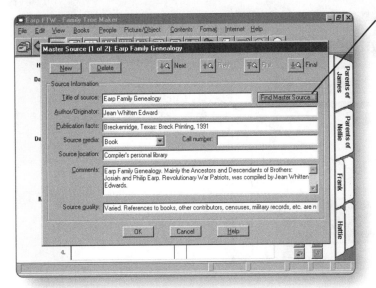

3. Click on the **Find Master Source button**. The Find Master Source dialog box will open.

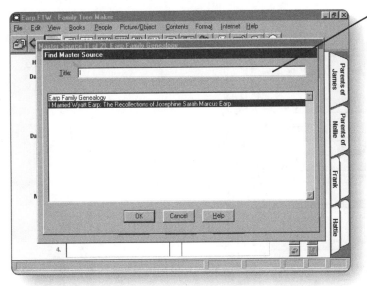

4. Type the **first word** of the title of the source. The first title containing that word will be highlighted.

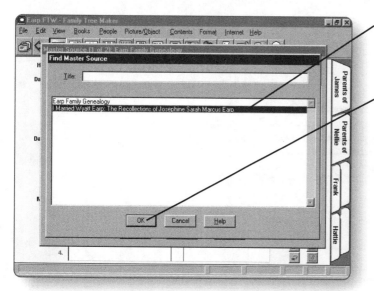

5. Click on the **title** of the desired source. The source will be selected.

6. Click on **OK**. The Find Master Source dialog box will close.

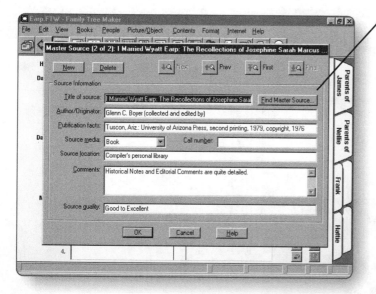

The selected source will now be in the Master Source dialog box, where you can view it or make changes, if necessary.

5

Using More About Options

Family history is much more than just names and dates of birth or death. As you research further into your family's generations, you will be keeping track of additional events and wanting to add family stories. In this chapter, you'll learn how to:

- Add and work with additional facts
- Add addresses for living relatives
- Track medical information
- Work with the More About Lineage window

Working with the More About Facts Window

Family Tree Maker offers you a way to track additional life events. As your research progresses, you will find that you are relying on such things as probate records and church records in addition to the more recognizable vital records. Family Tree Maker has included a variety of pre-defined facts (Family Tree Maker's name for the events in a person's life) to help you record this information.

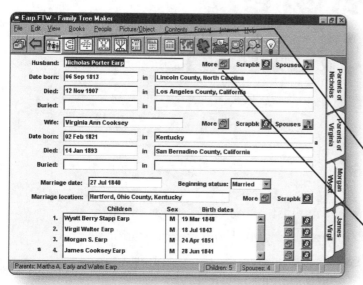

1. Click on the **Family Page button**. The Family Page will appear.

2. Click on the **More button**. The More About window will appear.

3. Click on the **Facts button**. The More About Facts window will appear.

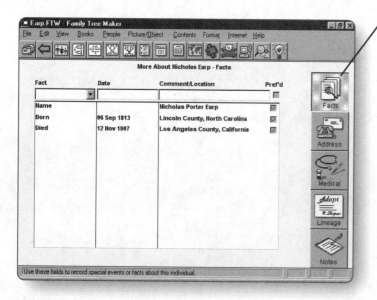

Adding Additional Facts

Much of the information you will record about your ancestors will be done in the More About Facts window. This is where you will record the variety of life events that you discover.

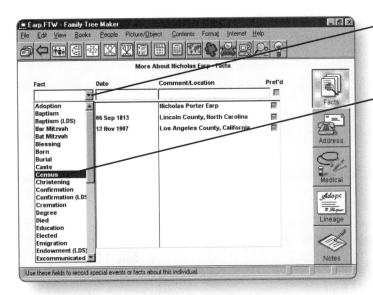

1. Click on the **Fact down arrow**. The Fact drop-down menu will appear.

2. Click on a **fact** in the menu. The fact will be selected and the menu will close.

3. Press the **Tab key** to advance to the Date field.

TIP

Many of the facts in the Fact drop-down menu are pertinent to specific religions. This allows you to select the appropriate religious event, rather than making do with a general christening event.

4. Type the **date** of the event in the Date field and **press** the **Tab key**. The cursor will move to the Comment/Location field.

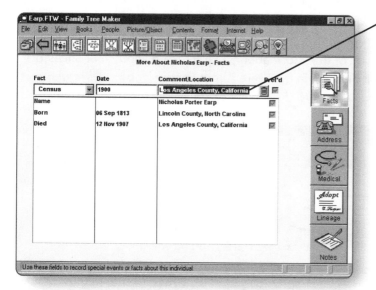

5. Enter the **event location** and **press** the **Tab key**. The new fact will be added to the list of facts for that individual, in chronological order.

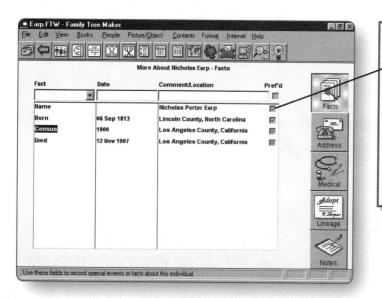

NOTE

The Pref'd check box is disabled for event type facts, unless you have conflicting or duplicated facts. If you had two death dates, you would select one of them as your preferred choice.

Adding Additional Names

At some point, you might discover that your ancestor had another name. It might have been a religious name or a nickname, or it might have been a variant of their given name. Family Tree Maker allows you to keep track of these different names with the Fact field.

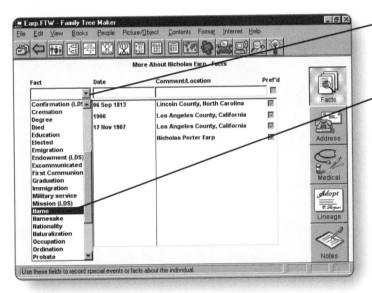

1. Click on the **Fact down arrow**. The Fact drop-down menu will appear.

2. Select the **Name fact** and **press** the **Tab key**. The cursor will move to Comment/Location field.

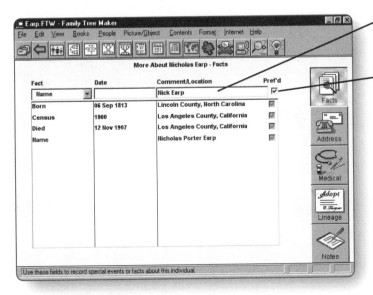

3. Enter the **new name** in the Comment/Location field.

4a. Click on the **Pref'd check box** if you want this name to be used in the Family Page and on reports.

OR

4b. Leave the **Pref'd check box** empty if you don't want this name used in the Family Page and on reports.

Selecting a Preferred Name

Even if you checked the Pref'd check box when you entered a name, you can always change that. For example, when sending reports to a cousin, you might want to use one name; when sharing with your brother or sister, you might want to use another name.

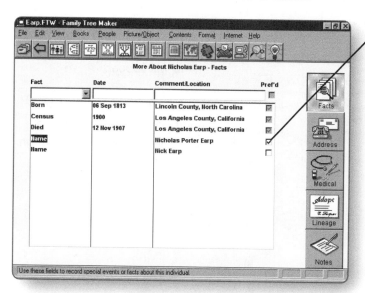

1. Click on the **Pref'd check box** next to the name you want to select. The name will be selected.

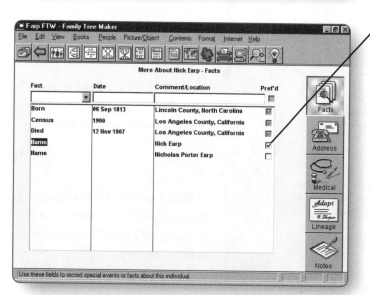

2. Click on the **Pref'd check box** next to another Name fact. Notice that in addition to the check mark, the preferred name will appear at the top of the list of name facts.

Creating a New Fact Name

Family Tree Maker includes 43 different facts, but you might need to record an event that is not covered by those facts. You can create a new fact name whenever you need one.

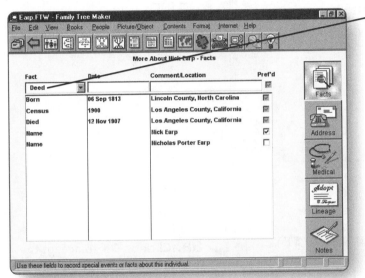

1. Click in the **Fact field**.

2. Type the **name** of the new event and **press** the **Tab key**. The cursor will move to the Date field.

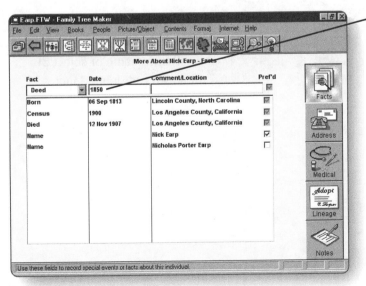

3. Enter the **date** and **press** the **Tab key**. The cursor will move to the Comment/Location field.

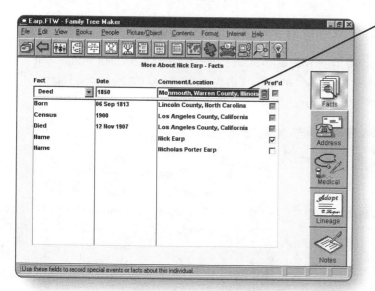

4. **Type** the **event location** and **press** the **Tab key**. Family Tree Maker will open a New Fact Name message box, verifying that you want to accept the new fact name.

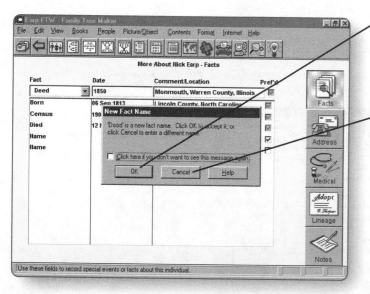

5a. **Click** on **OK** to accept the new fact name. The new fact name will be saved.

OR

5b. **Click** on **Cancel** to return to the Fact name field to type in a different name or select a different pre-defined fact.

Using the Address Window

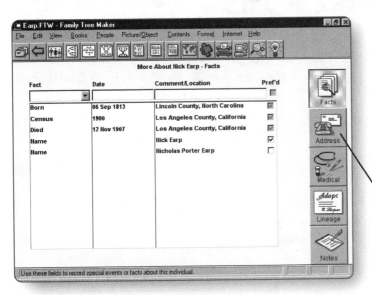

The Address window is useful when you're entering your living descendants. People involved with a family association rely heavily on this for mailing lists, as do those who want to keep track of relatives with whom they are exchanging information.

1. Click on the **Address button**. The More About Address and Phone(s) window will appear.

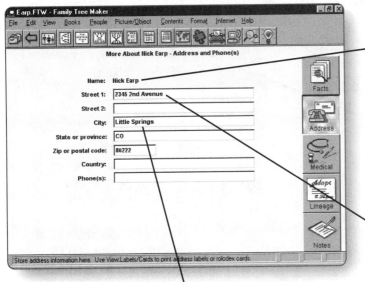

NOTE

Notice that the individual's name has already been supplied. Family Tree Maker assumes you are entering the address for the individual currently in the More About window.

2. Type the **street address** in the Street 1 field and **press** the **Tab key** twice. The cursor will move to the City field.

3. Enter the **city** and **press** the **Tab key**. The cursor will move to the State or province field.

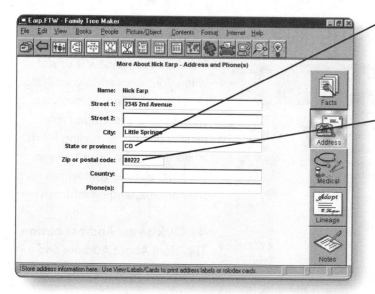

4. **Type** the **state or province** and **press** the **Tab key**. The cursor will move to the Zip or postal code field.

5. **Enter** the **zip or postal code** and **press** the **Tab key**. The cursor will move to the Country field.

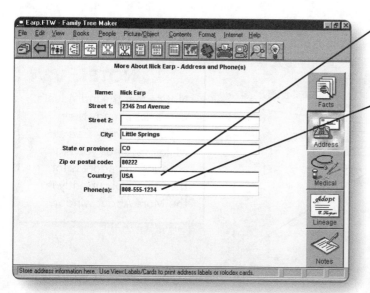

6. **Type** the **country** and **press** the **Tab key**. The cursor will move to the Phone(s) field.

7. **Enter** the **phone number** in the Phone(s) field.

TIP

Just because there are fields for all this information does not mean you need to supply it. You need only enter what is important for you to be able to contact the individual at a later date.

Working with Medical Information

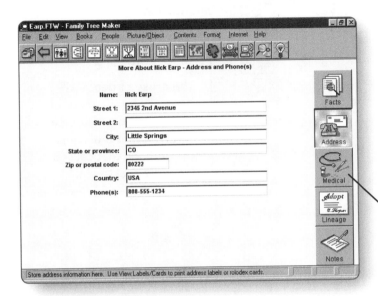

Modern medical technology has made understanding your medical family tree more important than ever before. Family Tree Maker provides you with space for recording pertinent medical information about your family members and ancestors.

1. **Click** on the **Medical button**. The More About Medical window will appear.

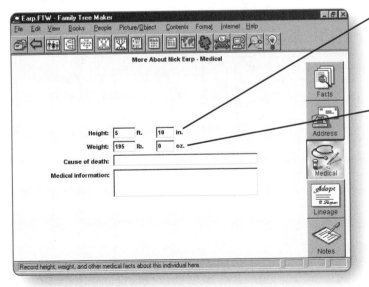

2. **Type** the **height** in feet and inches in the Height field and **press** the **Tab key**. The cursor will move to the Weight field.

3. **Enter** the **weight** in pounds and ounces and **press** the **Tab key**. The cursor will move to the Cause of death field.

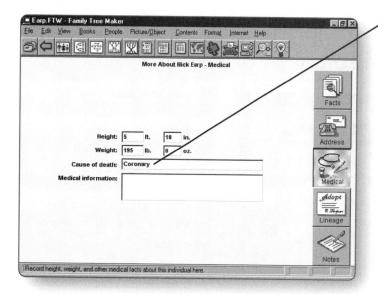

4. Type the **cause of death** and **press** the **Tab key**. The cursor will move to the Medical information field.

NOTE

The cause of death will generally be the medical term found on the death certificate, or the illness or condition that caused the individual to die.

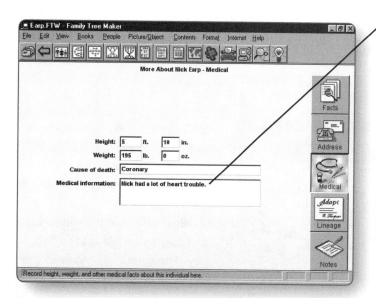

5. Enter the **details** you feel are important about your ancestor's medical history.

TIP

The Medical information field can hold up to 200 characters of information, which is about 5 lines of text.

Using the More About Lineage Window

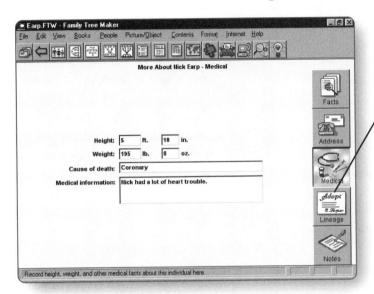

Family Tree Maker uses the Lineage window to organize information about relationships, titles, and aliases.

1. Click on the **Lineage button**. The More About Lineage window will appear.

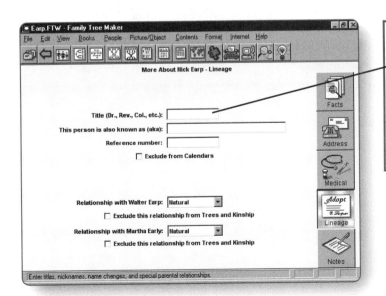

TIP

When entering a title, do not enter items such as Jr. or III. The titles entered here will be printed in front of the individual's name on reports.

Entering AKA Names

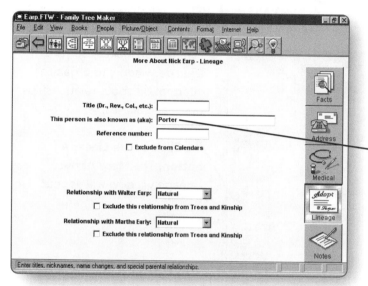

There will be times when you will discover a name change or an alternate name for your ancestor or family member. Legal name changes are just one way this field can be used.

1. **Click** in the **This person is also known as (aka) field** and **type** the **also known as name** for your ancestor.

TIP

When you print reports, you can elect to use the also known as name instead of or in addition to the name used in the Family Page. Such decisions are made when you are working in the report. For more on this, see Chapter 14, "Creating Genealogy Style and Genealogical Source Reports."

Working with Special Relationships

As you dig deeper in your family history, you are apt to discover mothers who died early, fathers who remarried, adoptions, and other unique relationship situations. You will want to record these in Family Tree Maker.

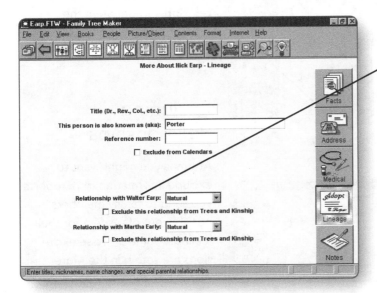

NOTE

Pay attention to the names in the Relationship section. How these individuals are connected to each other will be affected as you make changes in the Relationship section.

TIP

See Chapter 3, "Enhancing the Family," for a review of how to add a new parent (or parents) and how to specify the preferred parents.

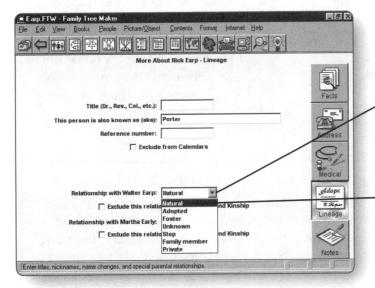

1. Click on the **Relationship with down arrow** for the father's name. The Relationship drop-down menu will appear.

2. Select the appropriate **relationship** between the father and the individual.

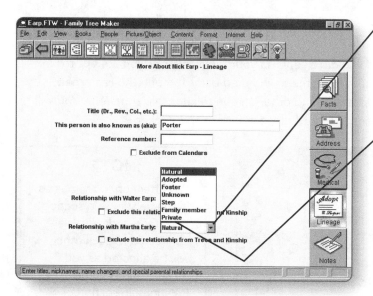

3. Click on the **Relationship with down arrow** for the mother's name. The Relationship drop-down menu will appear.

4. Select the appropriate **relationship** between the mother and the individual.

Excluding Relationships

At times you might want to exclude information from reports you send to family members, possibly out of respect for their feelings. Some of these exclusions are set up in the More About Lineage window.

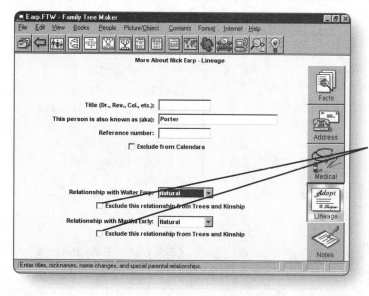

1. Click on the **Exclude this relationship from Trees and Kinship check box** for either the mother or the father of the individual. The option will be selected and that relationship will be excluded from your reports.

NOTE

Electing to exclude the relationship from Trees and Kinship will affect reports. Kinship reports and Ancestor Trees will exclude the paternal and/or maternal ancestors, depending on which relationship(s) you chose to exclude. Descendant trees will exclude the child and the child's descendants.

6

Understanding More About Notes

One way to make your family history interesting to other family members is to include family stories. With Family Tree Maker you can do just that. In this chapter, you'll learn how to:

- Enter notes and stories
- Copy and move notes and stories
- Find text in notes
- Format notes for printing
- Import and export notes
- Export notes

Working with Notes and Stories

Most of us have heard our grandparents, aunts, or uncles share stories about family members. As your research progresses, you will find additional stories. Family Tree Maker's More About Notes window allows you to incorporate these notes and stories into your research.

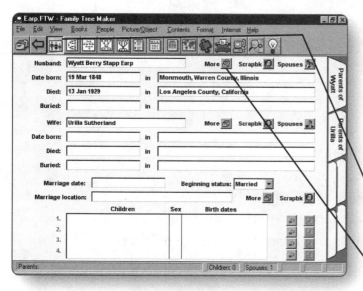

Entering Notes and Stories

The More About Notes window allows you to enter, in a narrative style, the stories or research notes you want to include in your reports.

1. Click on the **Family Page button**. The Family Page will appear.

2. Click on the **More button**. The More About window will appear.

3. Click on the **Notes button**. The More About Notes window will appear.

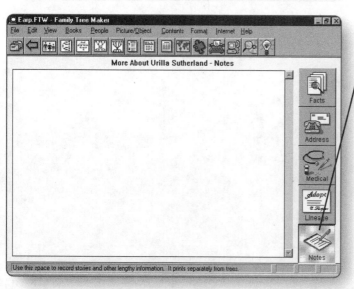

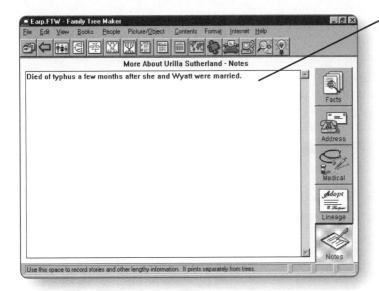

4. In the text box, **enter** the **text** you wish to include for this individual.

NOTE

The information typed into the More About Notes window will not print on the family tree styled reports. However, you can print this information on a family group sheet report or include it in a book.

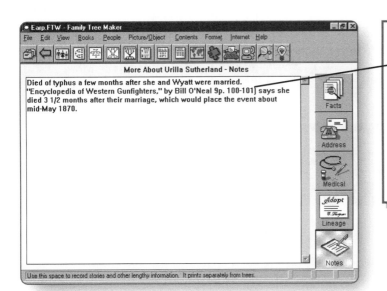

TIP

When quoting information from a source, be sure to include the source citation information. Always put quotation marks around any information that is a direct quote from a published source.

Copying Notes and Stories

Sometimes a particular note might apply to more than one individual. When you are working with such a note, you will want to take advantage of the copy and paste functions available in Family Tree Maker.

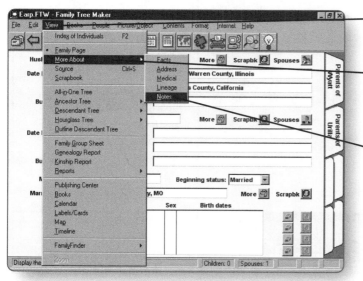

1. **Click** on **View**. The View menu will appear.

2. **Move** the **mouse pointer** to More About. The More About menu will appear.

3. **Click** on **Notes**. The More About Notes window will appear.

TIP

This is another method of getting to the More About Notes window for a particular individual.

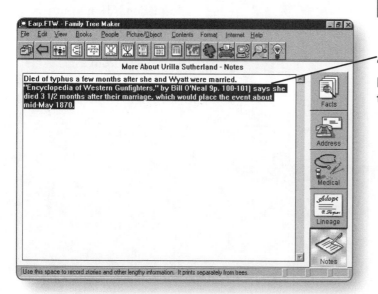

4. **Click and drag** the **mouse pointer** to highlight the desired text. The text will be selected.

5. Click on **Edit**. The Edit menu will appear.

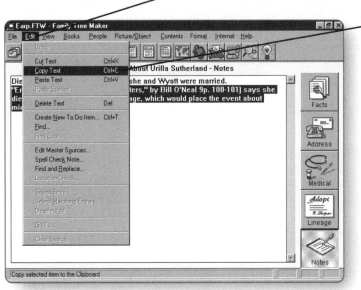

6. Click on **Copy Text**. The selected text will be placed on the clipboard.

TIP

Chapter 8, "Searching Your Family Tree File," explains how to locate someone in your database who is not included in the current Family Page. You can use these methods to locate the individual to whose Notes window you want paste the copied text.

Moving Notes and Stories

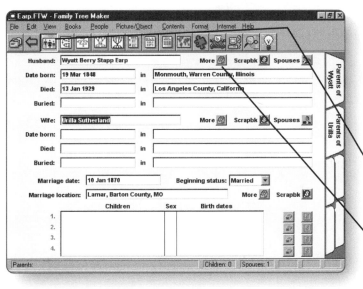

You might discover that a story you thought pertained to one individual was really about another. The easiest way to fix this is to move the story from one More About Notes window to another.

1. Click on the **Family Page button**. The Family Page will appear.

2. Click on the **More button**. The More About window will appear.

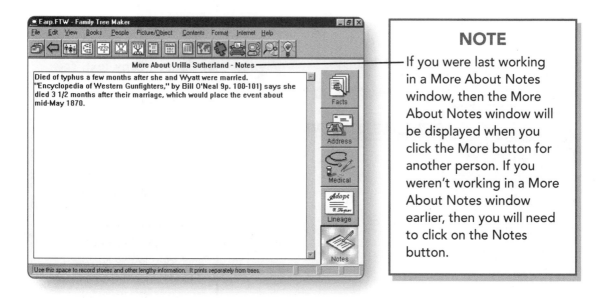

NOTE

If you were last working in a More About Notes window, then the More About Notes window will be displayed when you click the More button for another person. If you weren't working in a More About Notes window earlier, then you will need to click on the Notes button.

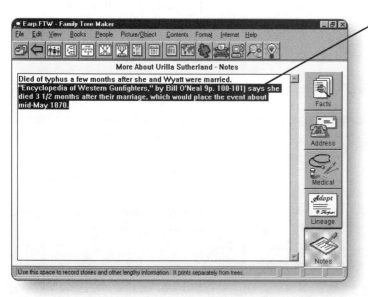

3. Click and drag the **mouse pointer** to highlight the selected text.

4. **Right-click** on the **selected text**. A menu will appear.

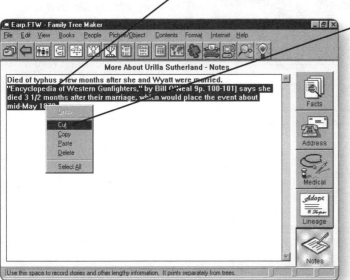

5. **Click** on **Cut**. The selected text will be removed from the More About Notes window and placed on the clipboard.

TIP

The menu that appears when you right-click is a shortcut that allows you to cut, copy, paste, or delete selected text. This is the same as clicking on the Edit menu and selecting the options there.

The selected text can now be placed in another individual's More About Notes window.

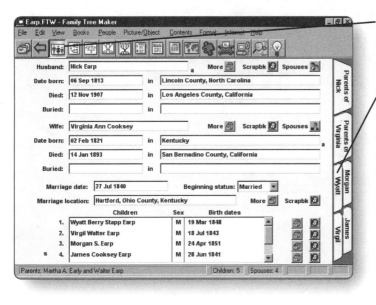

6. **Click** on the **Family Page button**. The Family Page will appear.

7. **Click** on the **Name tab** of the individual you want to select. The Family Page will change to reflect the new individual.

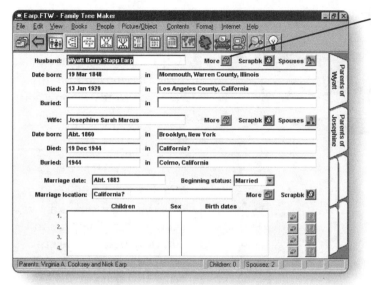

8. Click on the **More button**. The More About window will appear. The More About Notes window should be displayed because it was the last More About window used.

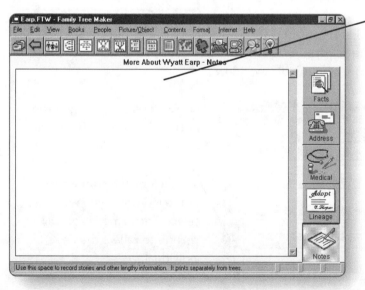

9. Click inside the **text box**.

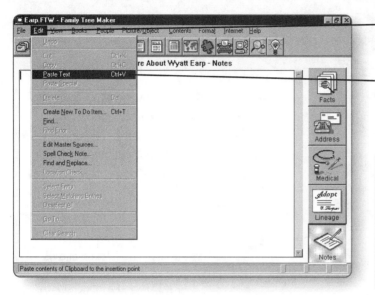

10. **Click** on **Edit**. The Edit menu will appear.

11. **Click** on **Paste Text**. The text will appear in the More About Notes window.

TIP

The keyboard shortcuts Ctrl+X for Cut, Ctrl+C for Copy, and Ctrl+V for Paste can be used instead of the menus.

Finding Text in Notes

It can be hard to find one particular sentence or thought when you have typed a large amount of text in the More About Notes window. Family Tree Maker offers a way to search for a specific word or phrase. Before you follow these directions, be sure the More About Notes window you want to search is open.

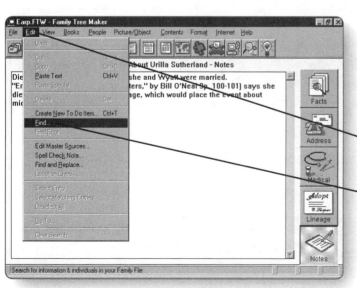

1. **Click** on **Edit**. The Edit menu will appear.

2. **Click** on **Find**. The Find dialog box will open.

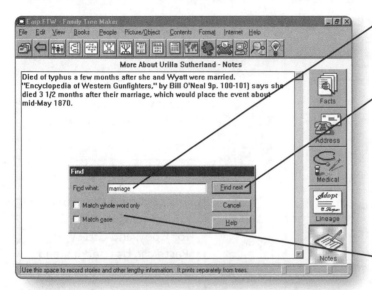

3. **Type** the **word or phrase** you want to search for in the Find what field.

4. **Click** on the **Find next button**. When Family Tree Maker finds the requested word or phrase, it will highlight it in the More About Notes window.

TIP

Family Tree Maker allows you to match whole words or match case. This allows you to eliminate those words that share consecutive letters with the word for which you are looking.

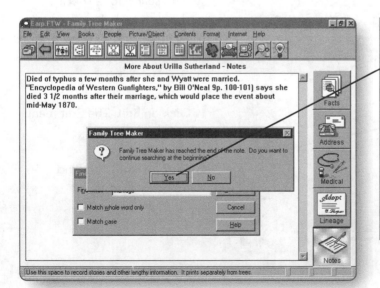

NOTE

If the cursor was not at the beginning of the text in the More About Notes window, then Family Tree Maker might ask you if you want to continue searching from the beginning. Click on Yes if you want to continue searching.

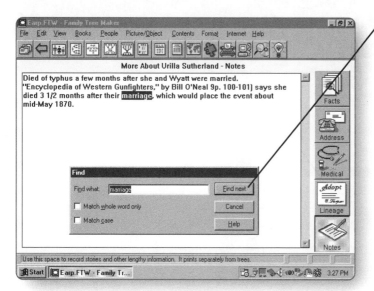

5. Click on the **Find next button** to continue searching the text.

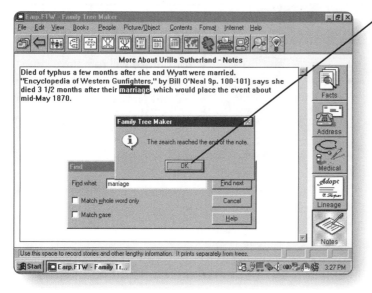

6. Click on **OK** when you see the message box telling you that Family Tree Maker has reached the end of the text. The message box will close and you will be returned to the Find dialog box.

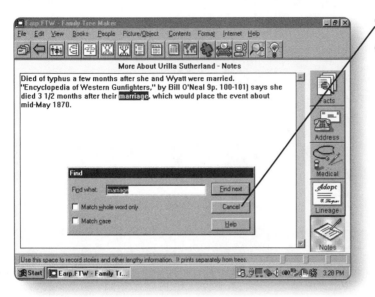

7. Click on **Cancel**. The Find dialog box will close.

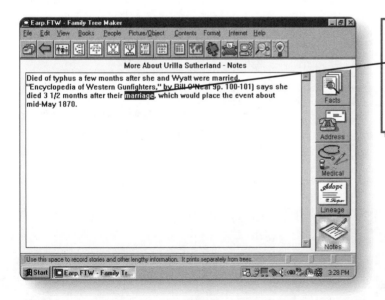

NOTE

The last highlighted word or phrase will remain highlighted in the More About Notes window.

Formatting Notes for Printing

With the More About Notes window open, you can format the text's chosen font, style, and size to alter how it appears when printed in the reports. This will make the notes stand out in your report.

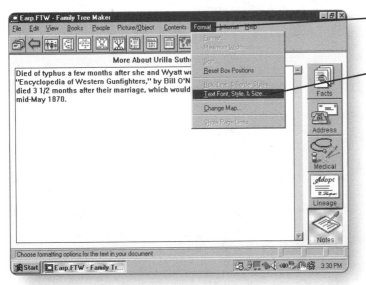

1. Click on **Format**. The Format menu will appear.

2. Click on **Text Font, Style, & Size**. A message box will appear, reminding you that the changes made will display only when you print the report, not on the screen.

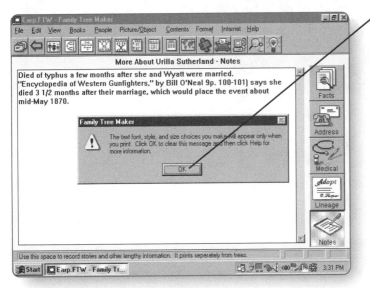

3. Click on **OK**. The message box will close and the Text Font, Style, & Size dialog box will open.

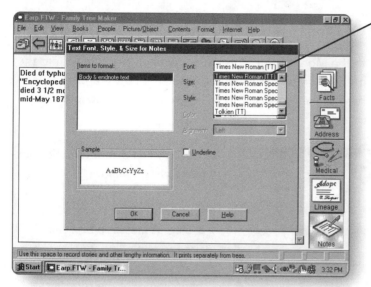

4. Select the desired **font** from the Font drop-down menu.

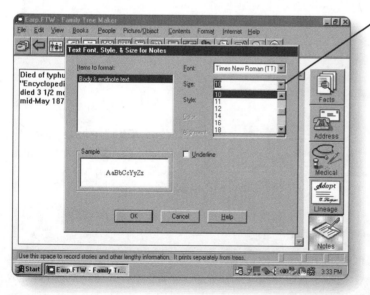

5. Select the **font size** from the Size drop-down menu.

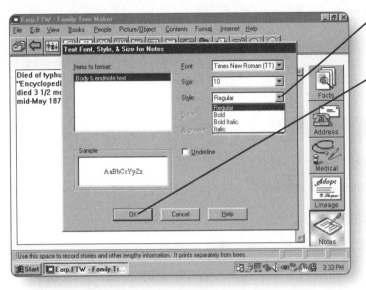

6. **Select** the **font style** from the Style drop-down menu.

7. **Click** on **OK**. The Text Font, Style, & Size dialog box will close.

NOTE

Formatting in the More About Notes window affects all the text in the Notes window. You cannot highlight a single paragraph and change the font or style.

Importing Text to Notes

At some point, you might want to import some text into Family Tree Maker. You might have received a write-up through e-mail, or you might have already typed up a family story that you now want to place in the More About Notes window. You can do so by importing the text or by copying and pasting.

Copying Text

The Windows operating system allows you to copy text from one application and paste it into another. Because Family Tree Maker is a Windows program, this option is available to you.

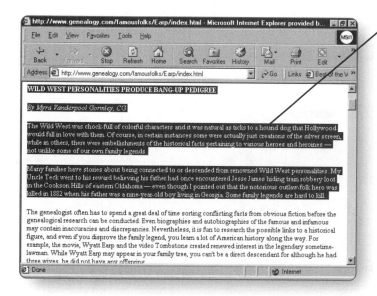

1. Highlight the **text** you want to copy from the e-mail message or word processing file.

2. Press Ctrl+C to copy the text. The text will be placed on the clipboard.

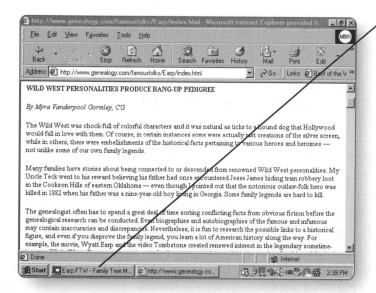

3. Click on **Family Tree Maker** in the Windows Taskbar. Family Tree Maker will be maximized.

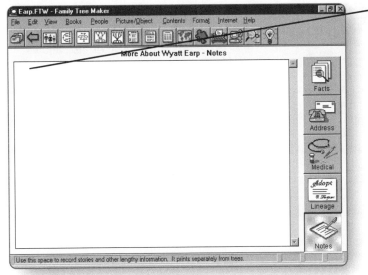

4. Click in the **More About Notes window**, at the location where you want the text to appear. The cursor will appear.

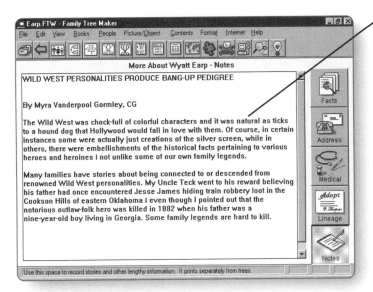

5. Press Ctrl+V. The copied text will appear in the More About Notes window.

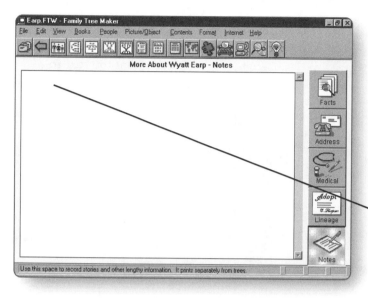

Importing Text

Family Tree Maker also allows you to import text. This can be done only when the file you want to import ends in a .txt extension, because that is the only file type that Family Tree Maker recognizes.

1. **Click** in the **More About Notes window**, at the location where you want the text to appear.

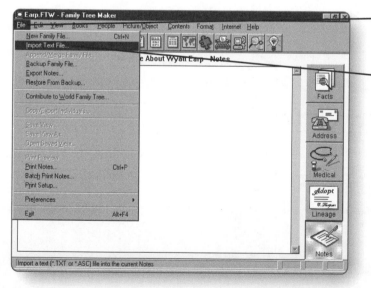

2. **Click** on **File**. The File menu will appear.

3. **Click** on **Import Text File**. The Import Text File dialog box will open.

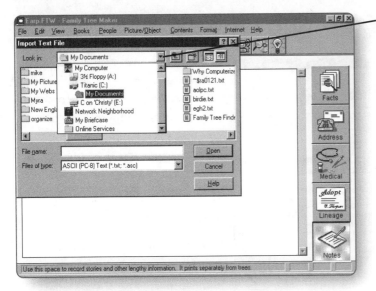

4. Click on the **Look in down arrow**. The Look in drop-down menu will appear.

5. Navigate to the **folder** where the text file is located.

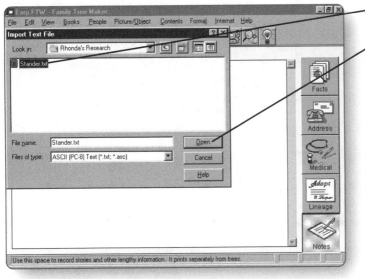

6. Click on the selected **file**.

7. Click on **Open**. The text will be placed in the More About Notes window.

Exporting Notes

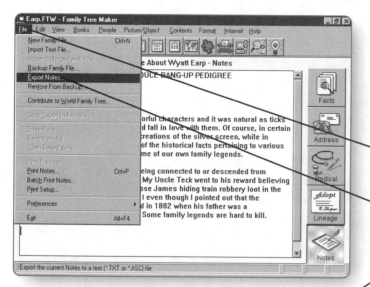

You might have notes that you have received from others and in turn, you might want to share your notes with a relative or fellow researcher. You can do so by exporting the notes.

1. Click on **File**. The File menu will appear.

2. Click on **Export Notes**. The Export Notes dialog box will open.

3. In the File name field, **type** the **name** of the file you want to export. You will want to pay attention to where the file is being saved so you can retrieve it later.

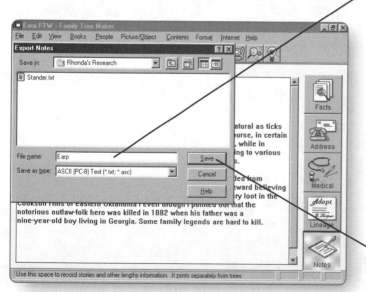

NOTE

Family Tree Maker will automatically assign the .txt extension to the file name.

---

4. Click on **Save**. The text in the More About Notes window will be saved to the file.

TIP

You can also use the copy and paste functions to place the desired text into another document.

7

Working with the More About Marriage Window

Much of what you have learned up to this point deals with a specific individual in your database. However, the marriage event is unique and Family Tree Maker understands that there are different ways to handle it. In this chapter, you'll learn how to:

- Select an ending status for the marriage
- Work with reference numbers
- Select the appropriate marriage fact
- Select a preferred date
- Work with the More About Marriage Notes window

Accessing the More About Marriage Window

The More About Marriage window allows you to include notes or pertinent additional dates about the marriage of two individuals. While the marriage date itself can be entered in the Family Page, the additional notes and details are entered in the More About Marriage window.

1. Click on the **Family Page button**. The Family Page will appear.

2. Click on the **Marriage More button**. The More About Marriage window will appear.

3. Click on the **Facts button**. The More About Marriage Facts window will appear.

Using the More About Marriage Facts Window

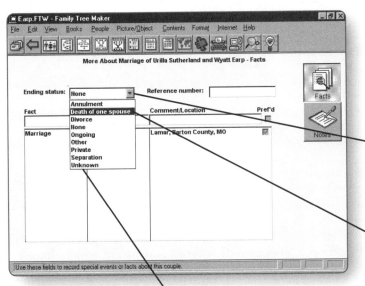

The More About Marriage Facts window is where you can include additional details about a marriage. This is where you would include a divorce fact or a conflicting marriage fact.

1. **Click** on the **Ending status down arrow**. The Ending status drop-down menu will appear.

2. **Select** the appropriate **ending status** from the menu. The option will be selected.

NOTE

If you don't know how the marriage ended, you can select Unknown from the drop-down menu.

Entering a Reference Number

The Reference number field allows you to enter any numbers or letters you choose. If you have a unique filing or pedigree system, you might use this field for that system's reference number.

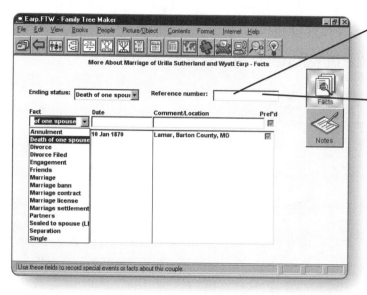

1a. Type a **Reference number** in the Reference number field.

OR

1b. **Leave** this **field** blank if you do not have a reference numbering system.

Adding a Marriage Fact

Although you have already entered one marriage fact, there are others that you might need to enter—possibly a conflicting marriage date or a fact that details the end of that marriage.

1. **Click** on the **Fact down arrow**. The Fact drop-down menu will appear.

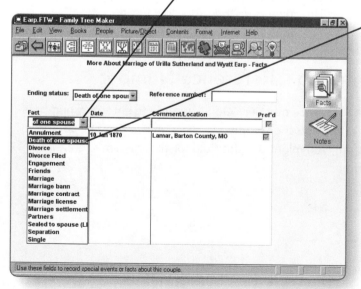

2. **Select** the **appropriate fact** from the menu and **press** the **Tab key**. The fact will be selected and the cursor will move to the Date field.

TIP

Remember that if you select something like the annulment, divorce, or death of one spouse, be sure to change the ending status to correspond with the fact.

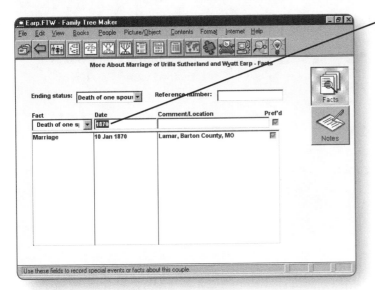

3. **Enter** the **date** of the event and **press** the **Tab key**. The cursor will move to the Comment/Location field.

4. **Type** the **location** of the event.

Using the Preferred Check Box

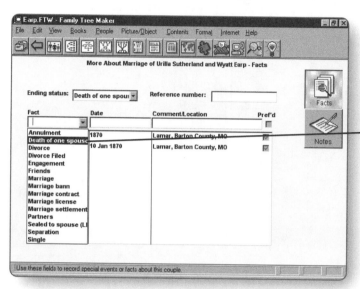

The Preferred check box is activated when you have selected a duplicate fact. This happens when you have two conflicting dates recorded.

1. Select a **duplicate fact** from the Fact drop-down menu.

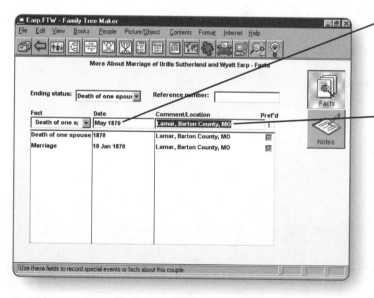

2. Type the **date** of the event in the Date field and **press** the **Tab key**. The cursor will move to the Comment/Location field.

3. Type the **location** of the event and **press** the **Tab key**. The new fact will appear in the Fact list.

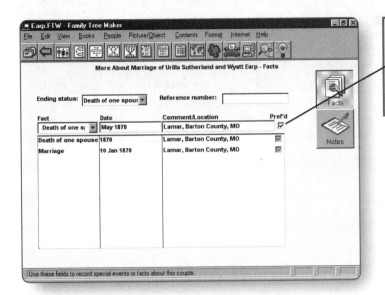

NOTE

At this point the Pref'd check box is automatically selected.

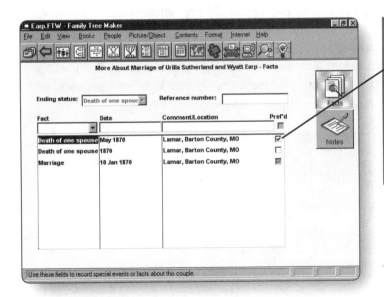

NOTE

The newly added fact has now become the preferred fact. This means it will be the marriage fact that appears in any reports that you print.

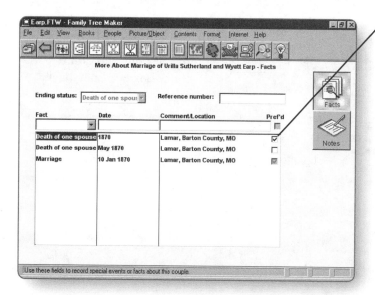

4. Click on the **Pref'd check box** for the second duplicated fact. The newly selected preferred fact will move to the top of the duplicated events and will have a check in the Pref'd check box.

Working with Marriage Notes

Just as you might include stories about an individual as a note, you might also want to record something about the marriage. As it does for individuals, Family Tree Maker supplies you with a More About Notes window for the marriage.

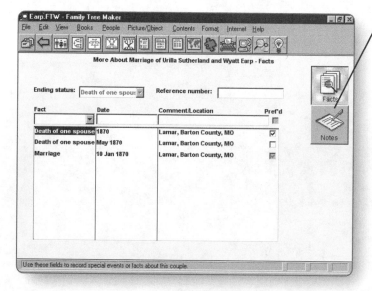

1. Click on the **Notes button**. The More About Marriage Notes window will appear.

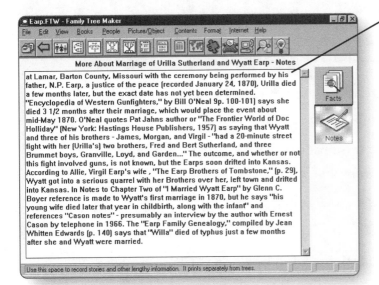

2. Type the **text** you want to include about the marriage.

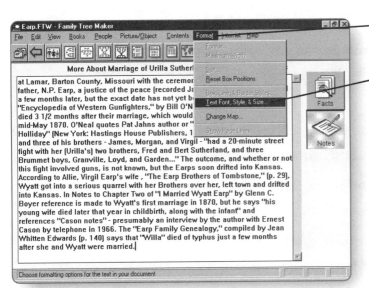

3. Click on **Format**. The Format menu will appear.

4. Click on **Text Font, Style, & Size**. The Text Font, Style, & Size dialog box will open, so you can format your newly added note.

NOTE

See Chapter 6, "Understanding More About Notes," to refresh your memory about changing the text in the More About Notes window.

Part II Review Questions

1. How do you add parents to the individual you have already entered? *See "Adding Parents" in Chapter 3*

2. How can you change the order in which children are listed? *See "Lining Up Children" in Chapter 3*

3. Where can you cite a source in Family Tree Maker? *See "Where Can You Cite Sources?" in Chapter 4*

4. What is the Source Citation Dialog box? *See "Citing a Source" in Chapter 4*

5. How can you include additional life events for an individual? *See "Adding Additional Facts" in Chapter 5*

6. What special relationships can you select in the More About Lineage window? *See "Working with Special Relationships" in Chapter 5*

7. Where can you enter notes and stories for an individual? *See "Entering Notes and Stories" in Chapter 6*

8. How can you copy and paste text in the Notes window? *See "Moving Notes and Stories" in Chapter 6*

9. How do you access the More About Marriage window? *See "Accessing the More About Marriage Window" in Chapter 7*

10. Can you include more than just the marriage event in the More About Marriage Facts? *See "Using the More About Marriage Facts Window" in Chapter 7*

PART III

Working in Family Tree Maker

Chapter 8
Searching Your Family Tree File 129

Chapter 9
Correcting Information 151

Chapter 10
Fixing Relationships and Duplicates . . . 169

8

Searching Your Family Tree File

When you first begin entering data, it is easy to use the tabs along the right side of the window to select an individual. However, after you have been researching for a while, you will discover that you have too many people to do this effectively. In this chapter, you'll learn how to:

- Locate individuals using the Quick Search
- Work with the Find feature
- Rearrange the index
- Search by name
- Search by other types of criteria
- Work in the FamilyFinder Center

Using Quick Search by Name

The Index of Individuals has a built-in quick search where you can easily type in the name of the individual for whom you are searching. This is the easiest way to locate an individual in your family tree file.

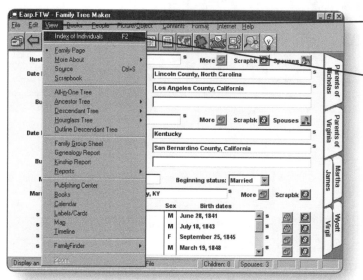

1. Click on **View**. The View menu will appear.

2. Click on **Index of Individuals**. The Index of Individuals dialog box will open.

TIP

There are two other ways to access the Index of Individuals dialog box. You can press the F2 key or click on the Index of Individuals button.

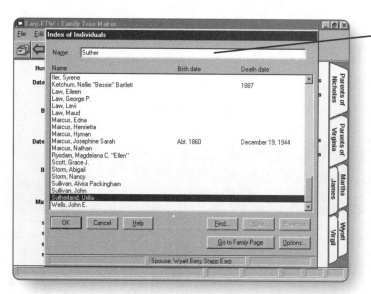

3. Click in the **Name field** and **type** the **surname** (last name) of the person you want to find. Family Tree Maker will move the highlight bar to different possible matches as you type.

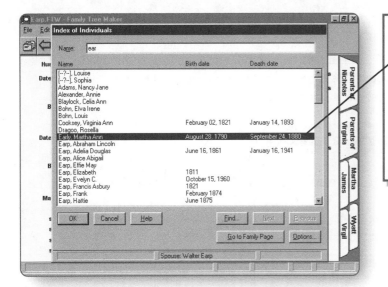

NOTE

Notice that the highlight bar locates and moves to the first name that fits the letters you have entered. It is usually not necessary to type in the complete surname.

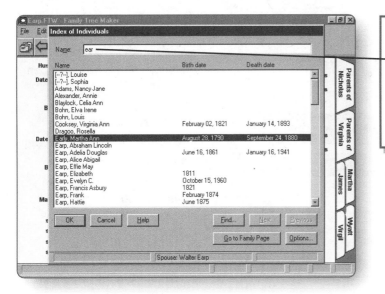

TIP

The Quick Search is not case sensitive. You can type the name in upper-case, lowercase, or mixed case.

Working with the Find Feature

There is a find feature built into the Index of Individuals dialog box. This is an alternative for those times when the Quick Search is not available.

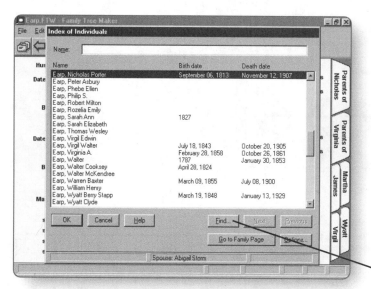

TIP

To find out more about when Quick Search does not work, see the "Rearranging the Index" section later in this chapter.

1. Press the **F2 key**. The Index of Individuals dialog box will open.

2. Click on the **Find button**. The Find Name dialog box will open.

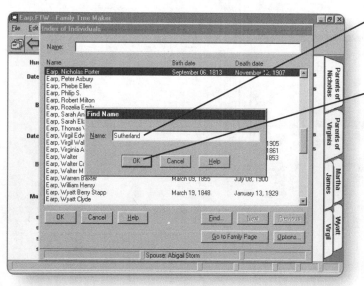

3. In the Name field, **type** the **name** of the individual you want to find.

4. Click on **OK**. The Find Name dialog box will close.

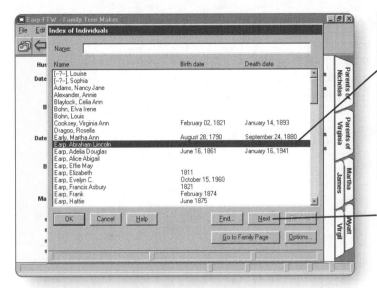

TIP

You do not need to type the entire name. You can type just the surname or the first name and Family Tree Maker will go to the first individual with that name.

5. Click on **Next**. Family Tree Maker will highlight the next individual who fits your search.

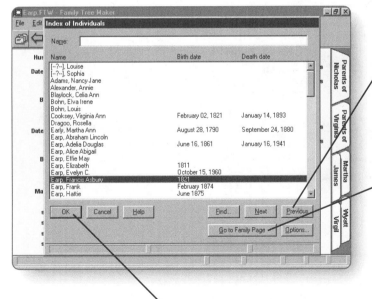

TIP

You can also click on the Previous button, and Family Tree Maker will highlight the previous individual who fit your search.

6. Click on the **Go to Family Page button**. The Index of Individuals dialog box will close and Family Tree Maker will display the Family Page for that individual.

TIP

Another way to go to the individual is to click on the OK button. This opens the last window you worked in for that particular person.

Rearranging the Index

The default arrangement of the Index of Individuals is alphabetical by last name in ascending order. However, you may want to view the list in a different format.

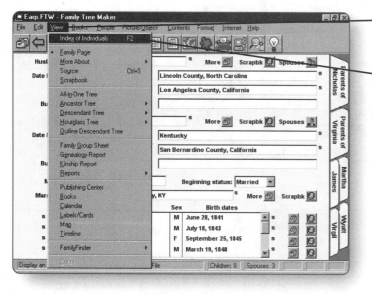

1. Click on **View**. The View menu will appear.

2. Click on **Index of Individuals**. The Index of Individuals dialog box will open.

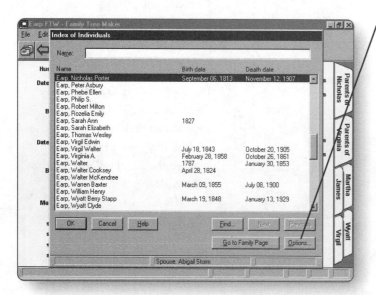

3. Click on **Options**. The Options dialog box will open.

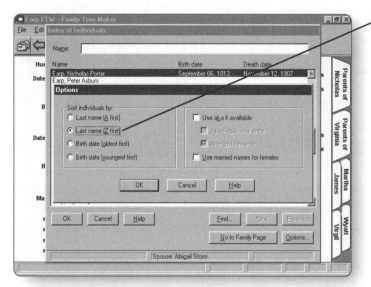

4. Select a different **radio button** in the Sort individuals by list. This will change the order of the Index of Individuals.

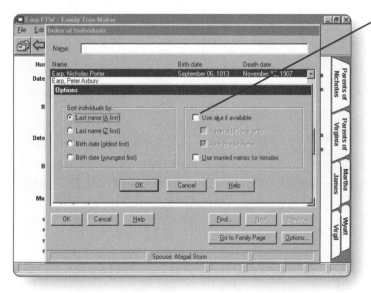

5. Click on the **Use aka if available check box** if you want the also known as name to display in the Index of Individuals.

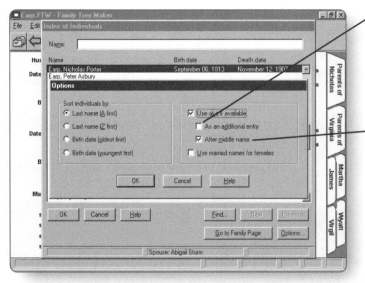

6. Click on the **As an additional entry check box**. Family Tree Maker will create a new entry in the Index using the nickname.

7. Click on the **After middle name check box**. Family Tree Maker will add the nickname to the original Index entry, placing it after the individual's middle name.

NOTE

The aka options are just another way Family Tree Maker allows you to format the Index of Individuals to make it work for you.

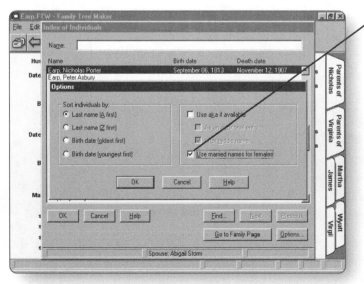

8. Click on the **Use married names for females check box**. Family Tree Maker will change the surname for each female in the Index to display her married surname.

NOTE

Selecting the married names changes all the females in the list, but it offers an easy way to list females for whom you don't have a maiden name.

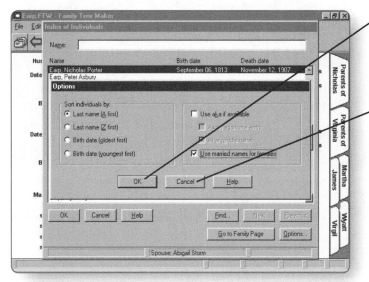

9a. **Click** on **OK**. The Options dialog box will close and your changes will take effect.

OR

9b. **Click** on **Cancel**. The Options dialog box will close, but the changes will not take effect.

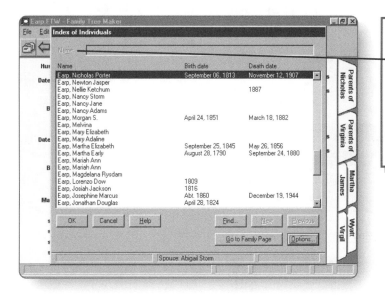

NOTE

If you have changed the sorting criteria to something other than Last name (A first), the Quick Search Name field will be disabled.

Using the Find Individual Feature

While you will often search for an individual by name or by scrolling through the Index of Individuals, Family Tree Maker understands that you might also need to look for individuals in a different manner. This is done using the Find Individual feature.

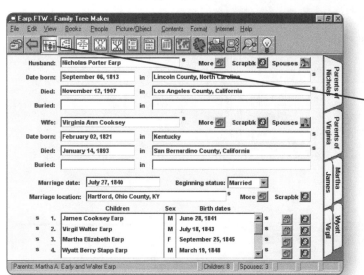

1. Click on the **Family Page button**. The Family Page will appear.

> **NOTE**
> The Find Individual menu option is available only when you are in the Family Page.

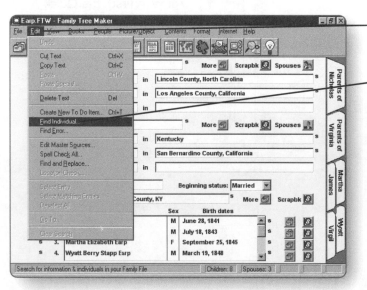

2. Click on **Edit**. The Edit menu will appear.

3. Click on **Find Individual**. The Find Individual dialog box will open.

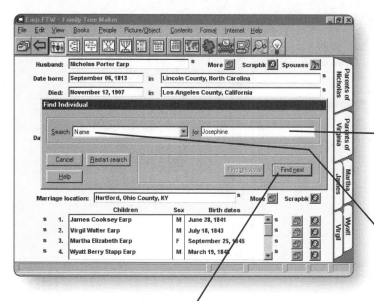

Searching by Name

Of course, you can still use the Find Individual feature to search for an individual by name.

1. **Type** the **name** for which you want to search in the for field.

NOTE

The Find individual dialog box defaults to a Name search.

2. **Click** on the **Find next button**. Family Tree Maker will locate the first individual in the database with the name for which you are searching.

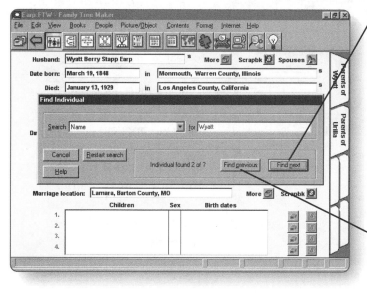

3. **Click** on the **Find next button** again. Family Tree Maker will display the next individual in the database with the name for which you are searching.

TIP

If you accidentally pass the individual you wanted, click on the Find previous button to go back in the search.

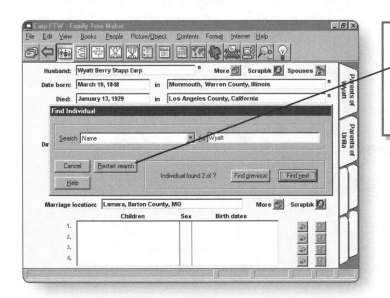

NOTE

You can recreate the same search by clicking on the Restart search button.

Searching by Date

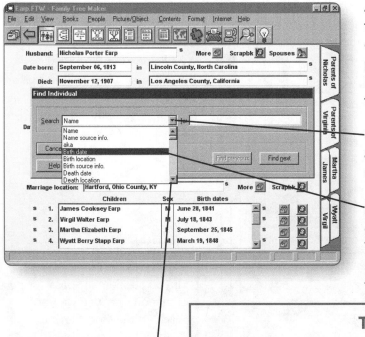

At some point, you might want to determine who in your database was born or married prior to a specific date. The Find Individual feature has the ability to search for dates.

1. Click on the **Search down arrow**. The Search drop-down menu will appear.

2. Click on the **Birth date option** and **press** the **Tab key**. The option will be selected and the cursor will move to the for field.

TIP

To select other search fields, use the scroll bar in the Search drop-down menu.

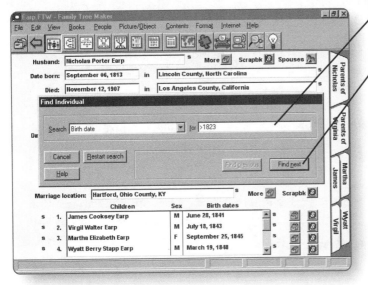

3. Type the **date** in the for field.

4. Click on the **Find next button**. Family Tree Maker will display the first More About Facts window with a date that fits the search criteria.

TIP

Continue to click on the Find next button until you find the individual in whom you are interested.

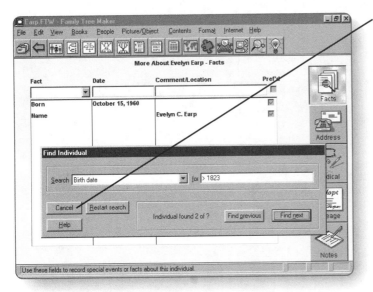

5. Click on **Cancel**. The Find Individual dialog box will close.

TIP

Click on Any and all date fields in the Search drop-down menu to search all events for a given date.

Searching by Location

After names and dates, the item researchers are most interested in is location. The Find Individual feature allows you to search for a specific location.

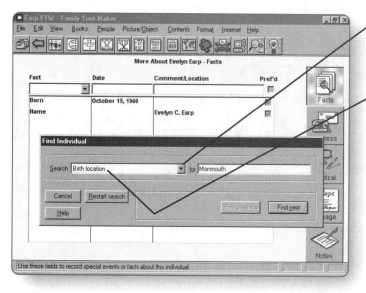

1. Click on the **Search down arrow**. The Search drop-down menu will appear.

2. Click on the **Birth location option** and **press** the **Tab key**. The option will be selected and the cursor will move to the for field.

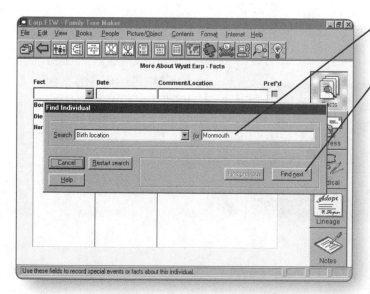

3. Type the **location** in the for field.

4. Click on the **Find next button**. Family Tree Maker will display the Family Page for the first individual who fits the search criteria.

> ### TIP
> Continue to click on the Find Next button until you find the individual in whom you are interested.

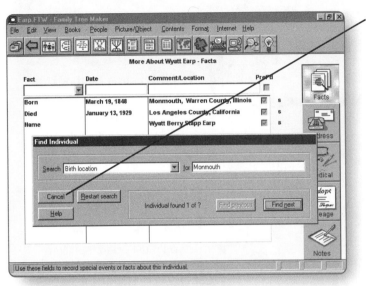

5. Click on **Cancel**. The Find Individual dialog box will close and the Family Page for the last individual found will be displayed.

Searching by Source

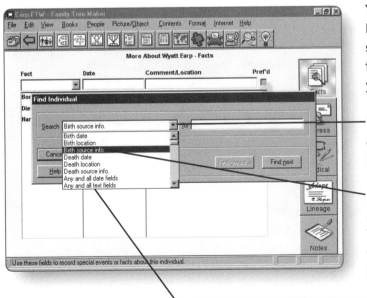

You can also use the Find Individual feature to search for a specific source or to determine for which events and individuals you have cited a source.

1. Click on the **Search down arrow**. The Search drop-down menu will appear.

2. Click on the **Birth source info option** and **press** the **Tab key**. The option will be selected and the cursor will move to the for field.

TIP

Selecting Any and all text fields is a quick way to look through all text fields for a word.

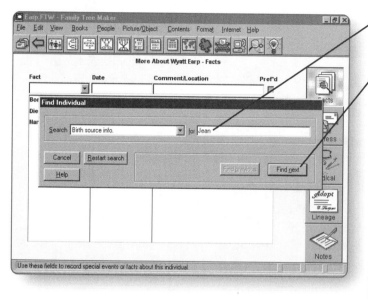

3. Type the **word** you are looking for in the for field.

4. Click on the **Find next button.** Family Tree Maker will display the first individual's record that contains the word for which you are searching.

NOTE

To see the text in question, you must open the More About window and look through the text fields.

Searching by Comment

You might be interested in discovering for which individuals you have entered medical information or other comments. This can be done using the Find Individual feature.

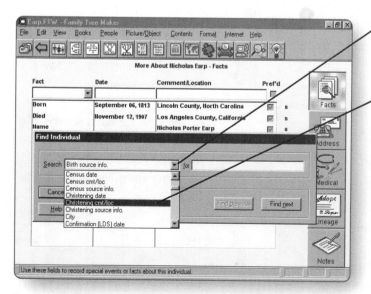

1. Click on the **Search down arrow.** The Search drop-down menu will appear.

2. Click on one of the **comment fields** and **press** the **Tab key.** The comment field you chose will appear in the Search field and the cursor will move to the for field.

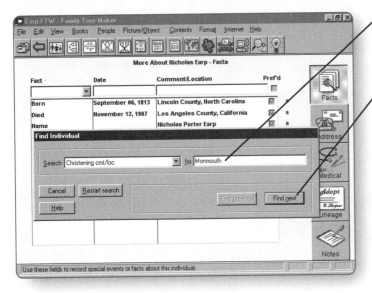

3. In the for field, **enter** the **word** for which you want to search.

4. Click on the **Find next button**. Family Tree Maker will display the Family Page for the first person who fits the search criteria.

TIP

To find comments with any text, replace the word with != and Family Tree Maker will show you everyone who has any text in that comment field.

Working with the FamilyFinder Center

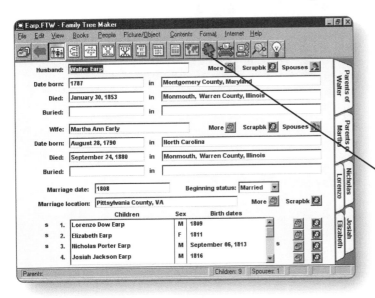

The FamilyFinder Center offers a number of different methods for searching and researching. In this book, we will concentrate on how to use the FamilyFinder Search and view the generated report.

1. Click on the **FamilyFinder Center button**. The FamilyFinder Center will appear.

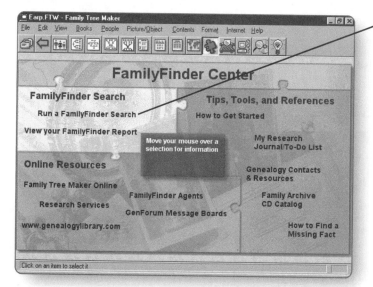

2. Click on **Run a FamilyFinder Search**. A message box will appear, asking you whether you want to create a FamilyFinder Report.

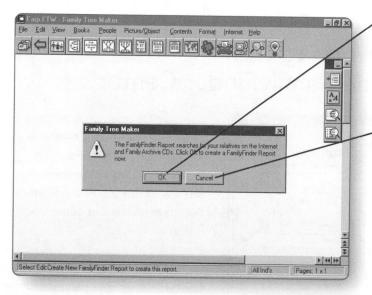

3a. Click on **OK**. The message box will close and the Create New FamilyFinder Report dialog box will open.

OR

3b. Click on **Cancel**. A blank FamilyFinder Report will be displayed.

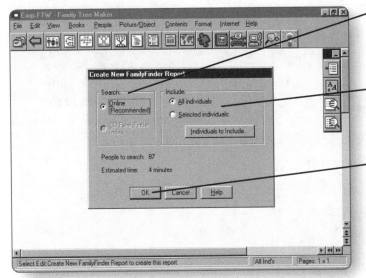

4. **Choose** between **Online** and **CD FamilyFinder Index** in the Search section.

5. **Choose** between **All individuals** and **Selected individuals** in the Include section.

6. **Click** on **OK**. Your browser will launch if you selected the Online option, which is the most thorough. When the search is complete, a message box will appear, telling you how many matches were found.

NOTE

If you click on the Individuals to Include button, the Individuals to Include dialog box will open. You may want to use this option when you have added some new individuals but do not want the report to be rerun for everyone in the family file.

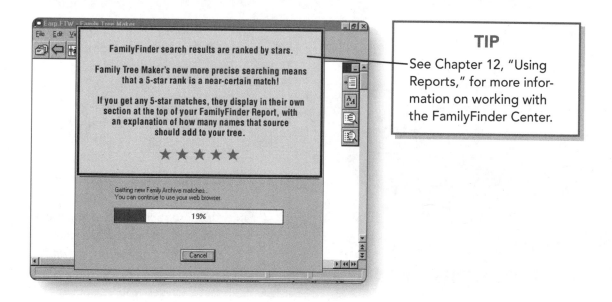

TIP

See Chapter 12, "Using Reports," for more information on working with the FamilyFinder Center.

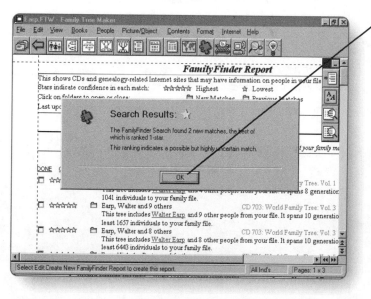

7. Click on **OK**. The FamilyFinder Report will be displayed.

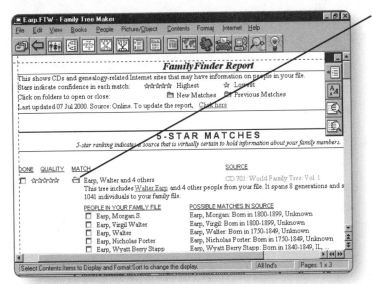

8. Click on the **File Folder** for one of your matches. The FamilyFinder Report will give you more details about the match.

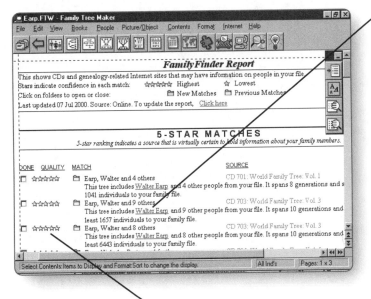

9. Double-click on the **ancestor's name**. The Family Page for that individual will appear.

TIP

The more stars next to an entry, the higher the probability of the match being your ancestor.

9

Correcting Information

In a perfect world, each piece of information you placed in your Family Tree file would be accurate and you would never need to make any changes. However, since no one is infallible when entering data, Family Tree Maker offers ways to undo family relationships, check your spelling, and delete individuals. In this chapter, you'll learn how to:

- Use the spell checker
- Undo a marriage
- Delete individuals from your Family Tree file
- Check for data entry errors

Working with the Family Tree Maker Spell Checker

While we'd like to think we won't make mistakes, there are times when, in typing the details of a will or the place of birth based on a faded record, we might not always get the spelling correct. However, you might not notice the error right away.

Checking Spelling in the Entry Screens

You can ask Family Tree Maker to spell check all the notes and text items in a book from the entry screens and report windows.

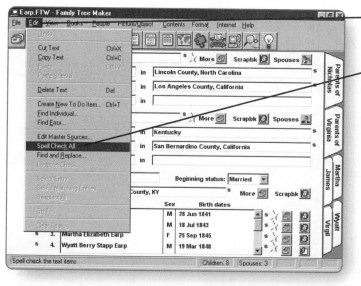

1. Click on **Edit**. The Edit menu will appear.

2. Click on **Spell Check All**. The Spell Check dialog box will open and Family Tree Maker will move to the first More About Notes screen.

NOTE

It is important to understand that the Spell Checker is going to go through all of your More About Notes screen.

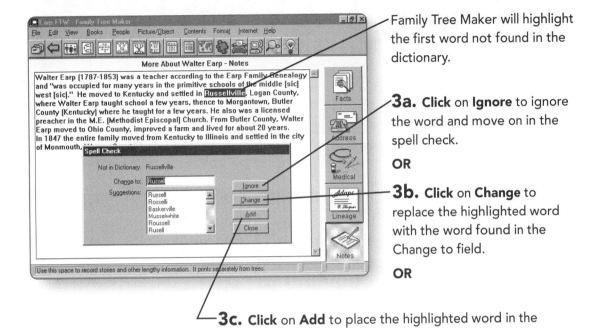

Family Tree Maker will highlight the first word not found in the dictionary.

3a. **Click** on **Ignore** to ignore the word and move on in the spell check.

OR

3b. **Click** on **Change** to replace the highlighted word with the word found in the Change to field.

OR

3c. **Click** on **Add** to place the highlighted word in the dictionary.

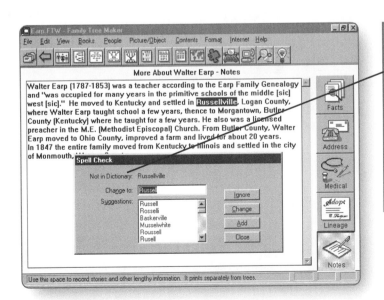

NOTE

When the Spell Checker highlights a word, it does not necessarily mean that the word is misspelled. It simply means that the word is not yet in its dictionary.

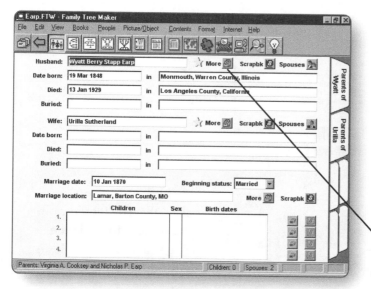

Checking Spelling in the Notes Windows

When you have finished entering details in a More About Note or a More About Marriage Note, you might want to make a habit of running the Spell Checker while you have the Note window open.

1. In the Family Page, **click** on the **More button**. The More About window will appear.

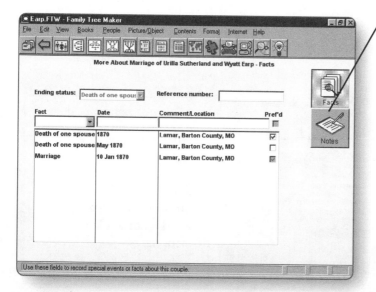

2. Click on the **Notes button**. The More About Notes window will appear.

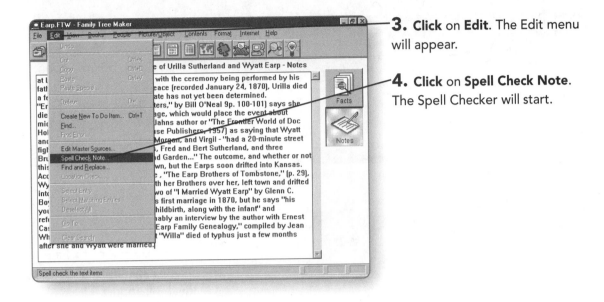

3. Click on **Edit**. The Edit menu will appear.

4. Click on **Spell Check Note**. The Spell Checker will start.

Untying the Marriage Knot

As you continue with your research, you might discover that your information about a marriage is inaccurate. This is especially likely when you get into areas where you have multiple generations of the same name (for instance, John Smith, son of John Smith). Family Tree Maker includes options for undoing a marriage if you discover that the individuals you listed as married are not the correct two people.

1. Click on the **Family Page button**. The Family Page will appear.

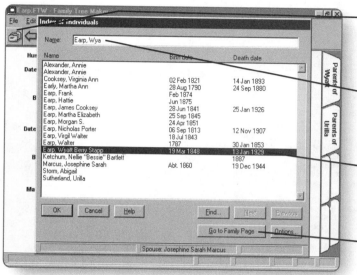

2. **Click** on the **Index of Individuals button**. The Index of Individuals dialog box will open.

3. **Type** the **name** of the individual for whom you need to untie a marriage.

4. **Click** on the correct **individual** in the list, if he or she is not already selected.

5. **Click** on **Go to Family Page**. The Family Page for that individual will appear.

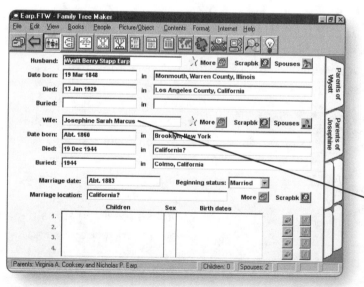

NOTE

You might need to select the appropriate spouse. See Chapter 2, "Entering Information into Family Tree Maker," for a quick review.

6. **Click** in the **Wife field** for the spouse you want to detach.

7. Click on **People**. The People menu will appear.

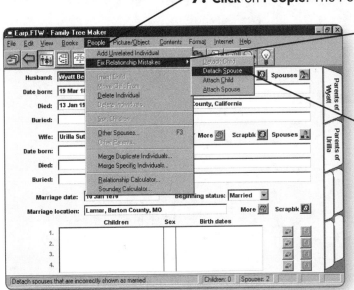

8. Move the **mouse pointer** to Fix Relationship Mistakes. The Fix Relationship Mistakes menu will appear.

9. Click on **Detach Spouse**. Family Tree Maker will open a message box, verifying that you want to detach the spouse.

10. Click on **OK** to confirm this change.

NOTE

Any children associated with the marriage will remain with the spouse that was not detached.

Removing People from Your Files

Detaching a spouse removes the individual from the marriage, but it does not remove the individual from your Family Tree file. However, you might discover that you do have an individual or group that needs to be deleted completely from the database.

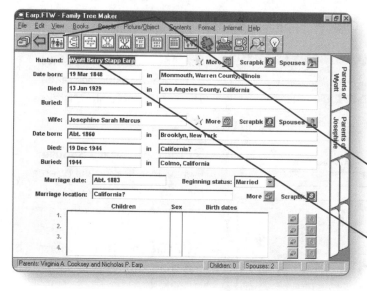

Deleting One Person

When you discover a single individual who should be removed from the database, you can delete that person in the Family Page.

1. Click on the **Family Page button**. The Family Page will appear.

2. Click in the **name field** for the individual you want to delete.

TIP

The individual you want to delete must be listed in the Family Page. Use the Index of Individuals or Find Individual options, if necessary, to select the person you want to delete.

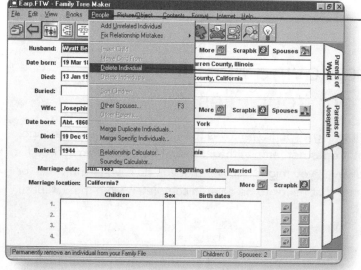

3. Click on **People**. The People menu will appear.

4. Click on **Delete Individual**. A message box will appear, verifying that you want to delete the individual.

5a. Click on **Yes** if you want to delete the individual.

OR

5b. Click on **No** if you do not want to delete the individual.

Deleting a Group of People

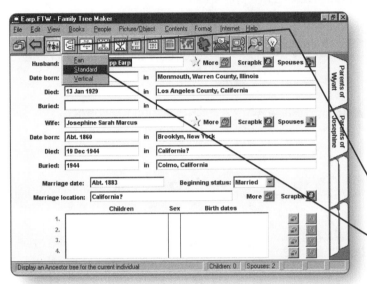

If you want to delete a group of individuals, you can select them in the Tree views and the Custom report. The group of individuals to be deleted must be visible on the report in order for you to delete them as a group.

1. Click on a **tree button**. The selected tree menu will appear.

2. Click on a **tree style**. The appropriate tree window will appear.

TIP

You can use the Custom report to select those individuals not related by blood or descent.

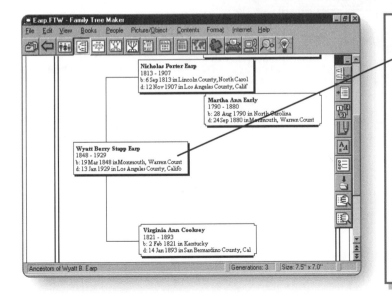

NOTE

Look at the primary person on the report. It is important to verify that the primary person and those related to that person and displayed on the report are indeed the individuals you wish to delete. If the person isn't the individual you want to delete, you can use the Index of Individuals to select a new person.

3. Click on the **Index of Individuals button**. The Index of Individuals dialog box will open.

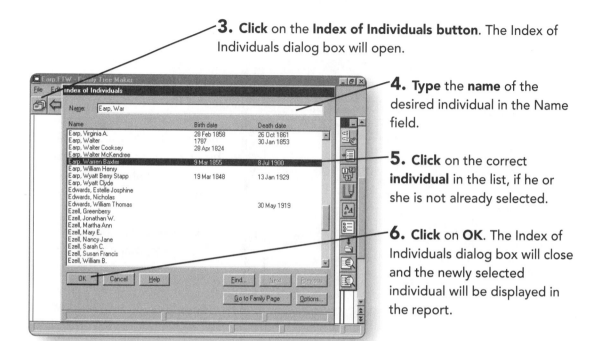

4. Type the **name** of the desired individual in the Name field.

5. Click on the correct **individual** in the list, if he or she is not already selected.

6. Click on **OK**. The Index of Individuals dialog box will close and the newly selected individual will be displayed in the report.

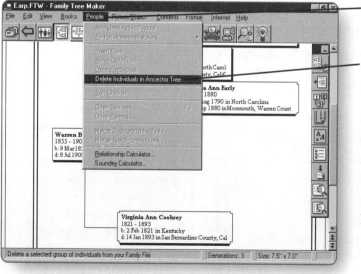

7. Click on **People**. The People menu will appear.

8. Click on **Delete Individuals in Ancestor Tree**. A message box will appear, verifying that you do indeed want to delete the individuals from your Family File. The actual wording of this menu item will differ, depending on the type of report or tree you selected.

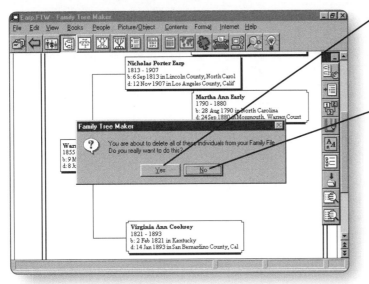

9a. Click on **Yes**. The individuals will be deleted from the Family File.

OR

9b. Click on **No**. The individuals will not be deleted from the Family File.

Checking the Family File for Errors

Family Tree Maker offers you three different ways to scan your Family File for errors. One is automatic, another runs a scan when you request it, and the third is a report of the errors that Family Tree Maker has found.

Data Entry Checking

Family Tree Maker offers a feature that works automatically after it is turned on. This data entry checking feature will let you know when you have entered a questionable date or a name error.

1. Click on **File**. The File menu will appear.

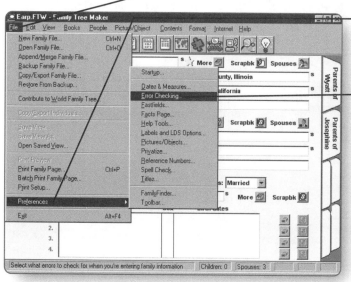

2. Move the **mouse pointer** to Preferences. The Preferences menu will appear.

3. Click on **Error Checking**. The Error Checking dialog box will open.

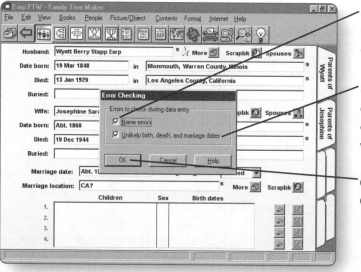

4. Click on the **Name errors check box**. Family Tree Maker will check for name errors.

5. Click on the **Unlikely birth, death, and marriage dates check box**. Family Tree Maker will check for date errors.

6. Click on **OK**. The Error Checking dialog box will close.

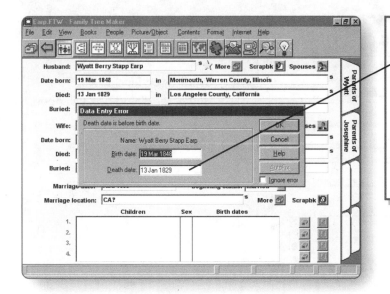

NOTE

When you type in a date that doesn't coincide with the other dates for an individual or family, Family Tree Maker will open a Data Entry Error dialog box to point out the problem.

Using the Find Error Command

The Find Error command is like a spell checker for the dates that have been entered. It will identify the errors and then allow you to fix the error or skip it.

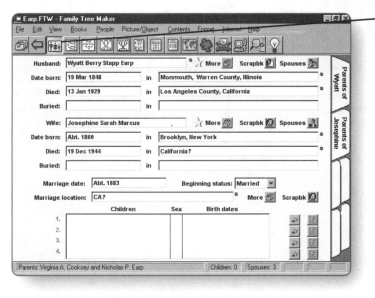

1. Click on the **Family Page button**. The Family Page will appear.

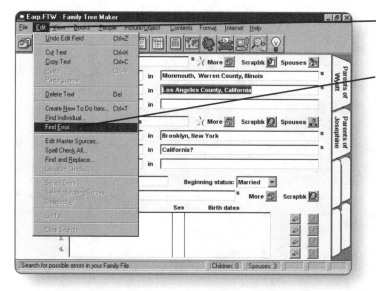

2. Click on **Edit**. The Edit menu will appear.

3. Click on **Find Error**. The Find Error dialog box will open.

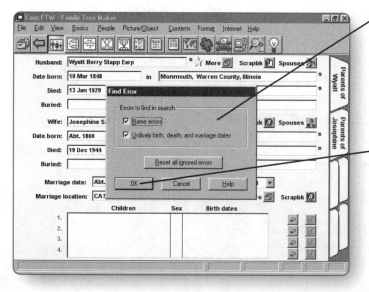

4. Select the **errors** you want to search for. You can search for name errors and/or unlikely birth, death, and marriage dates by selecting the appropriate check boxes.

5. Click on **OK**. Family Tree Maker will search your Family File for errors. When an error is found, you will have several options.

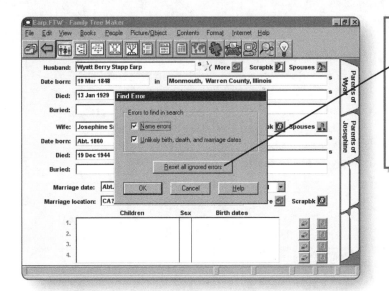

NOTE

The Reset all ignored errors button allows you to overwrite the Ignore Error check box you will be introduced to in the next set of steps.

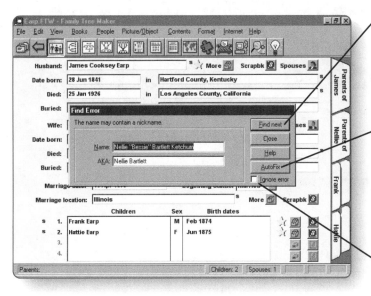

6a. Click on the **Find next button**. Family Tree Maker will bypass the error and find the next one.

OR

6b. Click on the **AutoFix button**. Family Tree Maker will change the error based on where it thinks the information should be placed.

OR

6c. Click on the **Ignore error check box**. Family Tree Maker will ignore the error now (and in the future, if you want it to).

NOTE

If you turn on the Ignore error check box, Family Tree Maker will ignore the error each time you run Find Error, until you click on the Reset all ignored errors button at the start of the Find Error search. The Ignore error check box can be used to have Family Tree Maker bypass those idiosyncrasies unique to the names or dates you are entering.

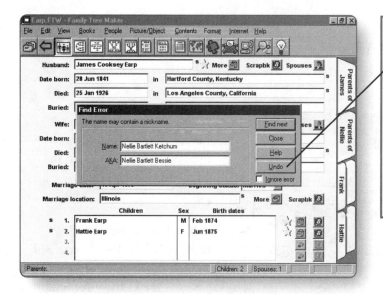

TIP

If you selected AutoFix in error, or if the change made by Family Tree Maker is not correct, click on Undo. If you use the Undo feature, you will not move to the next error until you click on the Find next button.

Working with the Data Errors Report

From time to time it is a good idea to run the Data Errors report. This lists all the potential errors that Family Tree Maker identifies in your Family File. After printing this report, you can take time to read through it and determine what in your Family File you might need to change.

1. Click on **View**. The View menu will appear.

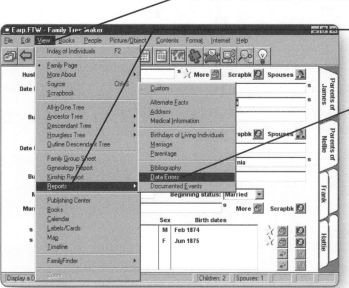

2. Move the **mouse pointer** to Reports. The Reports menu will appear.

3. Click on **Data Errors**. The Data Errors Report window will appear.

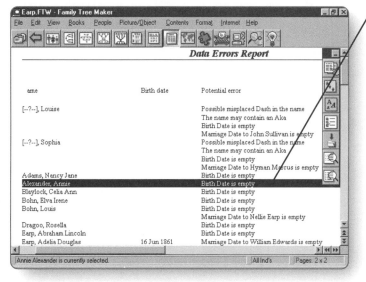

4. Click on an **individual** to highlight that person in the list. Notice the potential error.

5. Double-click on the **individual** to edit his or her information. The Family Page for that individual will appear.

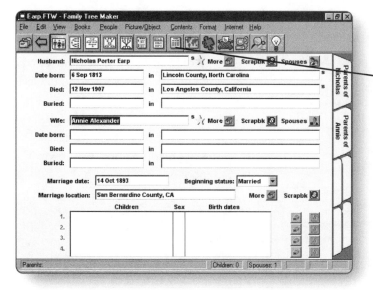

6. Correct the **error** in the Family Page.

7. Click on the **Report button** to return to the Data Errors report to work on the next error. The Data Errors report will reappear.

10

Fixing Relationships and Duplicates

Sometimes after you have imported a relative's GEDCOM (GEnealogical Data COMmunication) or data from Ancestral File®, you will discover that you have some duplicate individuals. At other times you might find that you need to adjust the relationship between a child and the parents. In this chapter, you'll learn how to:

- Link children to their parents
- Detach a child from the wrong parents
- Link individuals by marriage
- Merge duplicates
- Use the Find and Replace feature

Fixing Relationships

There are times when it will be necessary to change the relationships between the individuals in your Family File. Family Tree Maker recognizes that, as your research progresses, you will discover errors in how you have connected individuals in a family structure.

Linking Children to Their Parents

You might discover that you already have a child and his or her parents entered in your Family File, but did not realize they were related when you added them. It's easy to link children to parents in Family Tree Maker.

1. **Click** on the **Family Page button**. The Family Page will appear.

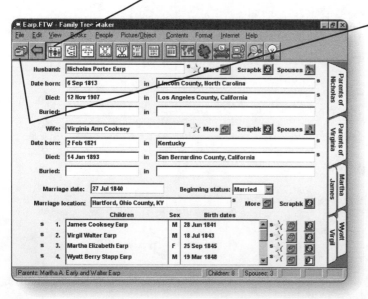

2. **Click** on the **Index of Individuals button**. The Index of Individuals dialog box will open.

TIP

You can also access the Index of Individuals dialog box by pressing F2.

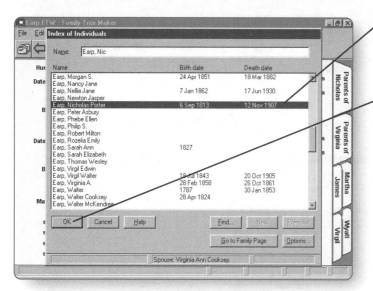

3. Click on the **individual** you want to include on the Family Page.

4. Click on **OK**. The Family Page will show the new individual.

NOTE

The individual you need to select is one of the parents of the child you wish to add.

5. Click on **People**. The People menu will appear.

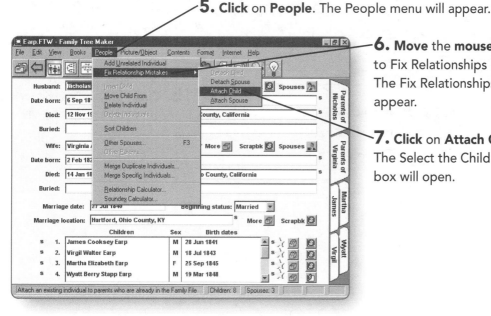

6. Move the **mouse pointer** to Fix Relationships Mistakes. The Fix Relationships menu will appear.

7. Click on **Attach Child**. The Select the Child dialog box will open.

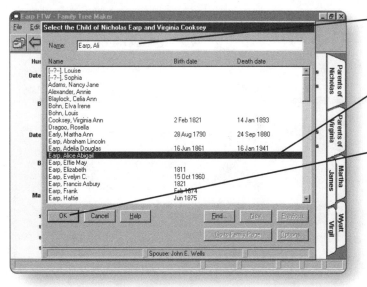

8. Type the **name** of the individual you want to add as a child.

9. Click on the **name** of the individual in the list.

10. Click on **OK**. A message box will appear, verifying that you want to attach the individual as a child on the Family Page.

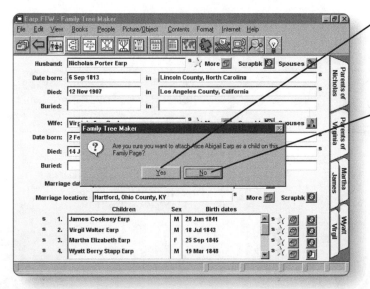

11a. Click on **Yes**. The child will be added to the Family Page.

OR

11b. Click on **No**. The child will not be added to the Family Page.

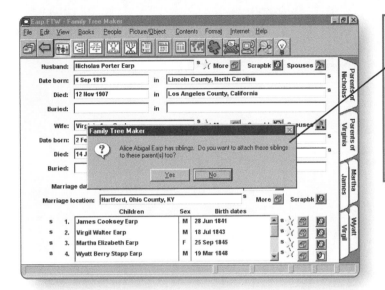

NOTE

If the child in question had siblings from another relationship, Family Tree Maker will ask whether the siblings should also be associated with the new parents.

Detaching a Child from the Wrong Parents

If you discover that a child has been linked to the wrong parents, you can easily detach the child from that family. This will not delete the child from the Family File.

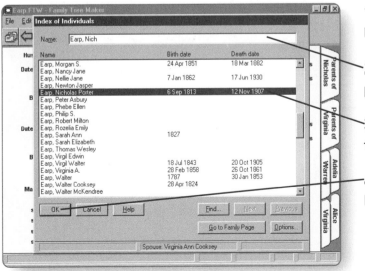

1. Press F2. The Index of Individuals dialog box will open.

2. Type the **name** of one of the parents in the Name field.

3. Click on the correct **name** in the list.

4. Click on **OK**. The family will be displayed in the Family Page.

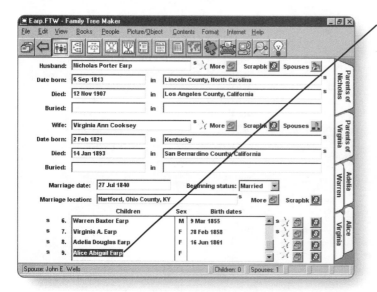

5. Click on the **child** you want to detach in the Children section.

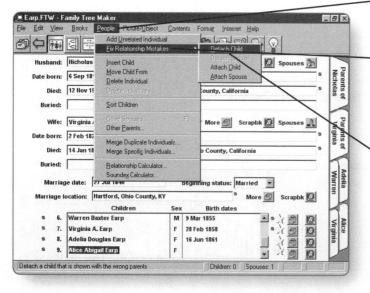

6. Click on **People**. The People menu will appear.

7. Move the **mouse pointer** to Fix Relationship Mistakes. The Fix Relationships menu will appear.

8. Click on **Detach Child**. A message box will appear, verifying that you want to detach the selected individual from his or her parents.

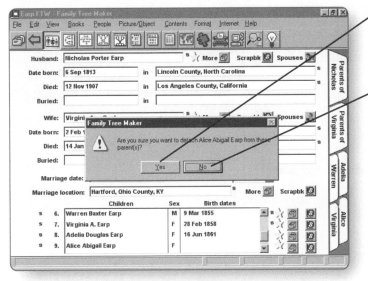

9a. Click on **Yes**. The siblings of the child will also be detached.

OR

9b. Click on **No**. The siblings of the child will not be detached.

Linking Individuals by Marriage

Unlike typing in the names of two spouses in the Family Page, the steps for linking two previously entered individuals require picking one of the individuals out of a list.

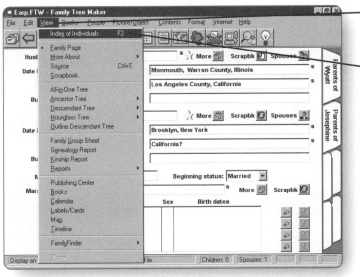

1. Click on **View**. The View menu will appear.

2. Click on **Index of Individuals**. The Index of Individuals dialog box will open.

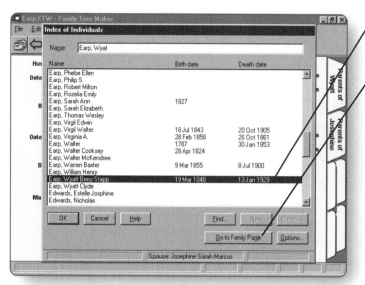

3. Click on the **individual** you want as one of the spouses.

4. Click on **Go to Family Page**. The Family Page will appear.

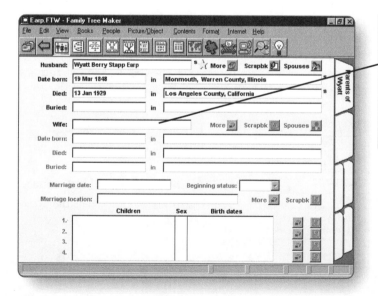

NOTE

There must be a place for the spouse to go. That means that in the Family Page, the spouse field must be empty.

5. Click on **People**. The People menu will appear.

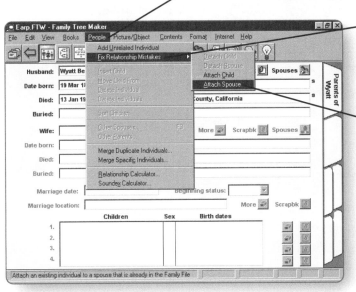

6. Move the **mouse pointer** to Fix Relationship Mistakes. The Fix Relationships menu will appear.

7. Click on **Attach Spouse**. The Select the spouse dialog box will open.

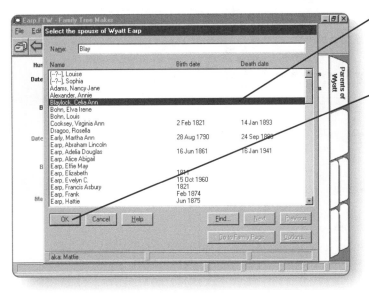

8. Click on the **name** of the individual you want to select as the spouse.

9. Click on **OK**. A message box will appear, asking if you're sure you want to make the selected individual the spouse.

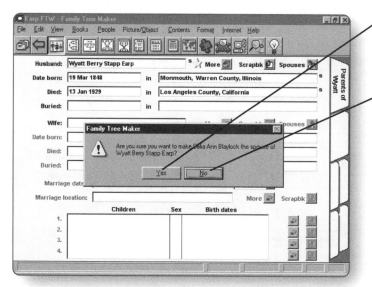

10a. **Click** on **Yes**. The spouse will be attached.

OR

10b. **Click** on **No**. The spouse will not be attached.

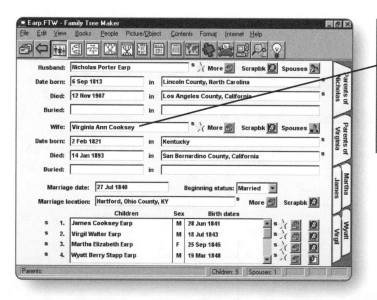

TIP

If the individual in question already has a spouse, you need to use the Spouses button to be able to add the spouse.

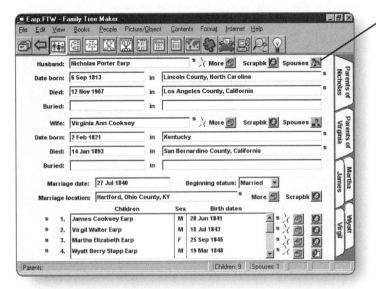

11. Click on the **Spouses button**. The Spouses of dialog box will open.

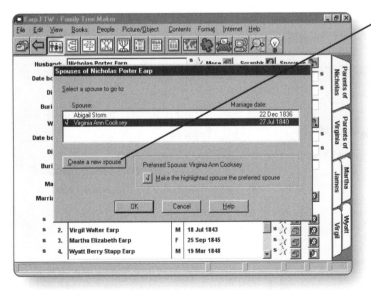

12. Click on the **Create a new spouse button**. A message box will appear, asking if you want to attach the children of the individual to the new spouse.

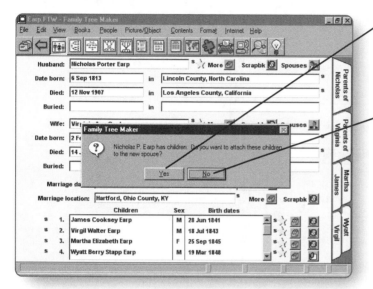

13a. Click on **Yes**. The children of the individual will be attached to the new spouse.

OR

13b. Click on **No**. The children of the individual will not be attached to the new spouse.

14. Click on **People**. The People menu will appear.

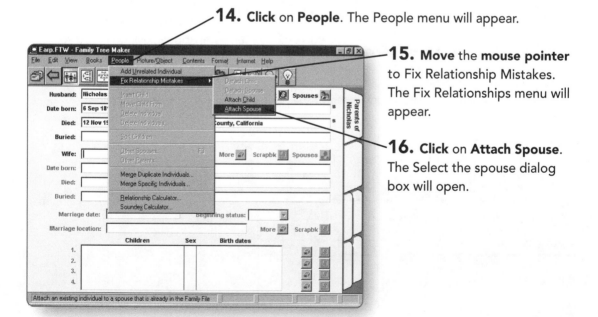

15. Move the **mouse pointer** to Fix Relationship Mistakes. The Fix Relationships menu will appear.

16. Click on **Attach Spouse**. The Select the spouse dialog box will open.

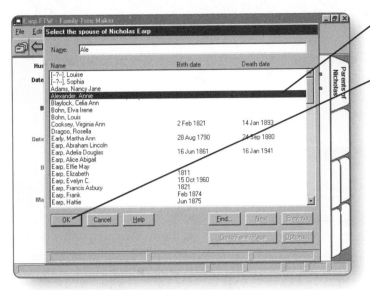

17. **Click** on the **name** of the spouse in the list.

18. Click on **OK**. A message box will appear, asking you whether you are sure you want to make the selected individual the spouse.

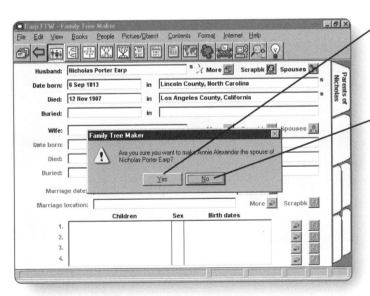

19a. Click on **Yes**. The selected individual will be added as a spouse.

OR

19b. Click on **No**. The selected individual will not be added as a spouse.

Fixing Duplicates

Often, when you are adding information from a fellow researcher, you will end up with duplicate individuals in your Family File. Sometimes the duplication is the result of entering an individual twice.

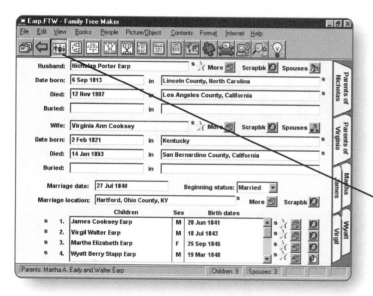

Fixing Duplicate Files

Family Tree Maker offers a method to merge individuals that looks not only at the name, but also at additional information, such as family relationships.

1. Click on the **Family Page button**. The Family Page will appear.

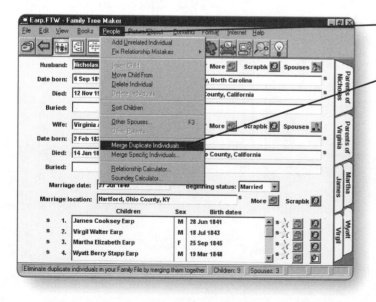

2. Click on **People**. The People menu will appear.

3. Click on **Merge Duplicate Individuals**. A message box will appear, reminding you to back up your file before you merge duplicate individuals.

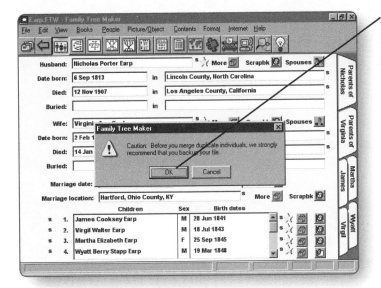

4. Click on **OK**. The Merge Duplicate Individuals dialog box will open.

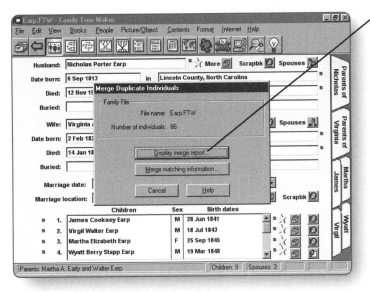

5. Click on **Display merge report**. The Merge Individuals Report dialog box will open.

NOTE

If Family Tree Maker cannot find duplicates, a message box will appear, telling you that none were found.

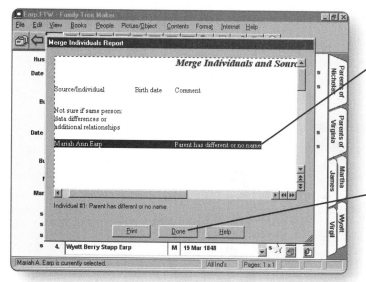

TIP

You can click on an individual in the list to get additional information about the differences between the two possible duplicates.

6. Click on **Done**. The Merge Duplicate Individuals dialog box will open.

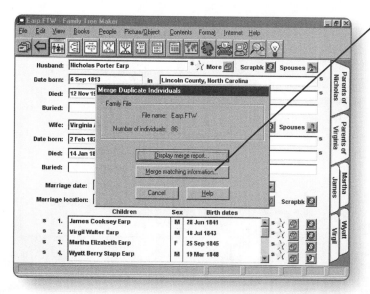

7. Click on **Merge matching information**. The Merge Individuals dialog box will open.

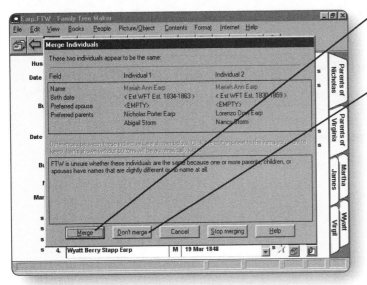

8a. **Click** on **Merge**. The two individuals will be merged.

OR

8b. **Click** on **Don't merge**. The two individuals will not be merged.

NOTE

Family Tree Maker automatically merges two individuals with the same information. You are given the option of whether to merge two individuals with differing information.

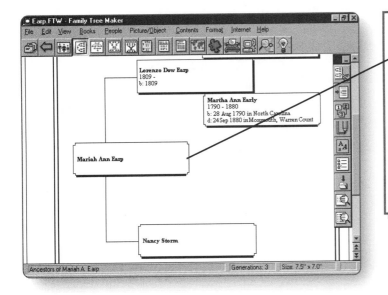

TIP

Be sure to view the individuals in the various views to verify that everything is correct. If it's not, you can use the Undo option to undo the merge. You must do this before you exit Family Tree Maker.

Merging Specific Individuals

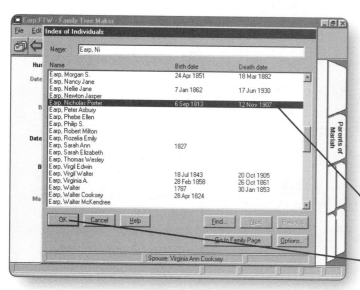

There are times when you will want total control over the individuals you want to merge. You gain this control using the Merge Specific Individuals menu option.

1. Press F2. The Index of Individuals dialog box will open.

2. Select one **individual** of those you wish to merge.

3. Click on **OK**. The Family Page will open.

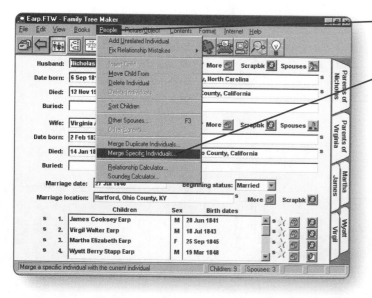

4. Click on **People**. The People menu will appear.

5. Click on **Merge Specific Individuals**. The Select the individual who is the same as dialog box will open.

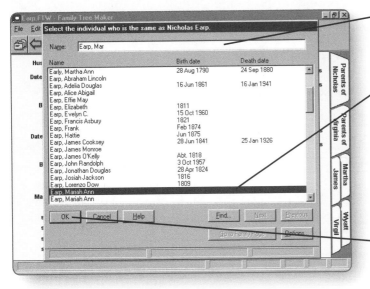

6. Enter the **name** of the second individual in the Name field.

7. Click on the **name** of the person with whom you wish to merge the first individual.

8. Click on **OK**. A message box will appear, verifying that the individuals should be merged.

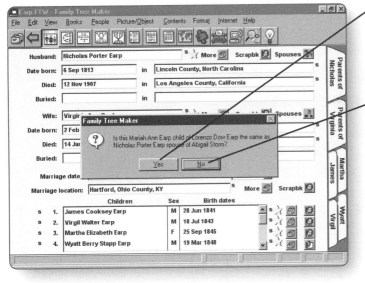

9a. Click on **Yes**. The two individuals will be merged.

OR

9b. Click on **No**. The two individuals will not be merged.

Using Global Search and Replace

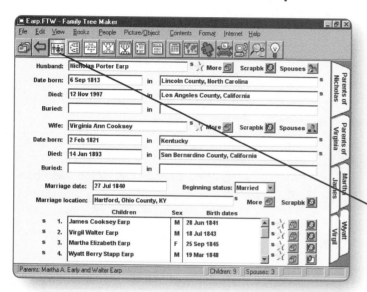

There will be times when you will discover that you have consistently misspelled a word or phrase. The Find and Replace feature allows you to have Family Tree Maker search for the wrong word or phrase and replace it with the correct word or phrase.

1. Click on the **Family Page button**. The Family Page will appear.

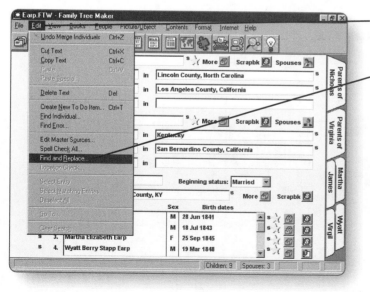

2. Click on **Edit**. The Edit menu will appear.

3. Click on **Find and Replace**. The Find and Replace dialog box will open.

4. In the Find field, **enter** the **word or phrase** you want to find.

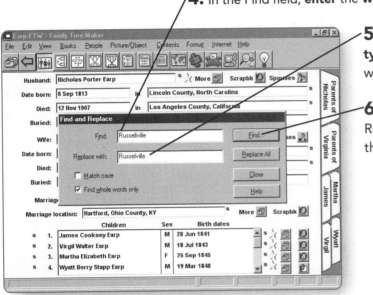

5. In the Replace with field, **type** the **word or phrase** with which you want to replace it.

6. Click on **Find**. The Find and Replace dialog box will show the first match.

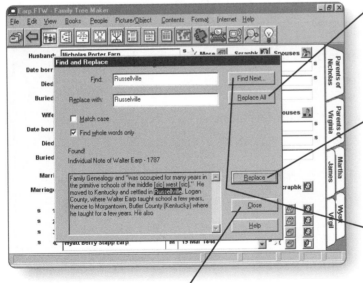

7a. Click on **Replace All**. Family Tree Maker will replace all occurrences of the Find word with the Replace word.

OR

7b. Click on **Replace**. Family Tree Maker will replace just that particular occurrence of the Find word with the Replace word.

OR

7c. Click on **Find Next**. Family Tree Maker will ignore the current occurrence and look for the next match.

8. Click on **Close**. Family Tree Maker will close the Find and Replace dialog box.

Part III Review Questions

1. How can you access the Index of Individuals? *See "Using Quick Search by Name" in Chapter 8*

2. What are the four ways you can arrange the index? *See "Rearranging the Index" in Chapter 8*

3. What are the other ways you can search for an individual in your Family File? *See "Using the Find Individual Feature" in Chapter 8*

4. How can you search for online research using Family Tree Maker? *See "Working with the FamilyFinder Center" in Chapter 8*

5. What are the two ways you can run the spell checker in Family Tree Maker? *See "Working with the Family Tree Maker Spell Checker" in Chapter 9*

6. How can you delete an individual from your Family File? *See "Deleting One Person" in Chapter 9*

7. What are the three ways you can check your Family File for errors? *See "Checking the Family File for Errors" in Chapter 9*

8. How can you link a child to parents? *See "Linking Children to Their Parents" in Chapter 10*

9. What two ways can you merge duplicate individuals in your Family File? *See "Fixing Duplicates" in Chapter 10*

10. How can you do a global search and replace of a word or phrase? *See "Using Global Search and Replace" in Chapter 10*

PART IV

Visualizing Your Family in Family Tree Maker

Chapter 11
  Managing Tree Reports
  in Family Tree Maker 193

Chapter 12
  Working with Reports. 211

Chapter 13
  Viewing and Printing
  Reports and Trees. 227

Chapter 14
  Creating Genealogy Style and
  Genealogical Reports 239

11

Managing Tree Reports in Family Tree Maker

After you have entered information about your family into Family Tree Maker, you will want to display that information in different formats. Family Tree Maker offers a number of different trees that show you ancestors, descendants, or both for a selected individual. In this chapter, you'll learn how to:

- Display Ancestor Trees
- Display Hourglass Trees
- Display Descendant Trees
- Display All-in-One Trees
- Enhance the tree views

Displaying Ancestor Trees

Ancestor Trees allow you to see how many direct line generations you have been able to carry your research back from a selected individual. Family Tree Maker offers three different versions of the Ancestor Tree.

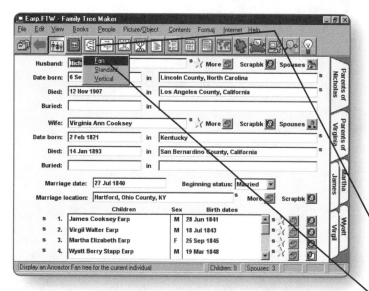

Creating Fan Charts

The fan chart of an Ancestor Tree begins with the selected individual. It then displays all the ancestors—parents, grandparents, great grandparents, and so on. You can control how the chart looks and how many generations to include.

1. Click on the **Ancestor Tree button**. The Ancestor Tree menu will appear.

2. Click on **Fan**. The fan chart will appear.

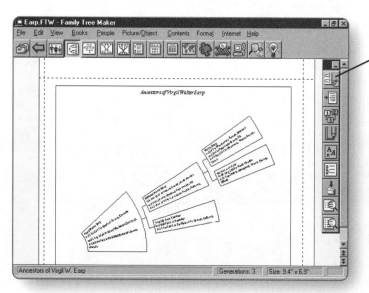

3. Click on the **Format button**. The Format for Ancestor Tree dialog box will open.

TIP

Family Tree Maker allows you to change the format of the chart with the tool bar along the right side of the tree.

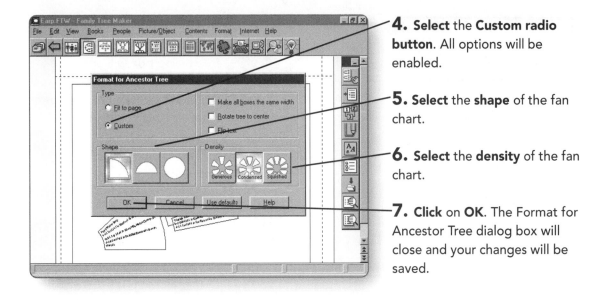

4. Select the **Custom radio button**. All options will be enabled.

5. Select the **shape** of the fan chart.

6. Select the **density** of the fan chart.

7. Click on **OK**. The Format for Ancestor Tree dialog box will close and your changes will be saved.

Creating a Pedigree Chart

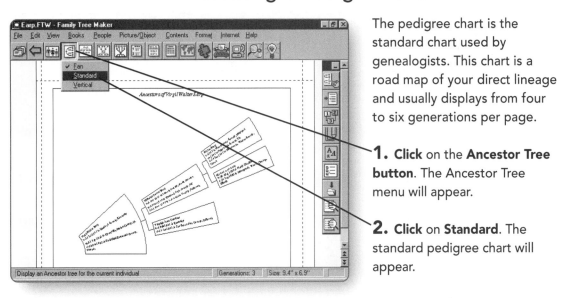

The pedigree chart is the standard chart used by genealogists. This chart is a road map of your direct lineage and usually displays from four to six generations per page.

1. Click on the **Ancestor Tree button**. The Ancestor Tree menu will appear.

2. Click on **Standard**. The standard pedigree chart will appear.

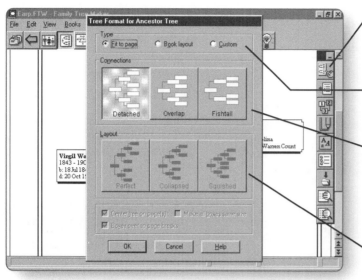

3. **Click** on the **Format button**. The Tree Format for Ancestor Tree dialog box will open.

4. **Select** the **type of pedigree chart** you want to display.

5. **Select** the **type of connections** you want to use in the chart.

NOTE

The Layout options are only active when you select the Custom type.

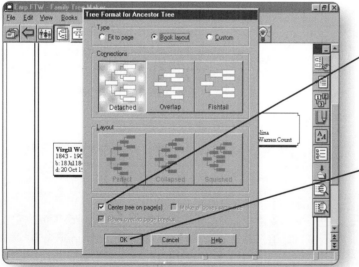

TIP

When selecting the Book layout type, you can elect to have each tree centered on the page.

6. **Click** on **OK**. The Tree Format for Ancestor Tree dialog box will close and your changes will be saved.

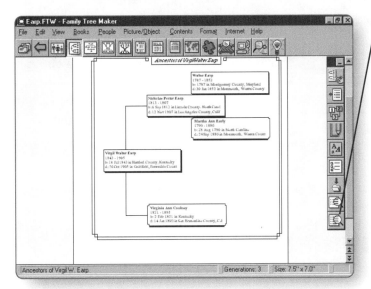

7. **Click** on the **Zoom Out button**. You will see more of the tree.

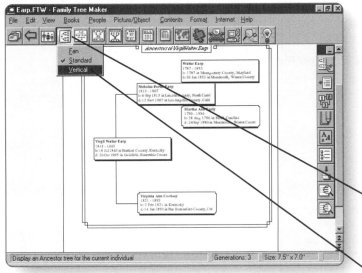

Creating a Vertical Ancestor Tree

The Vertical Ancestor Tree is a box-style chart. It starts at the bottom of a page or set of pages and goes up, showing the ancestors of the selected individual.

1. **Click** on the **Ancestor Tree button**. The Ancestor Tree menu will appear.

2. **Click** on **Vertical**. The Vertical Ancestor Tree will appear.

TIP

You can change what information is included in the boxes for each of the individuals.

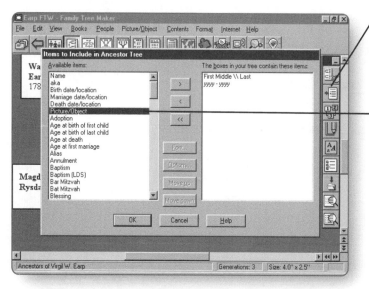

3. Click on the **Items to Include button**. The Items to Include in Ancestor Tree dialog box will open.

4. Click on an **item** in the Available items list.

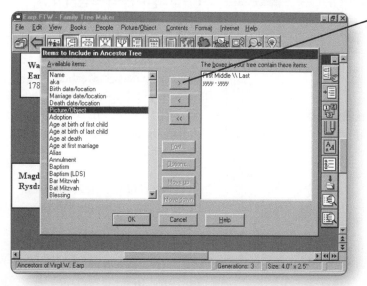

5. Click on the **inclusion button**. The item will move to the The boxes in your tree contain these items list.

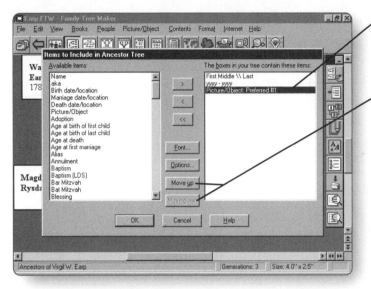

6. Click on an **item** in the The boxes in your tree contain these items list.

7. Click on the **Move Up or Move Down buttons**. The item will be moved to a new position.

> **TIP**
>
> The order in which the items appear in the The boxes in your tree contain these items list is the order in which they will appear in the boxes of the tree.

Displaying Hourglass Trees

Hourglass Trees allow you to view not only the ancestors, but also the descendants of the selected individual. The individual is in the center with the ancestors opening above and the descendants opening below, looking much like an hourglass.

Working with Fan Format

Like other fan-styled trees, the Hourglass Tree in fan format takes advantage of the fan shape. Keep in mind that with a large lineage, the fan style will use up a lot of paper.

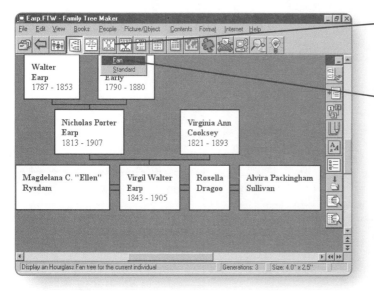

1. Click on the **Hourglass Tree button**. The Hourglass Tree menu will appear.

2. Click on **Fan**. The fan format of the Hourglass Tree will appear.

TIP

If the primary individual isn't the one that you want, you can use the Index of Individuals dialog box to select a different individual. See Chapter 8, "Searching Your Family Tree File," to review.

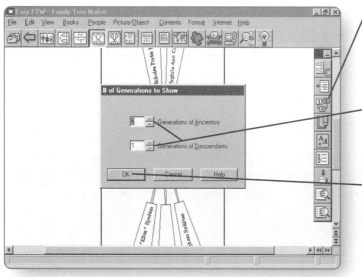

3. Click on the **Number of Generations button**. The # of Generations to Show dialog box will open.

4. Use the **arrows** to select the number of ancestors and descendants desired.

5. Click on **OK**. The # of Generations to Show dialog box will close.

Working with Standard Format

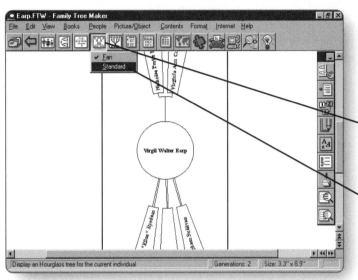

The standard format of the Hourglass Tree uses a box chart. The boxes can be as big or as small as you want, depending on the information you include.

1. Click on the **Hourglass Tree button**. The Hourglass Tree menu will appear.

2. Click on **Standard**. The standard format of the Hourglass Tree will appear.

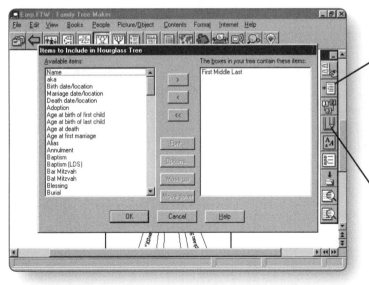

TIP

You can determine the events and comments included in each box; simply click on the Items to Include button.

3. Click on the **Box, Line, & Border Styles button**. The Styles for Hourglass Tree dialog box will open.

4a. Click on the **Boxes tab** to access style and color options for the boxes.

OR

4b. Click on the **Borders tab** to access style and color options for the border of the tree.

OR

4c. Click on the **Lines tab** to access style and color options for the lines connecting the boxes.

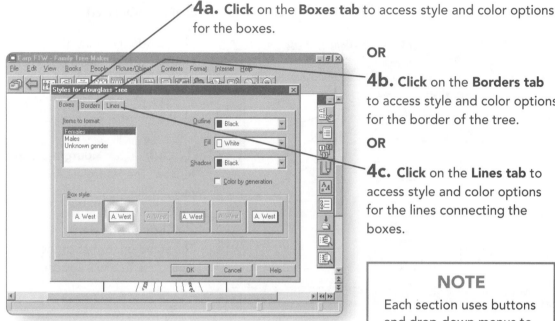

NOTE

Each section uses buttons and drop-down menus to make the selections available.

Displaying Descendant Trees

There will be times when you want to view the descendants of a given ancestor. Some research projects will require tracing the children and grandchildren. Descendant Trees allow you to see these in a simple format.

Creating a Standard Tree

As with the other trees you have looked at, there is a standard Descendant Tree. This standard tree is often known as a box chart. It details the descendants of a selected individual.

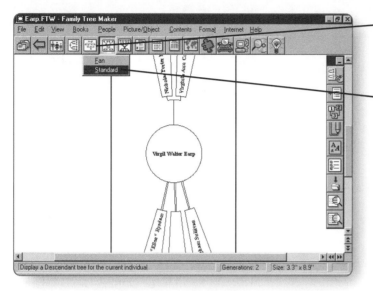

1. **Click** on the **Descendant Tree button**. The Descendant Tree menu will appear.

2. **Click** on **Standard**. The standard format of the Descendant Tree will appear.

Creating an Outline Tree

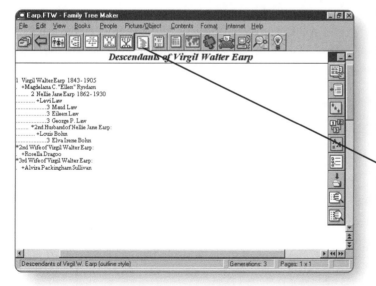

When you're working with the descendants of a given individual, Family Tree Maker offers an outline, or indented, tree. Each generation is indented, making it easy to distinguish them.

1. **Click** on the **Outline Descendant Tree button**. The outline report will appear.

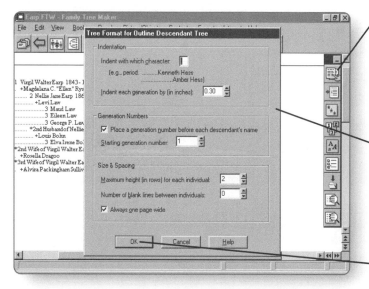

2. **Click** on the **Format button**. The Tree Format for Outline Descendant Tree dialog box will open.

NOTE

This dialog box allows you to change the indent character as well as the size and spacing.

3. **Click** on **OK**. The Tree Format for Outline Descendant Tree dialog box will close.

Displaying All-in-One Trees

You might want to view all the individuals in your database. Family Tree Maker makes this possible with the All-in-One Tree.

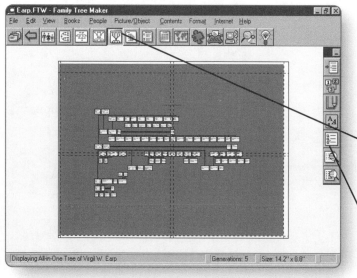

Creating an All-in-One Tree

The All-in-One Tree is easily created because Family Tree Maker does all the hard work.

1. **Click** on the **All-in-One Tree button**. The All-in-One Tree will appear.

2. **Click** on the **Options button**. The Options for All-in-One Tree dialog box will open.

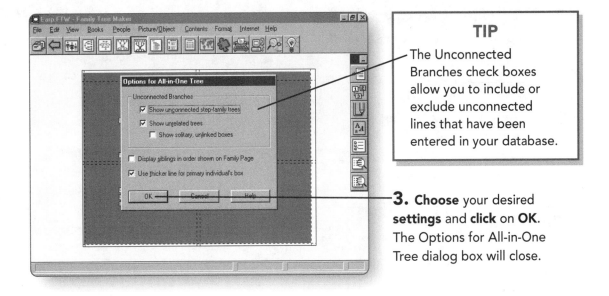

TIP

The Unconnected
Branches check boxes
allow you to include or
exclude unconnected
lines that have been
entered in your database.

3. Choose your desired
settings and **click** on **OK**.
The Options for All-in-One
Tree dialog box will close.

Setting Display Size

Because the All-in-One Tree displays all the individuals in your
database, its size can be cumbersome. Customizing the display
size can make it easier to understand the true scope of this view.

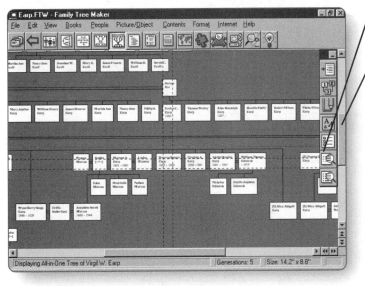

1. Click on the **Zoom In button**.
The All-in-One view will zoom in.

2. Use the **scroll bar** to see
the boxes not currently on the
screen.

TIP

You can also use the View
menu to select the Zoom
option you want. To see
the entire All-in-One Tree,
choose Size to Window.

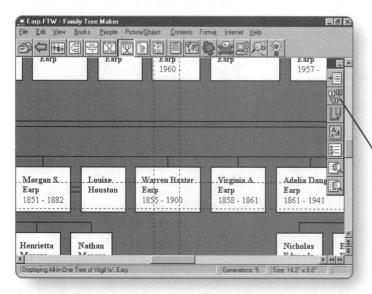

Pruning the Display

In addition to excluding the unrelated trees, you can control the number of generations included in the tree.

1. **Click** on the **Number of Generations button**. The # of Generations to Show dialog box will open.

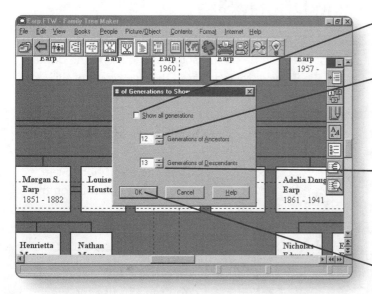

2. **Click** on the **Show all generations check box** to clear it.

3. **Use** the **arrows** in the Generations of Ancestors field to select the number of generations of ancestors.

4. **Use** the **arrows** in the Generations of Descendants field to select the number of generations of descendants.

5. **Click** on **OK**. The # of Generations to Show dialog box will close and the changes will appear on the tree.

Enhancing Tree Views

There are different ways to enhance the appearance of the different trees. With colors and different box styles you can make different lineages or genders stand out.

Emphasizing Relationships

With line styles and colors you can make a particular relationship clearer on a tree.

1. Click on the **Box, Line, & Border Styles button**. The Styles dialog box will open.

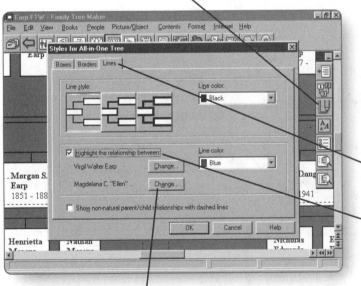

2. Click on the **Lines tab**. The Lines tab will move to the front.

3. Click on the **Highlight the relationship between check box** to select or deselect it. A check mark will appear when you select this option and will disappear when you deselect this option.

4. Click on the **Change button** to change one of the individuals currently selected. The Index of Individuals dialog box will open, and will include a list of those individuals already included in the tree.

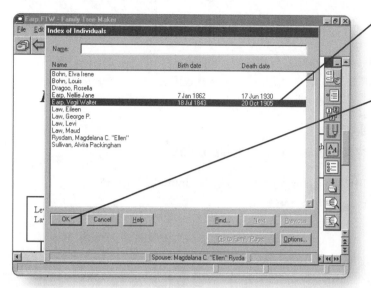

5. Click on the desired **individual** in the list. Your selection will be highlighted.

6. Click on **OK**. The Index of Individuals dialog box will close.

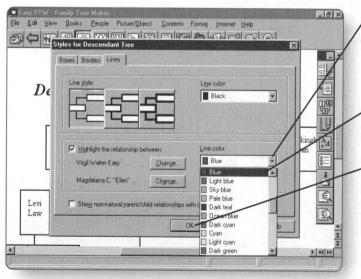

7. Click on the **Line color down arrow**. The Line color drop-down menu will appear.

8. Click on a **color**. The color will be selected.

9. Click on **OK**. The Styles dialog box will close and your changes will be saved.

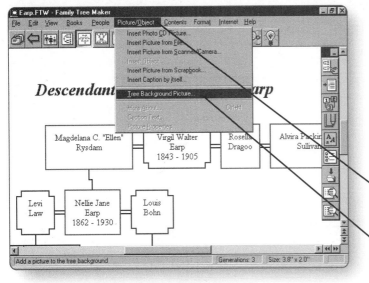

Adding a Background Image

Enhancing the overall appearance of your tree can be interesting and fun. One way to enhance your tree is to place a picture in the background.

1. Click on **Picture/Object**. The Picture/Object menu will appear.

2. Click on **Tree Background Picture**. The Background Picture dialog box will open.

3. Click on the **Display picture in background check box**. The option will be selected.

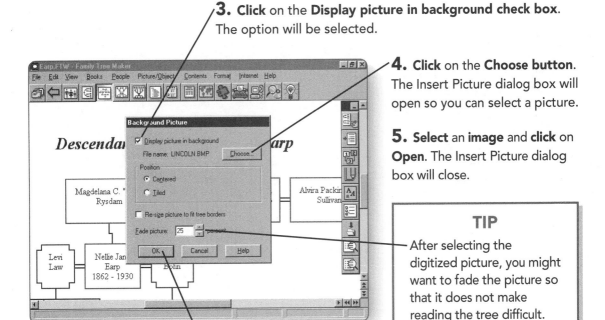

4. Click on the **Choose button**. The Insert Picture dialog box will open so you can select a picture.

5. Select an **image** and **click** on **Open**. The Insert Picture dialog box will close.

TIP

After selecting the digitized picture, you might want to fade the picture so that it does not make reading the tree difficult.

---

6. Click on **OK**. The Background Picture dialog box will close and the picture will appear in the background of the report.

12

Working with Reports

In addition to its many trees, Family Tree Maker also includes a number of other reports that allow you to understand what you have in your database and how the individuals may be related. In this chapter, you'll learn how to:

- Create a custom report
- Create a kinship report
- Create an address report
- Create a birthday report
- Use the Research Journal

Creating a Custom Report

Just as the name states, custom reports allow you to control the individuals and information included in reports.

1. Click on the **Report button**. The Report window will appear.

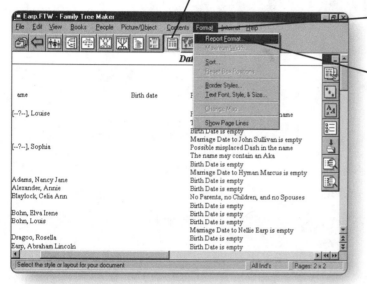

2. Click on **Format**. The Format menu will appear.

3. Click on **Report Format**. The Report Format dialog box will open.

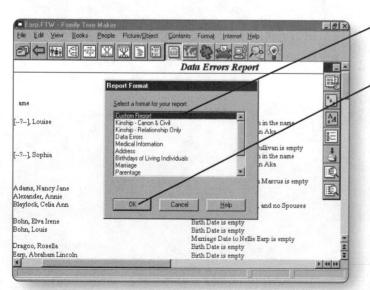

4. Click on **Custom Report**. The option will be selected.

5. Click on **OK**. The Report Format dialog box will close.

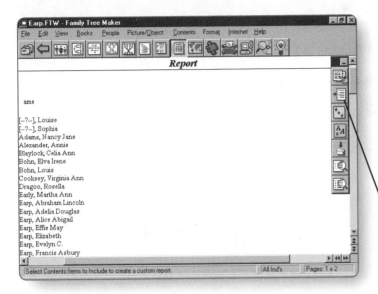

Adding Items to Include in Your Report

The custom report may not contain the information you want to include. However, this report is easy to adjust.

1. Click on the **Items to Include button**. The Items to Include in Report dialog box will open.

2. In the Available items list, **click** on an **item** that you want to include.

3. Click on the **Add button**. The item will be included in the Each row of your report will contain list.

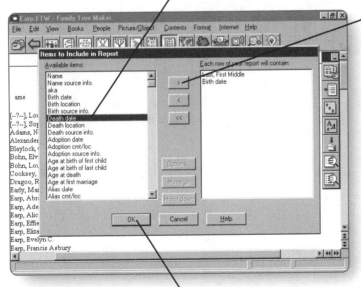

NOTE

Family Tree Maker might ask you about showing only preferred inform-ation. Click on OK in the message box that appears to include only preferred information.

4. Click on **OK**. The Items to Include in Report dialog box will close.

Choosing Individuals to Include in Your Report

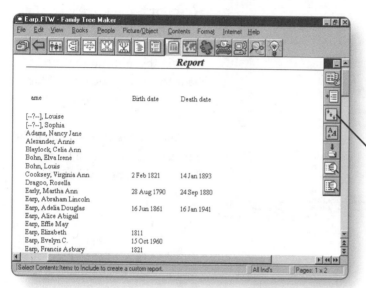

You may want to limit the individuals appearing in the report if you do not want to show your entire database. You can do this individually or by relationship.

1. Click on the **Individuals to Include button**. The Include dialog box will open.

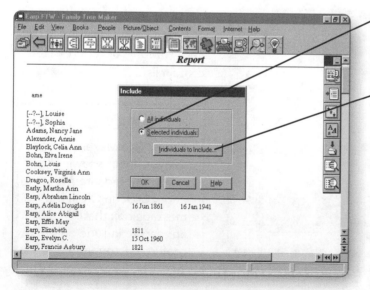

2. Click on the **Selected individuals radio button**. The option will be selected.

3. Click on the **Individuals to Include button**. The Individuals to Include dialog box will open.

4. In the Available individuals list, **select** the **individual** whom you want to include.

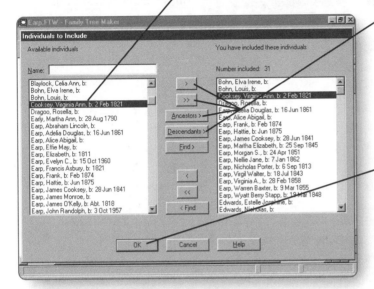

5. Click on the appropriate **inclusion button**. The individual you selected (and his or her ancestors or descendants, if applicable) will move to the You have included these individuals list.

6. Click on **OK**. The Individuals to Include dialog box will close and your changes will be saved.

NOTE

There are four major inclusion buttons. The ⟩ button tells Family Tree Maker to include the single highlighted individual. The ⟩⟩ button will include all the individuals. The Ancestors button will include the ancestors of the highlighted individual. The Descendants button will include the descendants of the highlighted individual.

Creating a Title and Footnote

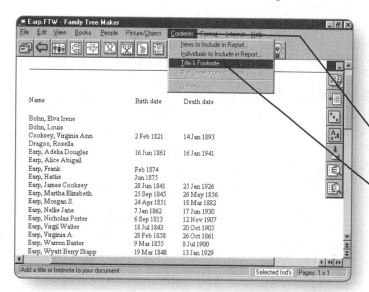

If you will be supplying this report to others, you may want to give it a title and include a footnote that will appear on each page.

1. Click on **Contents**. The Contents menu will appear.

2. Click on **Title & Footnote**. The Title & Footnote for Report dialog box will open.

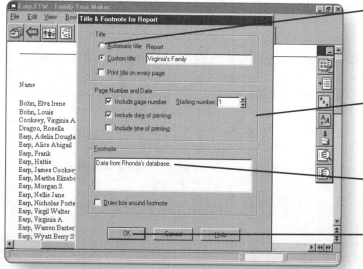

3. Click on a **radio button** to select the appropriate title option. The option will be selected.

4. Click on your desired **page number, date, and time options**. The options will be selected.

5. Type a **footnote** in the Footnote field.

6. Click on **OK**. The Title & Footnote for Report dialog box will close.

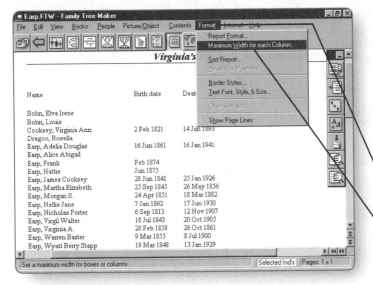

Adjusting Column Widths

Sometimes, in an effort to fit as much information onto a report as possible, it is necessary to adjust the column widths.

1. **Click** on **Format**. The Format menu will appear.

2. **Click** on **Maximum Width for each Column**. The Maximum Width for Each Column dialog box will open.

3a. **Click** on the **Set widths automatically radio button**. The option will be selected.

OR

3b. **Click** on the **Choose widths manually radio button**. The option will be selected.

4. **Adjust** the **width and spacing** for each column.

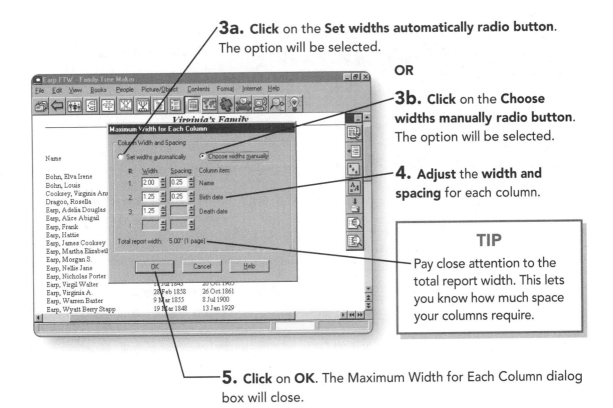

TIP

Pay close attention to the total report width. This lets you know how much space your columns require.

5. **Click** on **OK**. The Maximum Width for Each Column dialog box will close.

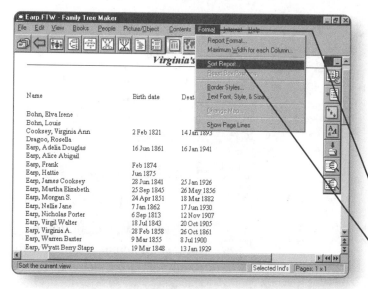

Sorting Reports

One benefit of putting your information into a database is your ability to manipulate the data after it has been entered. You can sort the report based on the columns included.

1. Click on **Format**. The Format menu will appear.

2. Click on **Sort Report**. The Sort Report dialog box will open.

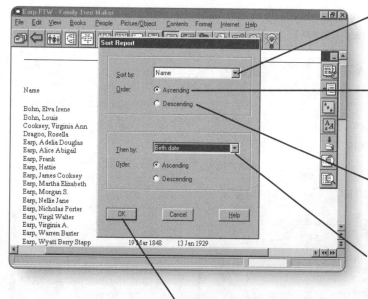

3. In the Sort by field, **select** the **first column** by which you want to sort.

4a. Click on the **Ascending radio button** to sort in ascending order.

OR

4b. Click on the **Descending radio button** to sort in descending order.

5. In the Then by field, **select** the **second column** by which you want to sort, if desired.

6. Click on **OK**. The Sort Report dialog box will close.

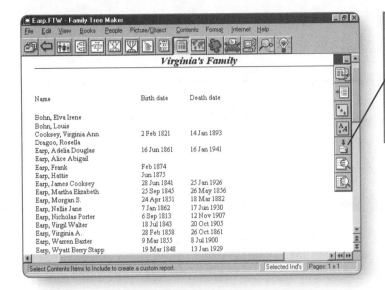

NOTE

You can save the style of this or any report or tree. Click on the Save View button and then give the view a name.

Creating a Kinship Report

Kinship reports help you to determine how individuals in your database are related. The people making up several generations might be related in more than one way.

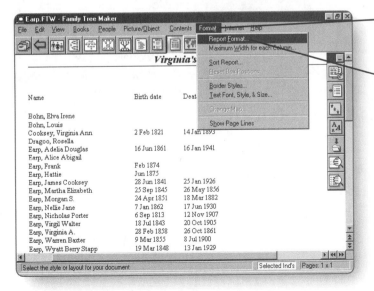

1. Click on **Format**. The Format menu will appear.

2. Click on **Report Format**. The Report Format dialog box will open.

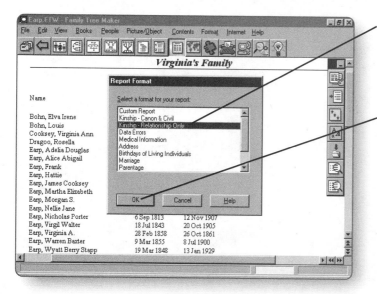

3. Click on **Kinship – Relationship Only**. The Kinship – Relationship Only report will be selected.

4. Click on **OK**. The Report Format dialog box will close.

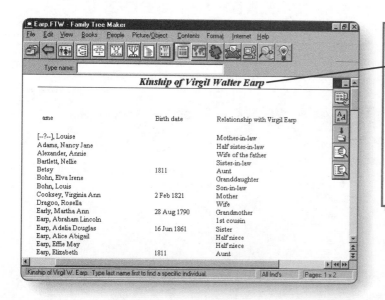

TIP

Remember that you can change the primary individual. Press F2 or click on the Index of Individuals button to open the Index of Individuals and select the person you want as the primary individual.

Working with Address and Birthday Reports

Whether you find yourself the keeper of addresses for the family association or you want to print out a report of birthdays so you will be sure to send cards, Family Tree Maker kept you in mind.

Creating an Address Report

If you have taken advantage of the More About Address option for living individuals, you can print out a report with those addresses.

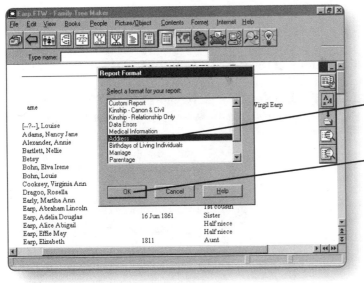

1. Open the **Report Format dialog box**, as you did in the previous section, "Creating a Kinship Report."

2. Click on **Address**. The Address report will be selected.

3. Click on **OK**. The Report Format dialog box will close.

TIP

You can determine which individuals are included in the address report. Simply click on the Individuals to Include button.

Creating the Birthday Report

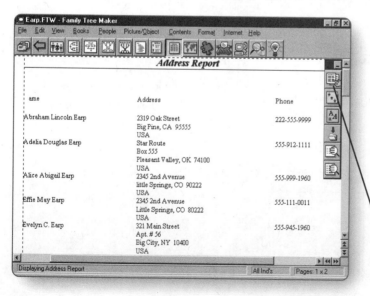

Thanks to the birthday report, you no longer need to look through all the pages of your living family members to find birthdays. The Birthday report will display the birthdays of all the living individuals in your database, or it can show just those you select.

1. Click on the **Format button**. The Report Format dialog box will open.

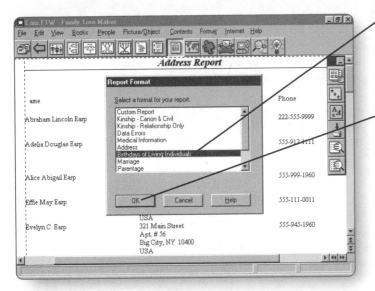

2. **Click** on **Birthdays of Living Individuals**. The option will be selected.

3. **Click** on **OK**. The Report Format dialog box will close.

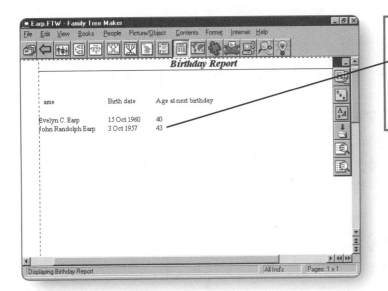

NOTE

Family Tree Maker omits anyone with a death date and anyone who is over 120 years old.

Using the Research Journal

Research journals offer a means for tracking your past research and for making notes on future research.

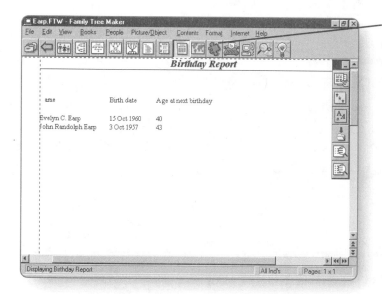

1. **Click** on the **FamilyFinder Center button**. The FamilyFinder Center will appear.

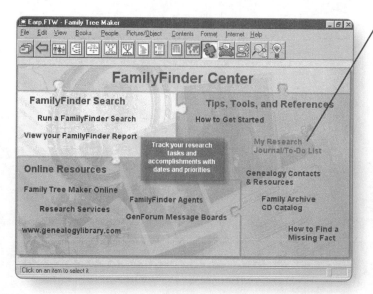

2. **Click** on **My Research Journal/To-Do List**. The Research Journal report will appear.

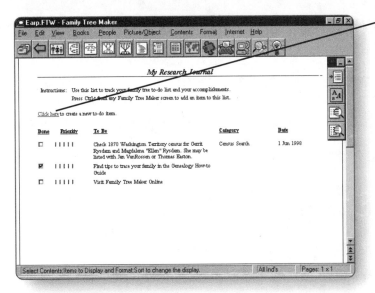

3. Click on the **Click here** link to add a To-Do item. The New To-Do Item dialog box will open.

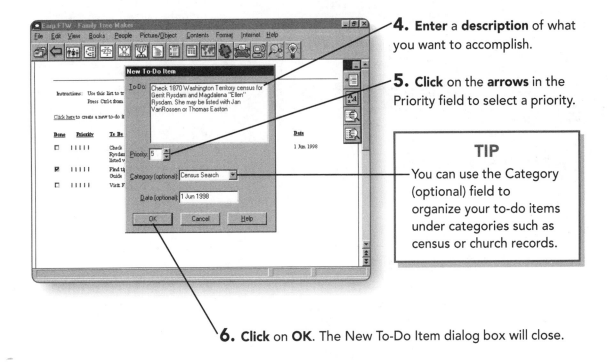

4. Enter a **description** of what you want to accomplish.

5. Click on the **arrows** in the Priority field to select a priority.

TIP

You can use the Category (optional) field to organize your to-do items under categories such as census or church records.

6. Click on **OK**. The New To-Do Item dialog box will close.

Working with the Genealogy How-To Guide

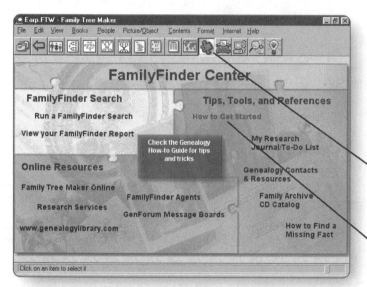

Whether you are just beginning or you have been involved in researching your family history for a while, there will be times when you will have questions about where to go with your research.

1. Click on the **FamilyFinder Center button**. The FamilyFinder Center will appear.

2. Click on **How To Get Started**. The Genealogy "How-To" Guide will appear.

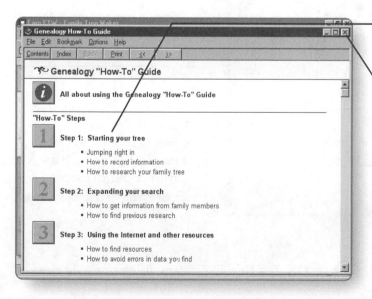

3. Click on the **item of interest**. Further instructions will appear.

4. Click on the **Close button** in the upper-right corner of the window. The Genealogy "How-To" Guide will close.

13

Viewing and Printing Reports and Trees

Now that you have learned how to enter information and view some of the reports and trees, you are probably interested in learning how to format and print them out. In this chapter, you'll learn how to:

- View the tree you want to print
- Customize the view of the tree
- Change the print setup
- Print the tree

Viewing the Tree You Want to Print

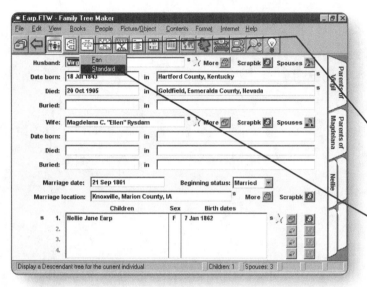

Family Tree Maker assumes that the tree or report you are interested in is the one on the screen, so you need to display the tree to print it.

1. Click on the **tree** you want to print. A menu might appear, depending on which tree you select.

2. If a menu does appear, **click** on the **tree type** you wish to print. The tree will appear.

Customizing the View

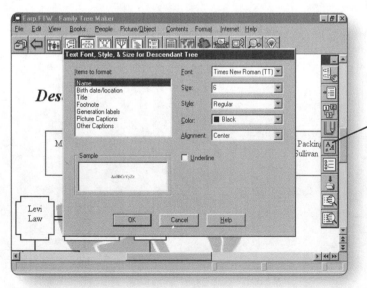

After you have displayed the tree you want to print, you can fine-tune the text style, font, and size. These features will only appear when the tree is printed.

1. Click on the **Text Font & Style button**. The Text Font, Style, & Size dialog box will open.

NOTE

The complete name of the dialog box will depend on the tree or report that you have selected.

Changing the Text Font

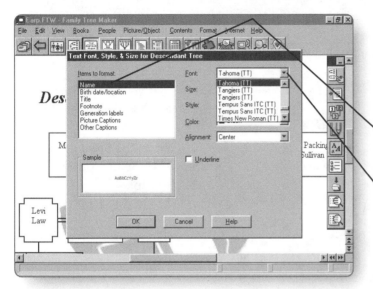

One wonderful aspect of computers and modern printers is that you can be creative with the fonts you use. You can go from formal to fun.

1. Click on an **item** in the Items to format list.

2. Click on the **Font down arrow**. The Font drop-down menu will appear.

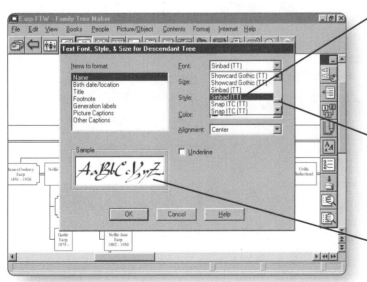

3. Click on the **font** you want to use. The font will be selected and the menu will close.

NOTE

Use the scroll bar to view the list of fonts.

TIP

If you use the keyboard arrow keys to move through the list of fonts, you will see a sample of each font in the Sample box.

Working with Text Style

In order to make things stand out, you might want to change the style of the text. For instance, you might decide that you want to italicize the dates to call attention to them.

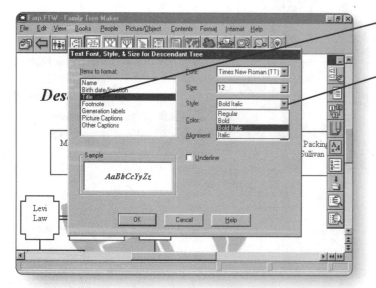

1. **Select** an **item** to format from the Items to format list.

2. **Click** on the **Style down arrow**. The Style drop-down menu will appear.

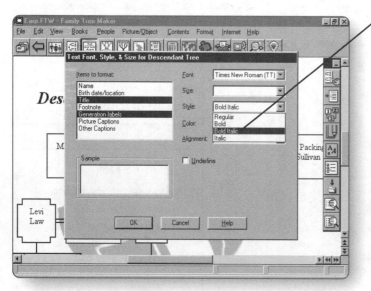

3. **Click** on the desired **style**. The style will be selected.

NOTE

If you want more than one item to have this style, press the Ctrl key and click on the additional items in the Items to format list. Then select the style from the Style drop-down menu.

Working with Text Size

Family Tree Maker has developed a number of default sizes for the fonts used in reports. You can change these if you want to, but in some cases it might make your report much larger.

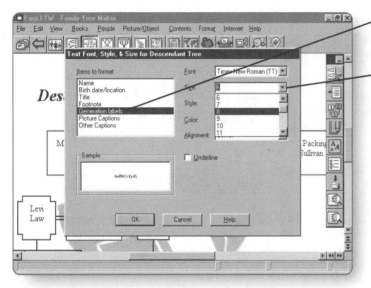

1. **Select** an **item** to format from the Items to format list.

2. **Click** on the **Size down arrow**. The Size drop-down menu will appear.

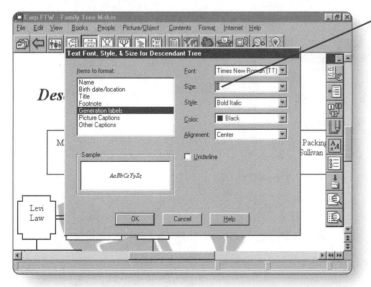

3. **Click** on the desired **size**. The size will be selected.

TIP

You can change the font, size, and style of an item all at once. Just select the item from the Items to format list and make your desired changes.

Text Color

If you are going to a family reunion or some other gathering where you want your chart to look extra special, you will want to take advantage of the color options Family Tree Maker offers.

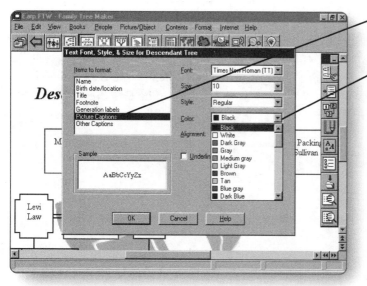

1. **Select** an **item** to format from the Items to format list.

2. **Click** on the **Color down arrow**. The Color drop-down menu will appear.

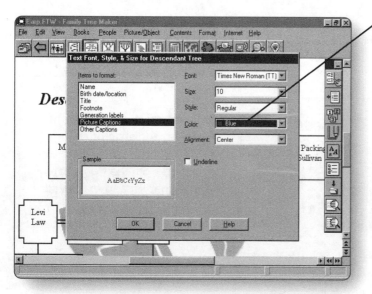

3. **Click** on the desired **color**. The color will be selected.

Changing the Print Setup

Family Tree Maker uses the printer settings you use in Windows, but you might want to change those settings if you are not happy with the way a particular report is printing.

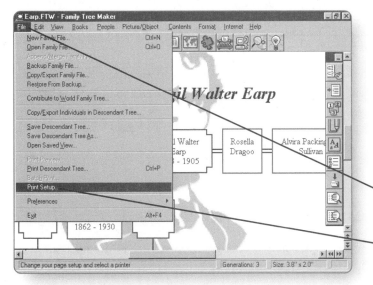

Changing the Paper Orientation

There are two ways to print on a piece of paper. Portrait uses the paper in the standard 8.5 by 11 inch mode; landscape uses the paper in 11 by 8.5 inch mode.

1. Click on **File**. The File menu will appear.

2. Click on **Print Setup**. The Print Setup dialog box will open.

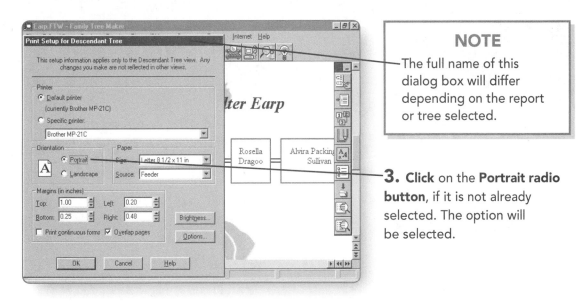

NOTE

The full name of this dialog box will differ depending on the report or tree selected.

3. Click on the **Portrait radio button**, if it is not already selected. The option will be selected.

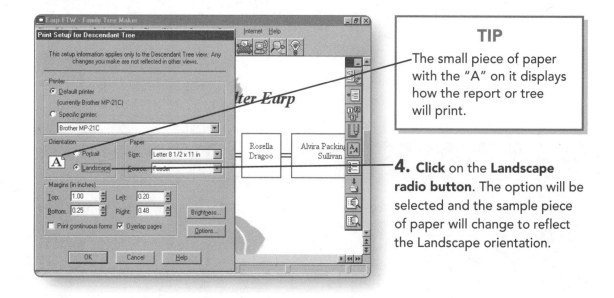

TIP

The small piece of paper with the "A" on it displays how the report or tree will print.

4. **Click** on the **Landscape radio button**. The option will be selected and the sample piece of paper will change to reflect the Landscape orientation.

Adjusting Margins

Usually the margins that have been set are at the optimum range for the reports and the printer used. However, you can change them.

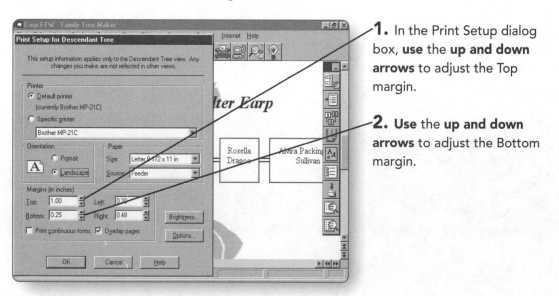

1. In the Print Setup dialog box, **use** the **up and down arrows** to adjust the Top margin.

2. **Use** the **up and down arrows** to adjust the Bottom margin.

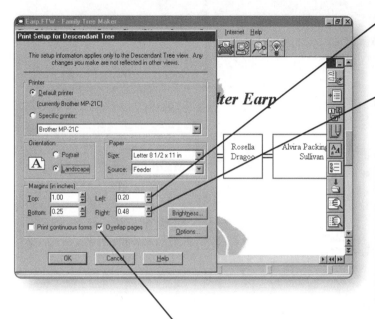

3. Use the **up and down arrows** to adjust the Left margin.

4. Use the **up and down arrows** to adjust the Right margin.

NOTE

Most printers have a minimum allowable margin. If you exceed this and get too close to the edge of the paper, Windows will let you know.

TIP

If you're printing one of the box charts or fan charts that will use more than one piece of paper, you will want to turn on the Overlap pages option.

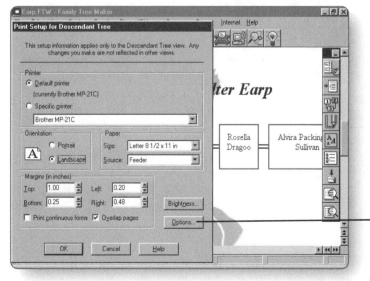

Changing Other Settings

You might want to adjust the features of your printer. This is especially useful when you're printing reports that have scanned images, because you can tell the printer to print at its peak quality for that report.

1. Click on the **Options button**. The printer Properties dialog box will open.

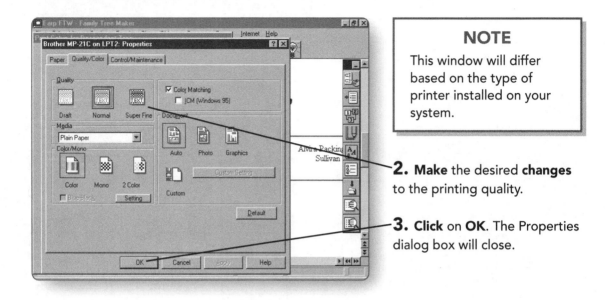

NOTE
This window will differ based on the type of printer installed on your system.

2. Make the desired **changes** to the printing quality.

3. Click on **OK**. The Properties dialog box will close.

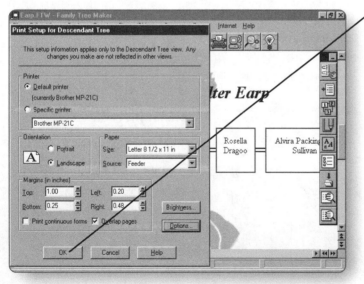

4. Click on **OK**. The Print Setup dialog box will close.

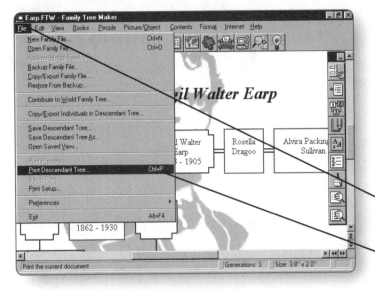

Printing the Tree

After you have made the necessary changes to the printer setup and you have formatted your tree the way you want it, it is time to print it.

1. **Click** on **File**. The File menu will appear.

2. **Click** on **Print Tree**. The Print Tree dialog box will open.

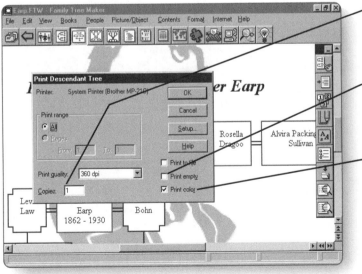

3. In the Copies field, **enter** the **number of copies** you wish to print.

4. **Select** the **Print empty check box** to print an empty report.

5. **Select** the **Print color check box** to print the report in color, if you have a color printer.

NOTE

Printing an empty report is an excellent way to have needed forms when you are on a research trip.

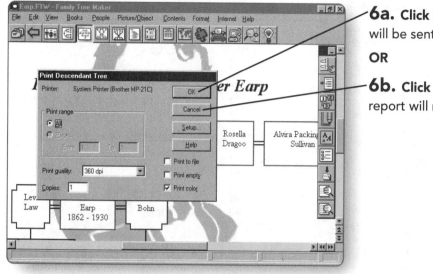

6a. **Click** on **OK**. The report will be sent to the printer.

OR

6b. **Click** on **Cancel**. The report will not be printed.

14

Creating Genealogy Style and Genealogical Reports

After you have entered all your information, you will want to share it with family members and other researchers. The genealogy style reports are one of the best ways to do this. In this chapter, you'll learn how to:

- Select a genealogy style
- Include sources in an endnote report
- Format the report
- Locate conflicting data
- Create a bibliography
- Create a documented events report

Using Genealogy Style Reports

Genealogy reports in Family Tree Maker are narrative reports containing genealogical information, basic facts, and biographical details. These are the most common formats you see in published family histories.

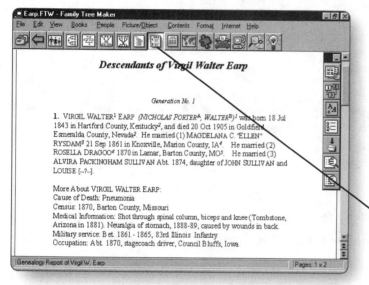

Working with Register Format

The Register format gets its name from the journal that devised it, *The New England Historic Genealogical Register*. This report lists individuals in order of descendants.

1. Click on the **Genealogy Report button**. The Genealogy report will appear.

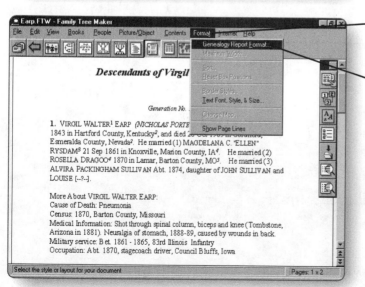

2. Click on **Format**. The Format menu will appear.

3. Click on **Genealogy Report Format**. The Genealogy Report Format dialog box will open.

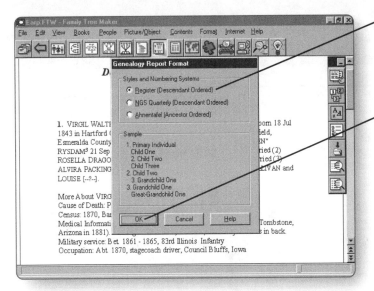

4. Select the **Register (Descendant Ordered) radio button**. The option will be selected.

5. Click on **OK**. The Genealogy Report Format dialog box will close.

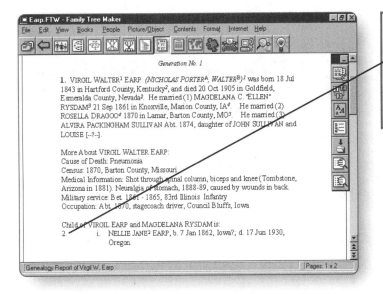

NOTE

The Register format assigns an identifying number to those who have offspring.

Working with NGSQ Format

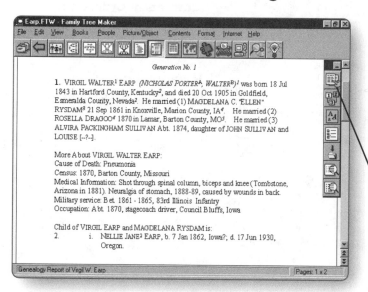

The NGSQ format also displays individuals in order of descendants. It was named after the *National Genealogical Society Quarterly*, the journal of the National Genealogical Society.

1. Click on the **Format button**. The Genealogy Report Format dialog box will open.

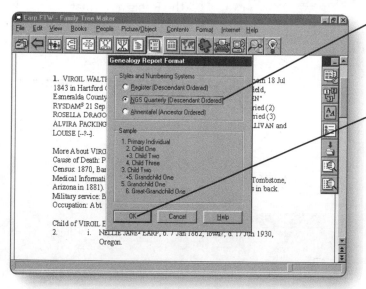

2. Select the **NGS Quarterly (Descendant Ordered) radio button**. The option will be selected.

3. Click on **OK**. The Genealogy Report Format dialog box will close.

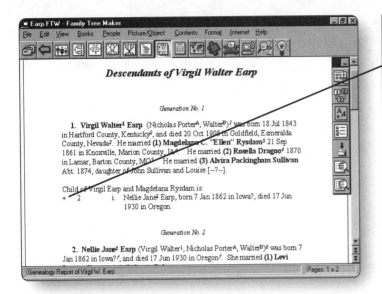

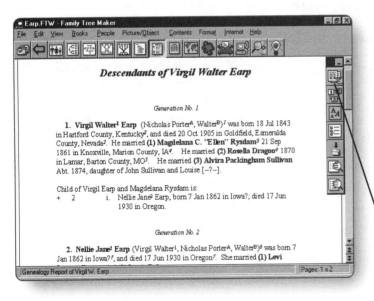

Using Ahnentafel Style

Ahnentafel is a German word that means "ancestor table" or "family table." This report lists individuals in an ancestral order. This is the opposite of the other two reports.

1. **Click** on the **Format button**. The Genealogy Report Format dialog box will open.

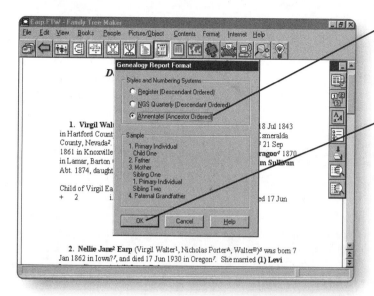

2. **Select** the **Ahnentafel (Ancestor Ordered) radio button.** The option will be selected.

3. **Click** on **OK**. The Genealogy Report Format dialog box will close.

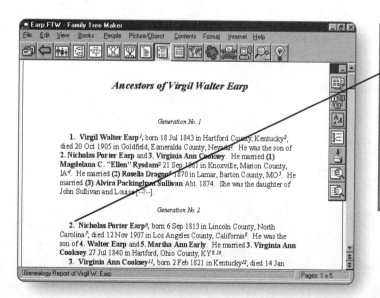

NOTE

The Ahnentafel style assigns the first individual the number 1. His or her father is number 2 and his or her mother is number 3. Men are always even numbers and women are always odd numbers.

Using Endnotes

Genealogy style reports include source citations. These can be included in the body of the report or they can be printed as endnotes.

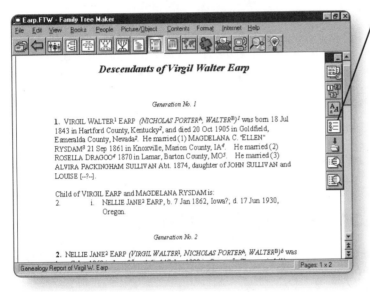

1. Click on the **Options button**. The Options for Genealogy Report dialog box will open.

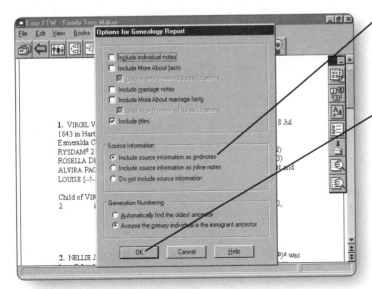

2. Click on the **Include source information as endnotes radio button**. The option will be selected.

3. Click on **OK**. The Options for Genealogy Report dialog box will close.

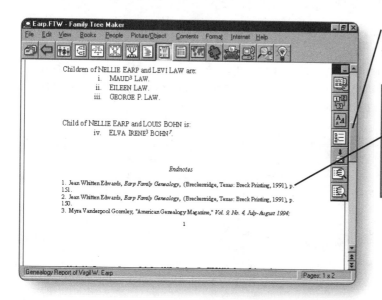

4. Use the **scroll bar** to scroll to the bottom of the report.

TIP

The endnotes are the source citations you learned about in Chapter 4, "Documenting Sources."

Formatting the Report

In addition to the different styles of reports, there are other items that need to be considered, such as page number and the type of notes to include.

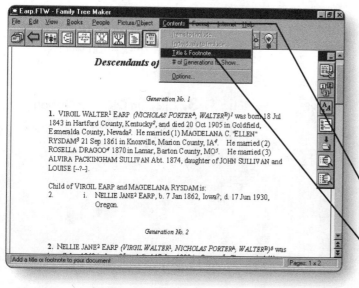

Adjusting Page Numbering and Title

Family Tree Maker has a default setting for the page number and title, but you can change these settings.

1. Click on **Contents**. The Contents menu will appear.

2. Click on **Title & Footnote**. The Title & Footnote dialog box will open.

3a. **Click** on the **Automatic title radio button**. The option will be selected.

OR

3b. **Click** on the **Custom title radio button**. The cursor will move to the empty field where you can type the title as you want it to display in the report.

4. In the Page Number and Date section, **click** on the **page number and date options** you want to set.

5. **Use** the **up and down arrows** to change the starting page number.

6. **Click** on **OK**. The Title & Footnote for Genealogy Report dialog box will close.

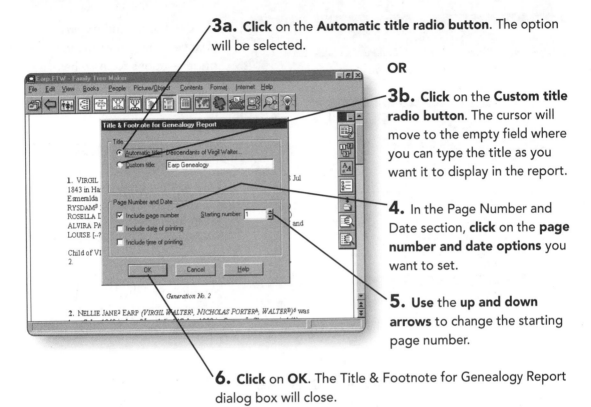

Changing the Number of Generations

As you can with the trees, you can control the number of generations that are included in the genealogy report.

1. **Click** on the **Number of Generations button**. The # of Generations to Show dialog box will open.

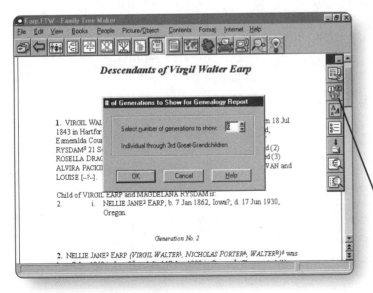

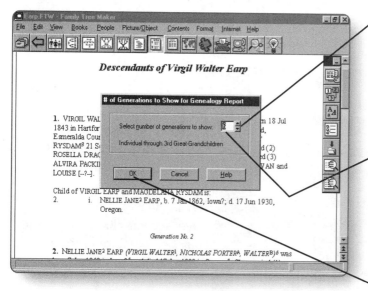

2. **Use** the **up and down arrows** in the Select number of generations to show field to adjust the number.

TIP

You can double-click on the number to highlight it and then type the number of generations to include in the report.

3. **Click** on **OK**. The # of Generations to Show dialog box will close.

Including Notes and Other Options

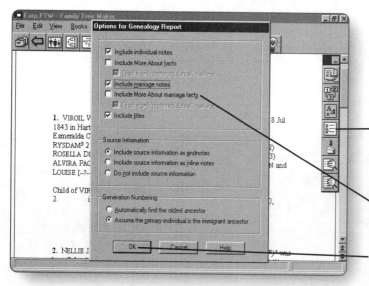

In Chapter 6, "Understanding More About Notes," you learned to include family stories. These stories can be included in printed reports.

1. **Click** on the **Options button**. The Options for Genealogy Report dialog box will open.

2. **Click** on the **check boxes** for the options you want to set.

3. **Click** on **OK**. The Options for Genealogy Report dialog box will close.

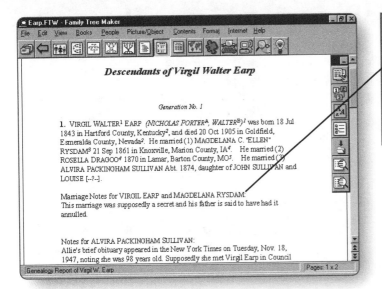

TIP

It is a good idea to read through the report to see if the notes are appropriate and should be included.

Locating Conflicting Facts

Family Tree Maker allows you to enter duplicate facts. This is by design, because you will find dates in your research that conflict with each other and you will want to record each of them. Family Tree Maker also lets you conduct a search based on these conflicting facts.

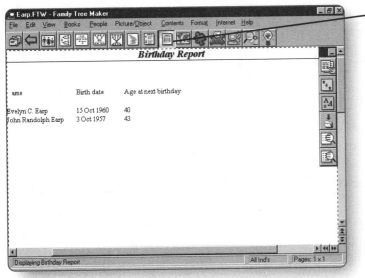

1. Click on the **Reports button**. A miscellaneous Report will appear.

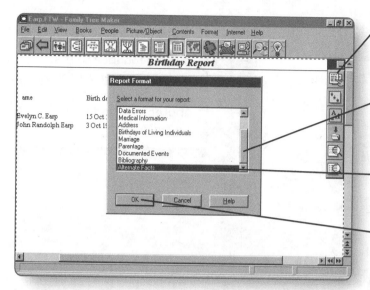

2. Click on the **Format button**. The Report Format dialog box will open.

3. Scroll down until you reach the bottom of the Select a format for your report list.

4. Click on **Alternate Facts**. The option will be selected.

5. Click on **OK**. The Report Format dialog box will close and the Alternate Facts Report will be displayed.

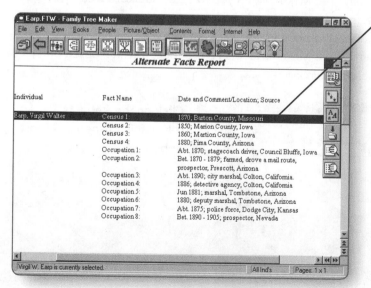

6. Click on an **individual** from the report. The individual will be selected.

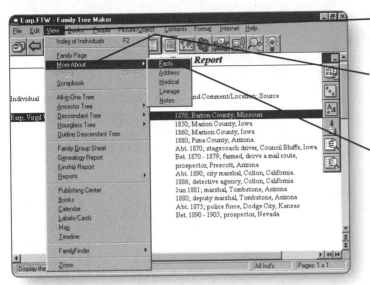

7. Click on **View**. The View menu will appear.

8. Move the **mouse pointer** to More About. The More About menu will appear.

9. Click on **Facts**. The More About Facts window will appear, so you can view the facts for the individual.

Creating a Bibliography Report

A bibliography is a list of books and sources. These are the sources you have used in compiling your family tree file. A bibliography report is a useful reference tool.

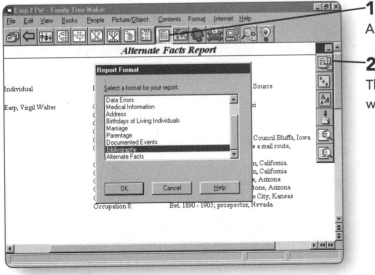

1. Click on the **Report button**. A report will appear.

2. Click on the **Format button**. The Report Format dialog box will open.

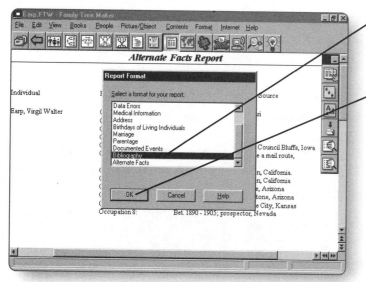

3. Click on **Bibliography** in the Select a format for your report list. The option will be selected.

4. Click on **OK**. The Report Format dialog box will close.

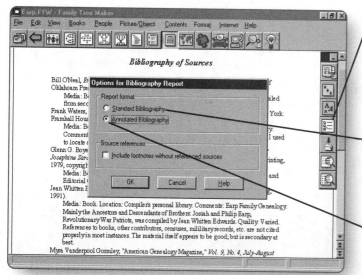

5. Click on the **Options button**. The Options for Bibliography Report dialog box will open.

6a. Click on **Standard Bibliography** to create a standard bibliography.

OR

6b. Click on **Annotated Bibliography** to create an annotated bibliography.

NOTE

The annotated bibliography includes the full source citation and comments by the researcher about the source.

Creating a Documented Events Report

Understanding how you came to the conclusions you did in your family tree file is usually directly related to the sources used. The Documented Events report is a clear list of the individuals and events you have documented.

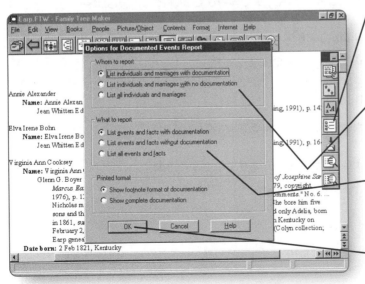

1. Click on the **Format button**. The Report Format dialog box will open.

2. Click on **Documented Events**. The option will be selected.

3. Click on **OK**. The Report Format dialog box will close.

4. Click on the **Options button**. The Options for Documented Events Report dialog box will open.

5. Click on the desired **Whom to report radio button**. The option will be selected.

6. Click on the desired **What to report radio button**. The option will be selected.

7. Click on **OK**. The Options for Documented Events Report dialog box will close.

Part IV Review Questions

1. What three types of Ancestor Trees can you display?
    See "Displaying Ancestor Trees" in Chapter 11

2. Which Descendant Tree indents the individuals?
    See "Creating an Outline Tree" in Chapter 11

3. How do you view a complete All-in-One Tree?
    See "Setting Display Size" in Chapter 11

4. How do you select the items to include in a custom report?
    See "Adding Items to Include in Your Report" in Chapter 12

5. How can you record plans for future research?
    See "Using the Research Journal" in Chapter 12

6. Where can you turn for guidance in your research?
    See "Working with the Genealogy How-To Guide" in Chapter 12

7. How do you alter the view of the trees in Family Tree Maker?
    See "Customizing the View" in Chapter 13

8. Can you print in both landscape and portrait modes?
    See "Changing the Paper Orientation" in Chapter 13

9. What three types of Genealogy reports are available?
    See "Using Genealogy Style Reports" in Chapter 14

10. What can you format in the report?
    See "Formatting the Report" in Chapter 14

PART V

Publishing Your Family History

Chapter 15
      Creating a Scrapbook **257**

Chapter 16
      Creating a Family History Book **277**

Chapter 17
      **Creating Your Personal Family
      Tree Maker Home Page** **293**

15

Creating a Scrapbook

With present technology it is possible to create beautiful reports and enhance them by adding scanned and digitized photographs. Family Tree Maker calls these reports scrapbooks. In this chapter, you'll learn how to:

- ● Create a scrapbook
- ● Insert images into a scrapbook
- ● Enter information about scrapbook items
- ● Rearrange scrapbook objects
- ● Edit pictures or objects
- ● Search for objects
- ● Share your scrapbook

Using the Scrapbook

In the scrapbook, you can work with digitized files such as scanned photographs. There are scrapbooks for individuals and for marriages.

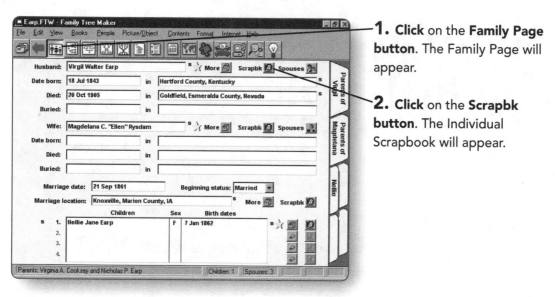

1. Click on the **Family Page button**. The Family Page will appear.

2. Click on the **Scrapbk button**. The Individual Scrapbook will appear.

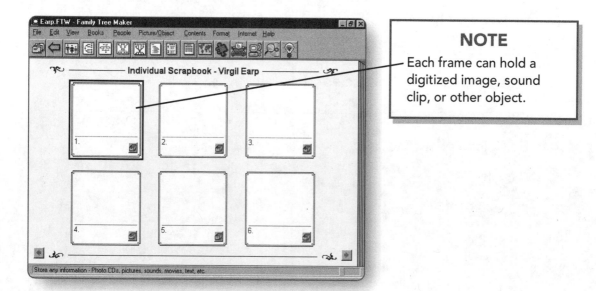

NOTE

Each frame can hold a digitized image, sound clip, or other object.

Inserting Scrapbook Images

While most of the items you will work with in Family Tree Maker will be scanned photographs, Family Tree Maker does support sound clips and OLE (*Object Linking and Embedding*) objects.

Using Images

Scanning photographs helps to preserve them, and they can then be included in the reports you print from Family Tree Maker. But first you need to import the image files.

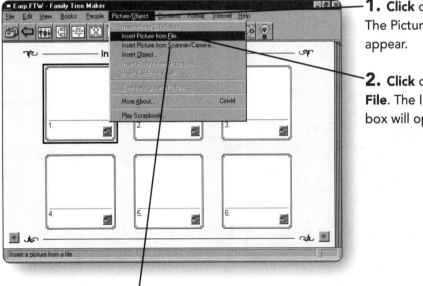

1. **Click** on **Picture/Object**. The Picture/Object menu will appear.

2. **Click** on **Insert Picture from File**. The Insert Picture dialog box will open.

NOTE

It is also possible to scan the picture directly into the scrapbook. Click on Insert Picture from Scanner/Camera. Remember, though, that images can take up a great deal of space on your hard drive. For scanned images, it is recommended that you set the resolution to a maximum of 200 DPI (*Dots Per Inch*). This will produce a good picture and keep the file size down at the same time.

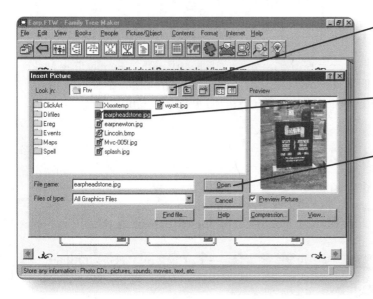

3. Use the **Look in drop-down menu** to locate the folder that holds the images.

4. Click on the desired **image**. The image will be selected.

5. Click on **Open**. The Insert Picture dialog box will close and the picture will appear in the Edit Picture dialog box.

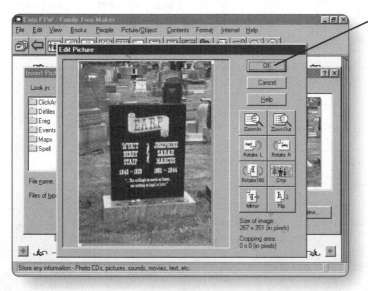

6. Click on **OK**. The Edit Picture dialog box will close.

Using Sound Clips

There is something fascinating about hearing the voice of a relative. Family Tree Maker offers a way of including sound clips in the scrapbook.

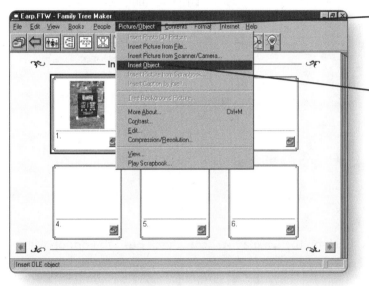

1. Click on **Picture/Object**. The Picture/Object menu will appear.

2. Click on **Insert Object**. The Insert Object dialog box will open.

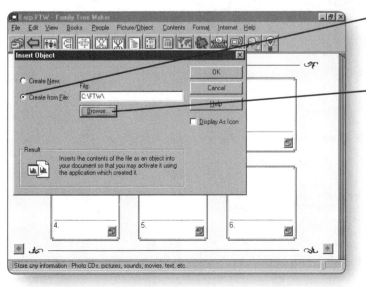

3. Click on the **Create from File radio button**. The option will be selected.

4. Click on the **Browse button**. The Browse dialog box will open.

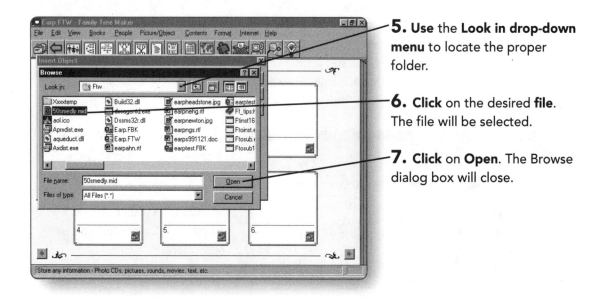

5. Use the **Look in drop-down menu** to locate the proper folder.

6. Click on the desired **file**. The file will be selected.

7. Click on **Open**. The Browse dialog box will close.

8. Click on the **Display As Icon check box**. The option will be selected.

9. Click on **OK**. The Insert Object dialog box will close.

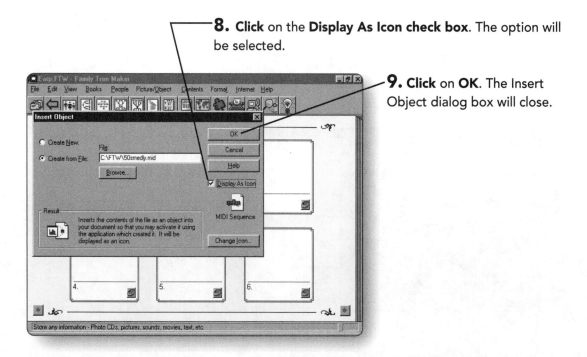

Using OLE Objects

Object linking and embedding (OLE) allows you to launch another program from within Family Tree Maker. You might want to do this so that you can open a word processor file to display a detailed family story.

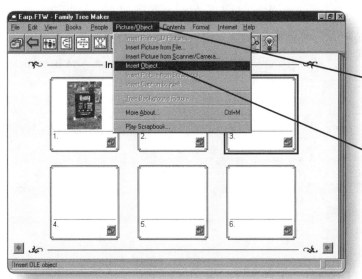

1. Click on **Picture/Object**. The Picture/Object menu will appear.

2. Click on **Insert Object**. The Insert Object dialog box will open.

---

3. Click on the **Create from File radio button**. The option will be selected.

4. Click on the **Browse button**. The Browse dialog box will open.

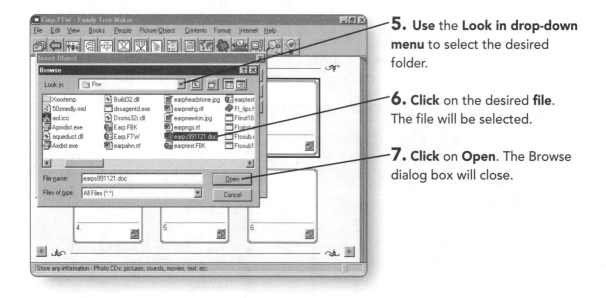

5. Use the **Look in drop-down menu** to select the desired folder.

6. **Click** on the desired **file**. The file will be selected.

7. **Click** on **Open**. The Browse dialog box will close.

8. **Click** on the **Display As Icon check box**. Family Tree Maker will insert an icon in the scrapbook.

9. **Click** on **OK**. The Insert Object dialog box will close.

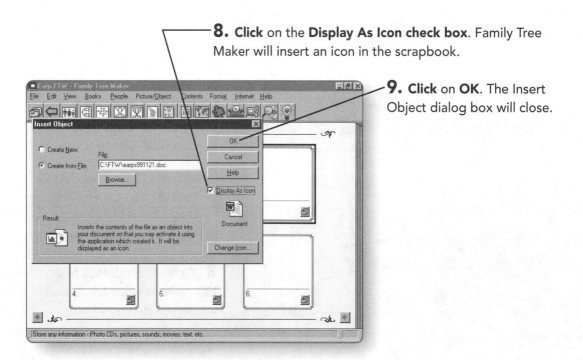

Entering Information about Scrapbook Objects

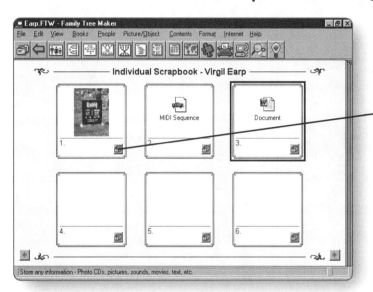

To help you know what you have in your scrapbook, Family Tree Maker offers a More About screen for each scrapbook entry.

1. **Click** on the **More About button** for the selected scrapbook item. The More About Picture/Object dialog box will open.

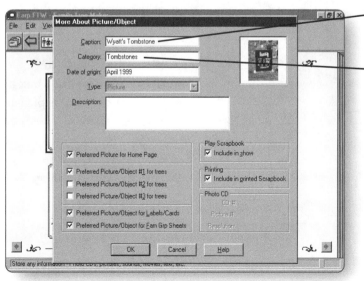

2. **Type** a **caption** in the Caption field.

3. **Type** a **category** in the Category field.

TIP

Plan ahead before you use the Category field. Family Tree Maker allows you to categorize your scrapbook objects, making them easier to search.

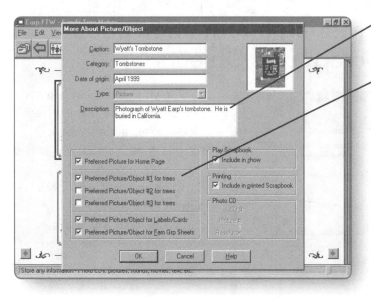

4. Type a **description** for the object in the Description field.

5. Select the desired **Preferred check boxes**. The option(s) will be selected.

TIP

Remember that while Family Tree Maker can display sound clips and OLE objects, in a printed report you will only get the digitized images.

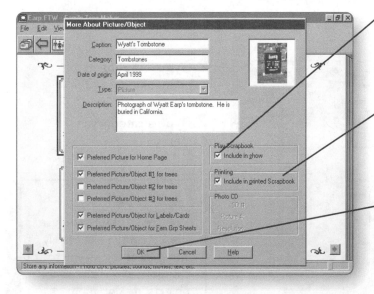

6. Click on the **Include in show check box** if you want the object to display when you play the scrapbook.

7. Click on the **Include in printed Scrapbook check box** if you want the object to display in the printed scrapbook.

8. Click on **OK**. The More About Picture/Object dialog box will close.

Rearranging Scrapbook Objects

There might be a time when you want the items or objects in the scrapbook to display in a particular order that's different from the way you originally entered them.

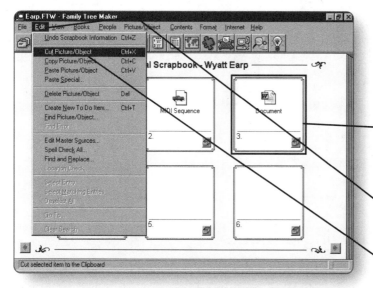

Moving Objects

One way to rearrange the objects inserted in a scrapbook is to move them.

1. **Click** on the **object** you want to move. The object will be selected.

2. **Click** on **Edit**. The Edit menu will appear.

3. **Click** on **Cut Picture/Object**. The picture will move to the clipboard.

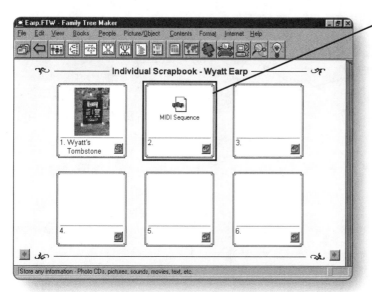

4. **Click** in the **frame** where you want to place the object. The frame will be selected.

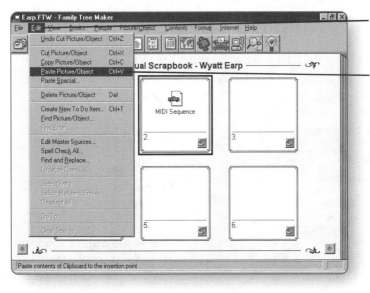

5. **Click** on **Edit**. The Edit menu will appear.

6. **Click** on **Paste Picture/ Object**. The object will be pasted in the new position.

Copying Objects

You can copy and paste a scrapbook item from the scrapbook of one individual to that of another.

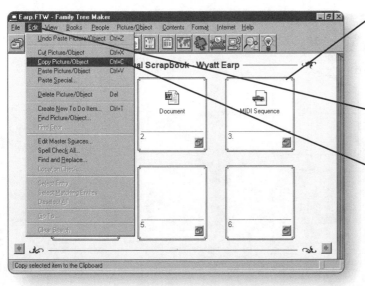

1. **Click** on the **object** you want to copy. The object will be selected.

2. **Click** on **Edit**. The Edit menu will appear.

3. **Click** on **Copy Picture/ Object**. The object will be copied to the clipboard.

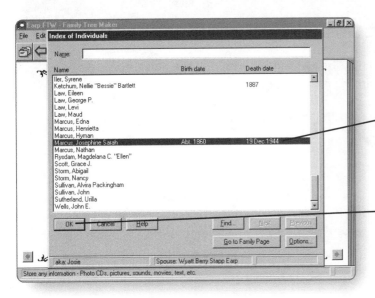

4. Click on the **Index of Individuals button**. The Index of Individuals dialog box will open.

5. Click on the **individual** to whose scrapbook you want to paste the object. The individual will be selected.

6. Click on **OK**. The new individual's scrapbook will appear.

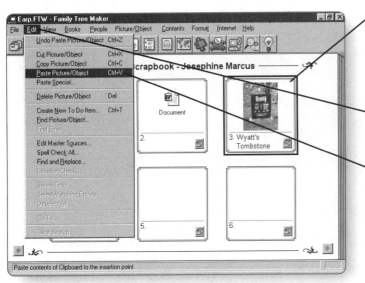

7. Click on the **frame** where you want to place the object. The frame will be selected.

8. Click on **Edit**. The Edit menu will appear.

9. Click on **Paste Picture/Object**. The copied object will be placed in the scrapbook.

Editing Pictures and Objects

Family Tree Maker has included the ability to rotate, crop, mirror, and flip images.

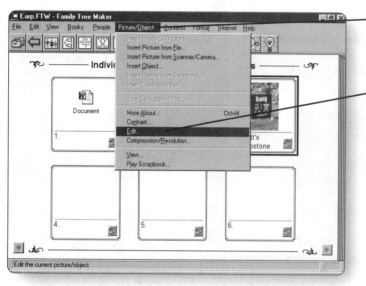

1. Click on **Picture/Object**. The Picture/Object menu will appear.

2. Click on **Edit**. A message box will appear, encouraging you to use the original picture.

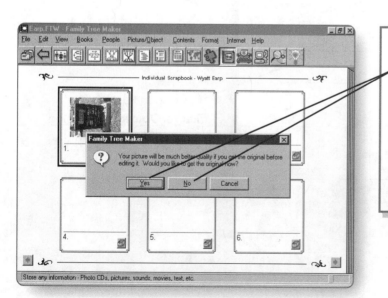

TIP

Family Tree Maker encourages you to edit the original file rather than a copy. If you click on Yes, the Insert Picture dialog box will open. If you click on No, the Edit picture dialog box will open.

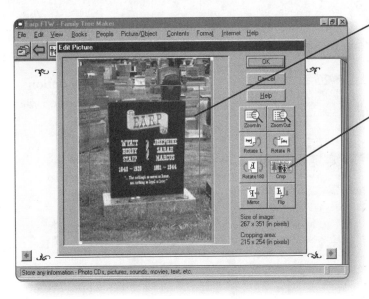

3. Click and drag the **mouse pointer** to highlight the area of the image you want to edit. The area will be selected.

4. Click on the **Crop button**. The picture will be cropped.

TIP

You can undo the changes by clicking on the Cancel button. The Edit Picture window will close without making the changes.

Searching for Objects

While it may not seem possible now, the more objects you add, the quicker you will need to rely on the abilities of the Find features to locate specific scrapbook objects.

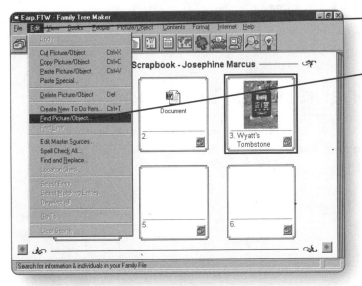

1. Click on **Edit**. The Edit menu will appear.

2. Click on **Find Picture/Object**. The Find Picture/Object dialog box will open.

TIP

You must have the Scrapbook open to use the Find Picture/Object menu command.

3. Click on the **Search down arrow**. The Search drop-down menu will appear.

4. Click on the **search option** you want to use. The option will be selected.

5. In the for field, **type** the **term** for which you want to search.

6. Click on the **Find next button**. The Family Page will appear.

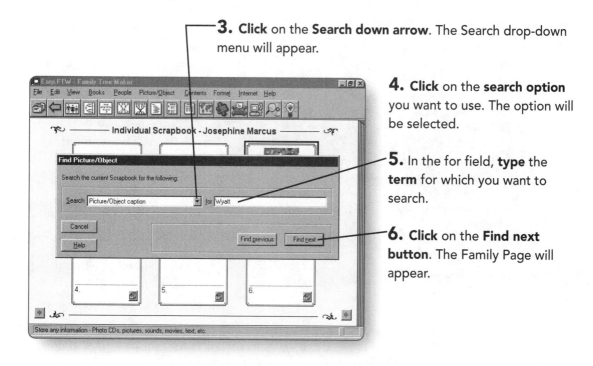

7. Click on the **Scrapbk button** for the individual who appears. The individual's scrapbook will appear, and you will be able to view the scrapbook objects, one of which must fit your search criteria.

Sharing Your Scrapbook

When you have put together the digitized images with the digitized interview of your relative, you will want to share it with others.

Playing a Scrapbook

Family reunions are a great place to share scrapbooks. If you have Family Tree Maker set up on a computer with speakers, there is no limit to what you can do.

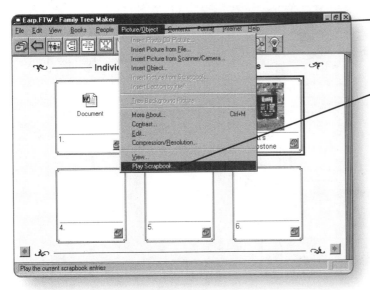

1. Click on **Picture/Object**. The Picture/Object menu will appear.

2. Click on **Play Scrapbook**. The Play Scrapbook dialog box will open.

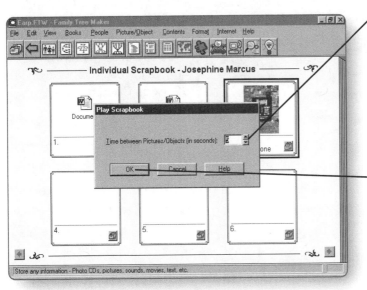

3. Use the **up and down arrows** in the Time between Pictures/Objects (in seconds) field to adjust the delay between objects.

4. Click on **OK**. The scrapbook will be played.

Printing a Scrapbook

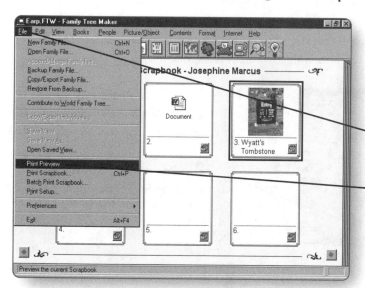

Most of the time, you will share your scrapbook by printing it out. Remember, the printed scrapbook includes only digitized images.

1. Click on **File**. The File menu will appear.

2. Click on **Print Preview**. The Scrapbook Print Preview window will appear.

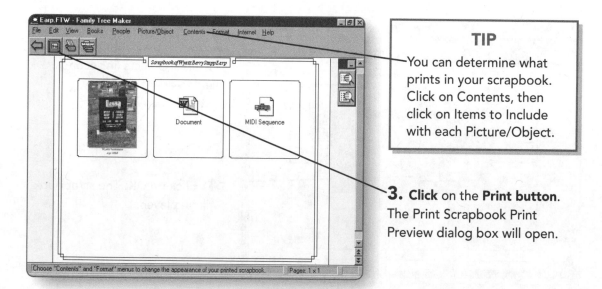

TIP

You can determine what prints in your scrapbook. Click on Contents, then click on Items to Include with each Picture/Object.

3. Click on the **Print button**. The Print Scrapbook Print Preview dialog box will open.

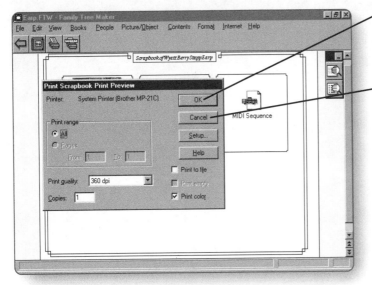

4a. **Click** on **OK**. The scrapbook will be printed.

OR

4b. **Click** on **Cancel**. The scrapbook will not be printed.

16

Creating a Family History Book

For many researchers, the ultimate goal is to publish a record of their ancestry. Family Tree Maker has long kept this in mind and offers one of the easiest ways to put a variety of reports together to share with family, friends, or colleagues. In this chapter, you'll learn how to:

- Select specific reports and trees
- Organize the selected items
- Work with images
- Add page breaks
- Create a customized index

Selecting Available Items

You have looked at many of the trees and reports that Family Tree Maker can create, but you might have been unaware that you can select these and put them together to create a book. One of the first things you have to do is decide what items to select. Following is a list of possible items to include in the book, from the title page to the index, including lots of family trees and narrative reports.

- Front matter (title page, copyright notice, and so on)
- Introduction
- Ancestor Trees
- Descendant Trees
- Hourglass Trees
- Kinship reports
- Narrative reports
- Timelines
- Calendars
- Bibliography
- Index

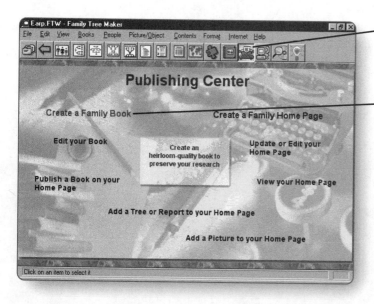

1. Click on the **Publishing Center button**. The Publishing Center will appear.

2. Click on **Create a Family Book**. The New Book dialog box will open.

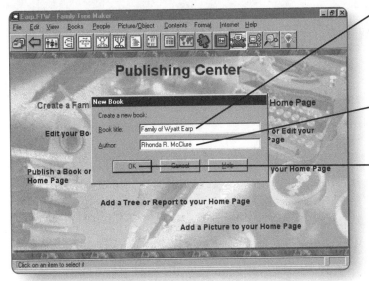

3. Type the **book title** in the Book title field and **press** the **Tab key**. The cursor will move to the Author field.

4. Type the **author's name** in the Author field.

5. Click on **OK**. The Books window will appear.

TIP

Another way to begin putting together a new book is to click on Books. After the Books menu appears, click on New Book.

Selecting Front Matter

When you open any book, the first pages you look at contain what Family Tree Maker refers to as the front matter. The title page, copyright notice, dedication, and table of contents are such items. When you first create your book, you will need to decide which of these you want to include.

NOTE

When the Books window appears, there is only one item already included in the Outline for list. The Title Page was created when you filled in the information in the New Book dialog box.

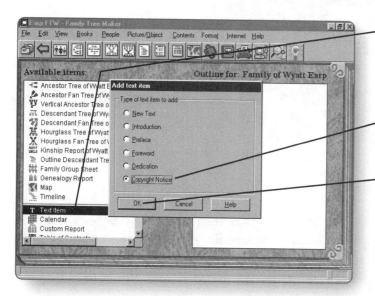

1. In the Available items list, **double-click** on **Text Item**. The Add text item dialog box will open.

2. Click on the desired **text item**. The item will be selected.

3. Click on **OK**. The selected text item will be added to the Outline for list.

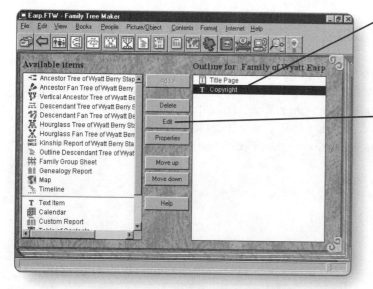

4. In the Outline for list, **click** on the newly added **text item**. The option buttons will be activated.

5. Click on **Edit**. The text editor window will appear and display the selected item.

6. Use the **toolbar buttons** to make changes to the item.

7. Click on the **Close button** and **click** on **OK** when you are prompted to save the file.

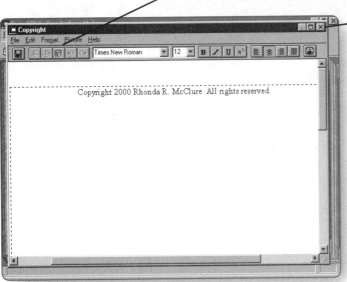

Adding Trees and Reports

A book of your ancestors should contain a number of different trees and reports. It is important to keep your audience in mind when you're deciding what to include. You can create different books for different groups of individuals, so that the one you share with your family is more personal and less formal than the one you share with another genealogist.

1. Click on the **tree or report** you want to include. The tree or report will be highlighted.

2. Click on **Add**. The tree or report will be added to the Outline for list.

NOTE
You can select any of the reports, trees, or other options in the Available items list. You will learn to organize them later in this chapter, in "Organizing the Items" section.

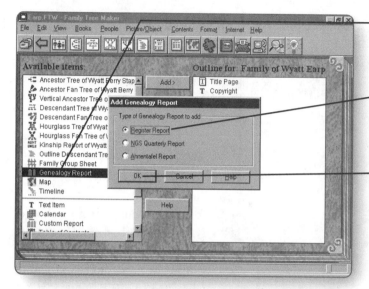

3. Double-click on **Genealogy Report**. The Add Genealogy Report dialog box will open.

4. Select the **type of Genealogy Report** to add. The option will be selected.

5. Click on **OK**. The Add Genealogy Report dialog box will close and the Genealogy Report will appear in the Outline for list.

Including Text with Pictures

Most of your family will want to see pictures in the book you share with them. While you can include them in some of the trees and reports, there are other times when you might want to have more control over the image. You can take this control by adding a text item with pictures.

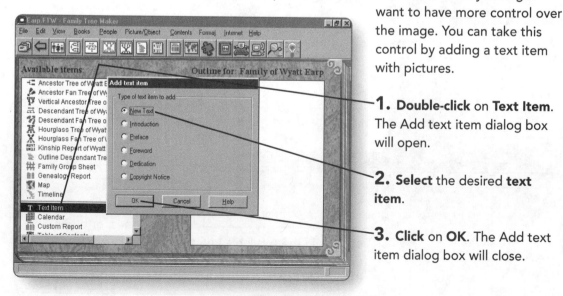

1. Double-click on **Text Item**. The Add text item dialog box will open.

2. Select the desired **text item**.

3. Click on **OK**. The Add text item dialog box will close.

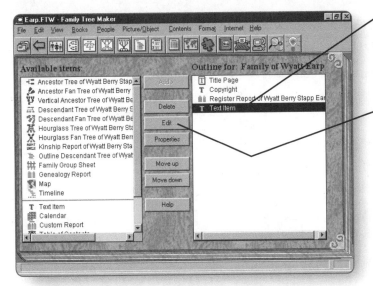

4. In the Outline for list, **click** on the newly added **text item**. Additional option buttons will be activated.

5. **Click** on **Edit**. The Text Item edit window will appear.

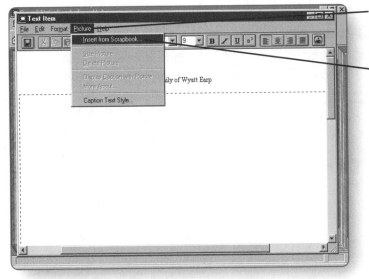

6. Click on **Picture**. The Picture menu will appear.

7. Click on **Insert from Scrapbook**. The Individuals with Scrapbook Pictures dialog box will open.

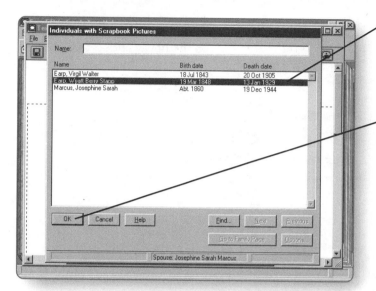

8. **Click** on the **individual** whose scrapbook you want to access. The individual will be highlighted.

9. **Click** on **OK**. The Insert Scrapbook Picture dialog box will open.

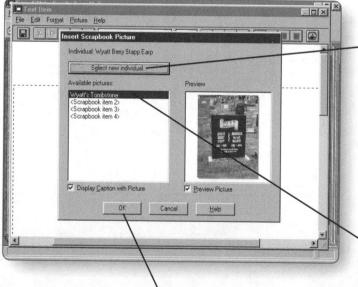

NOTE

If the displayed individual's scrapbook does not include the picture you were expecting, you can click on Select new individual and the Individuals with Scrapbook Pictures dialog box will open again.

10. **Click** on the **picture** you want to include. The picture will be displayed in the Preview box if you have the Preview Picture box checked.

11. **Click** on **OK**. The Insert Scrapbook Picture dialog box will close and the picture will be included in the Text Item window.

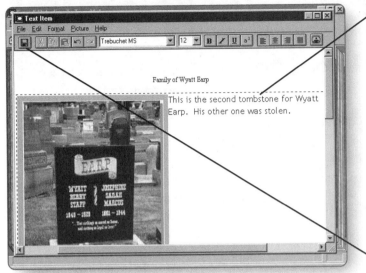

12. **Type** the **text** you want to associate with the image.

> **TIP**
>
> The Text Item window is similar to a word processing program. You can alter the font and format of the text and the image.

13. **Click** on the **Save button**. The changes to the text item will be saved.

14. **Click** on the **Close button**. The Text Item window will close.

Working with Outline Items

After you have decided which reports and trees you want to include in your book, you can begin to organize their order in the Outline for list. This is the order in which they will print when you send your book to the printer. You can also control which of your reports will start a new chapter in the book.

Organizing the Items

When you added to the Outline for list, Family Tree Maker simply placed the newly added tree or report at the bottom of the list. However, this may not be the order you want them in for the reports. You can add them in the order you want them to appear, or you can simply move them around after they are in the list.

1. In the Outline for list, **click** on the **tree or report** you want to move. The item will be highlighted.

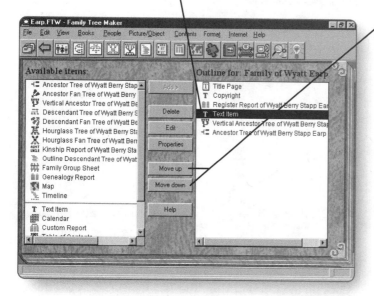

2. Click on the **Move up or Move down button** to move the highlighted item.

NOTE

Although Family Tree Maker doesn't disable the buttons, you cannot move the Title Page. Family Tree Maker will tell you that the Title Page must be the first item in the book.

TIP

It is a good idea to have a plan before you start moving the reports around. For more information about publishing your family history with Family Tree Maker, and for some ideas about different types of family book projects, read *Create Your Family History Book with Family Tree Maker Version 8: The Official Guide* (Prima, 2000) by Marthe Arends.

Working with Item Properties

As you were putting your reports and trees into the order they now appear, you were probably visualizing divisions of your book. If you look at any of the published family histories in your local genealogy library, you will see that they are broken into chapters to make using the book easier.

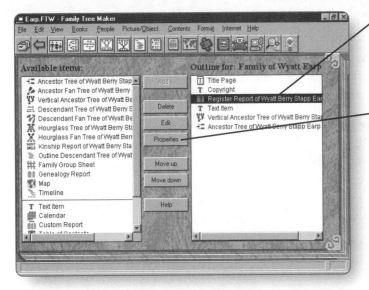

1. Click on the **report or tree** with which you want to work. The report or tree will be highlighted.

2. Click on the **Properties button**. The Item Properties dialog box will open.

3. Select the **This item begins a Chapter check box** if you want the item to be the first item in a new chapter. A check mark will appear in the check box.

4. Select the **Start this item on odd numbered page check box** if you want to control on what page the item will begin. A check mark will appear in the check box.

5. Click on **OK**. Your changes will be saved and the Item Properties dialog box will close.

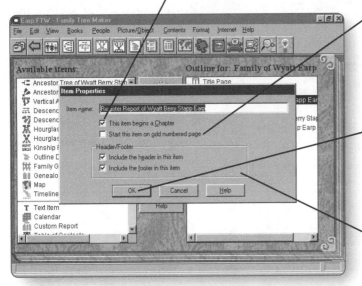

NOTE

You can use the Header/ Footer options to determine which of your reports and trees will include the header or footer information. The header is usually the title of the book. The footer is the page number.

Finalizing the Book

Family Tree Maker offers a few enhancements to help to define your book and make it easier to read. After all, you want those who read the book to find it easy to use.

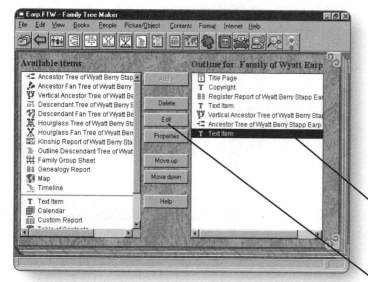

Adding Page Breaks

There might be times when you're working with one of the text items that you want to break up the text or put your images on separate pages. To do this, you will need to add a page break.

1. **Click** on the **text item** you want to edit. The text item will be highlighted.

2. **Click** on the **Edit button**. The Text Item window will appear.

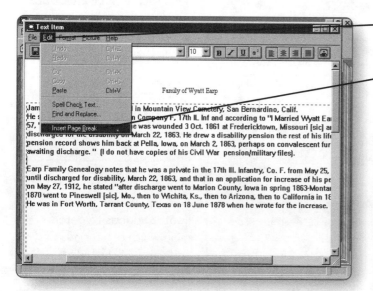

3. **Click** on **Edit**. The Edit menu will appear.

4. **Click** on **Insert Page Break**. A new page will be added in the Text Item window.

> **TIP**
>
> You can undo the page break by putting the insertion point at the top of the page and pressing the Backspace key.

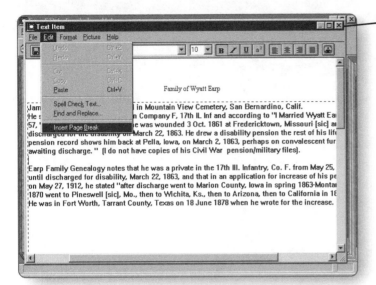

5. Click on **Close**. Family Tree Maker will prompt you to save the changes and the Text Item window will close.

Creating a Customized Index

Family Tree Maker allows you to include an index in your family history book. Genealogists for years to come will be pleased to find that your book has an index. While Family Tree Maker does the hard work of organizing the page numbers, you control the look and feel of the index.

1. Click on **Index** in the Available items list. The option will be highlighted.

2. Click on **Add**. The Index will be added to the end of the Outline for list.

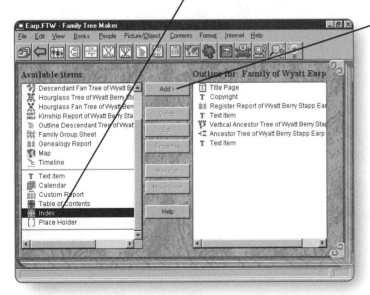

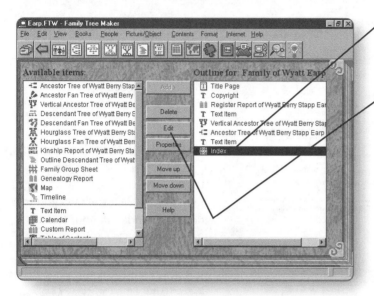

3. In the Outline for list, **click** on **Index**. The option will be highlighted.

4. Click on **Edit**. The Index of Individuals report will appear.

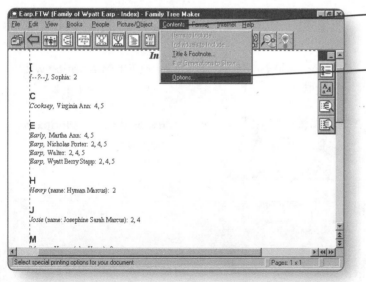

5. Click on **Contents**. The Contents menu will appear.

6. Click on **Options**. The Options for Book Index dialog box will open.

7. **Select** the **number of columns** to include in the index. The radio button will appear next to the number of columns you select.

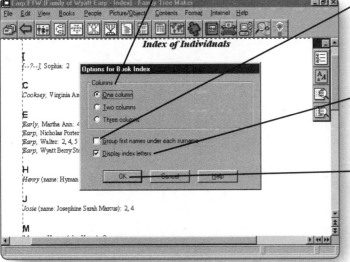

8. **Click** on the **Group first names under each surname check box**. A check mark will appear.

9. **Click** on the **Display index letters check box**. A check mark will appear.

10. **Click** on **OK**. Family Tree Maker will make the requested changes to the report.

NOTE

You may want to view the index with all possible combinations of these choices to determine how they affect the ease of reading of the index.

17

Creating Your Personal Family Tree Maker Home Page

While publishing a family history is still traditionally done by putting it on paper, the Internet has brought about a marvelous new way for people to publish their family histories. When publishing to paper, we tend to hold off publishing, in an effort to get everything perfect. The Internet saves us from this need to delay, as we can always upload a revised version of our pages. In this chapter, you'll learn how to:

- Create your first home page
- Register your home page
- Add reports to your home page
- Add trees to your home page
- Remove items from your home page

Creating Your First Home Page

Computers can intimidate genealogists, and many genealogists consider the Internet to be the biggest computer of them all—though it is not really a single computer. So, it is understandable that you might be hesitant when contemplating creating a family history Web page.

Working with the Wizard

Family Tree Maker is following the lead of many other software programs by adding wizards that help you perform certain tasks. The Family Home Page wizard walks you through putting together a basic home page.

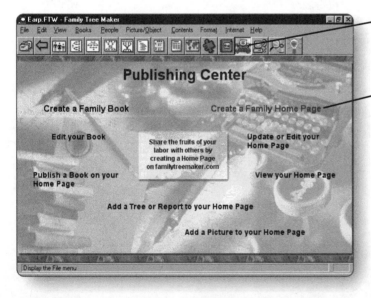

1. **Click** on the **Publishing Center button**. The Publishing Center will appear.

2. **Click** on **Create a Family Home Page**. The Family Home Page wizard will start.

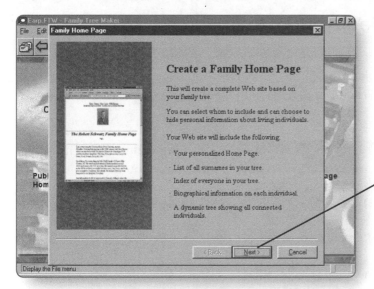

NOTE

The Family Home Page wizard helps you learn how to create a family history home page on the Family Tree Maker Web site.

3. Click on the **Next button.** The wizard will begin to ask you questions.

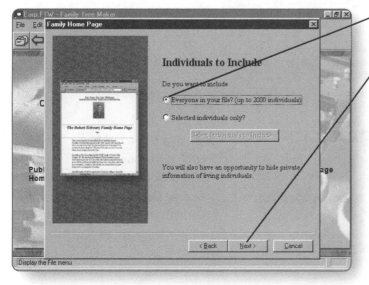

4. Answer the **question** asked. The wizard will record the answer.

5. Click on **Next**. The wizard will ask its next question.

6. Continue to answer the wizard's **questions**. When it has asked all the questions, the wizard will tell you it's time to go online.

NOTE

You may need to first go online to register. If so, see the following section, "Registering Your Home Page," and then return and rerun the wizard so that it can upload your page to your site.

Registering Your Home Page

The wizard has put together a general page for you to upload. Since this is the first Web page you have created, you will need to register with the Family Tree Maker site before the page can be uploaded.

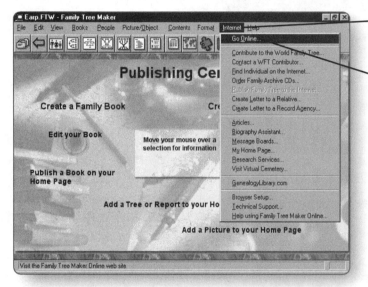

1. Click on **Internet**. The Internet menu will appear.

2. Click on **Go Online**. Your Web browser will open.

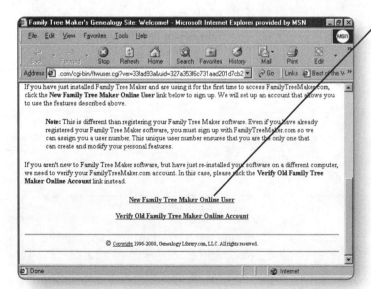

3. Use the **scroll bar** to scroll to the bottom of the Web page and **click** on **New Family Tree Maker Online User**. The Family Tree Maker Online Sign-Up screen will appear.

4. **Type** your **first name** in the First Name field and then **press the Tab key**. The insertion point will move to the next field.

5. **Supply** the requested **information** for the rest of the form and **click** on the **Submit button** at the bottom of the page. Your registration will be sent and you will be able to begin adding pages to your home page.

Working with Your Home Page

After the wizard has helped you upload that first Web page, you can enhance it by adding additional reports, an InterneTree, and even a book. The beauty of your home page is that you can change what is available whenever you wish. Most of the reports that you can print to paper can be used on the Family Tree Maker site.

Adding Reports

Adding reports to your family home page will make them viewable to anyone who visits your Web page. These pages will be added to the indexing and search abilities found on Family Tree Maker's Web site and to the Genealogy.com search page. The following is a list of reports and trees that you can publish to your family home page.

- Outline Descendant Trees
- Custom reports
- Genealogy Reports (Register, NGSQ, or Ahnentafel)
- Family Tree Maker book

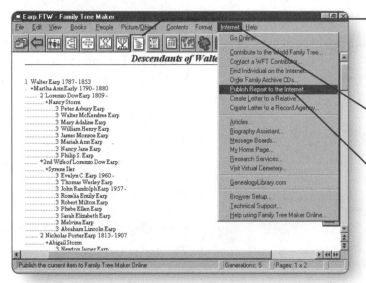

1. Click on the **report button** of the tree or report you want to add to your home page. The report will appear.

2. Click on **Internet**. The Internet menu will appear.

3. Click on **Publish Report to the Internet**. Family Tree Maker will open a message box, letting you know that it is preparing the report for publication to your home page.

NOTE

Family Tree Maker will begin to upload the report. It will keep you informed of its progress. After the information has been uploaded, you can have Family Tree Maker take you to your home page.

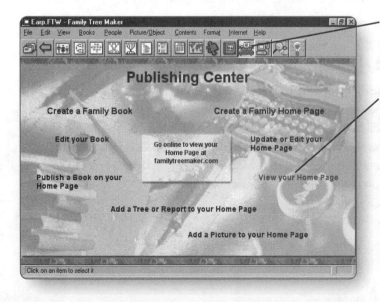

4. Click on the **Publishing Center button**. The Publishing Center will appear.

5. Click on **View your Home Page**. Your browser will appear.

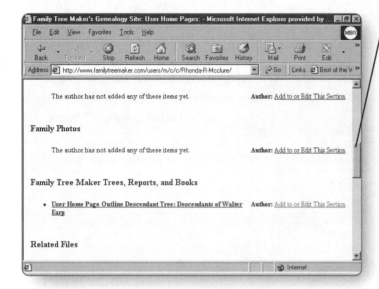

6. Use the **scroll bar** to scan through your Web page.

NOTE

You will see that in addition to working in the Family Tree Maker program, you can also upload other items to your home page, including pictures and Web links. Click on the Add to or Edit This Section link to customize your home page.

Adding an InterneTree

The InterneTree is a box-style tree. However, unlike the normal box-style reports, this one is interactive. Visitors to your home page can use an index and move through the generations. For each person in the tree, they will see the name of the individual, the birth date, and the death date.

TIP

You must be in the Family Page before you add your InterneTree.

1. Click on **Internet**. The Internet menu will appear.

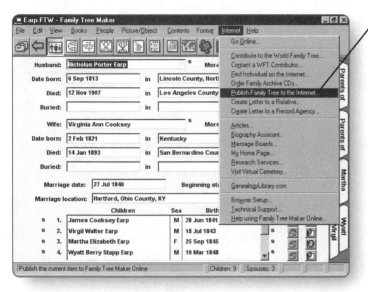

2. Click on **Publish Family Tree to the Internet**. Family Tree Maker will remind you that you need to be connected to the Internet. Click on OK and the Include dialog box will open.

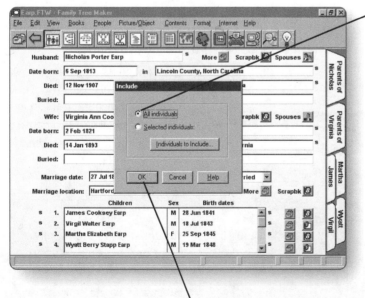

3. Select the **individuals** you want to include. The radio button will reflect your choice.

NOTE

If you choose Selected individuals, you will need to click on Individuals to Include to select the specific individuals you want to include.

---

4. Click on **OK**. The tree information will be uploaded to your home page.

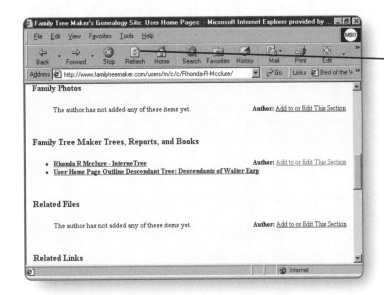

NOTE

You may need to click on the Refresh button to see the InterneTree in the list of reports on your home page.

Adding a Book

Just as you can print your family history book on paper and publish it to send to your family and fellow researchers, you can now include it on your home page. This offers you the chance to publish it while it's still a work in progress. As you find new information or correct inaccurate conclusions, you can simply upload a new version of the book to your home page.

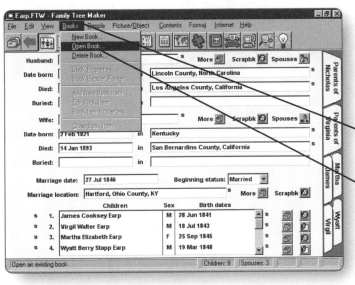

1. **Click** on **Books**. The Books menu will appear.

2. **Click** on **Open Book**. The Open Book dialog box will open.

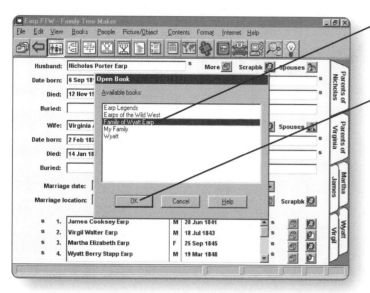

3. Select the desired **book** from the Available books list. The book will be highlighted.

4. Click on **OK**. The Book window will appear.

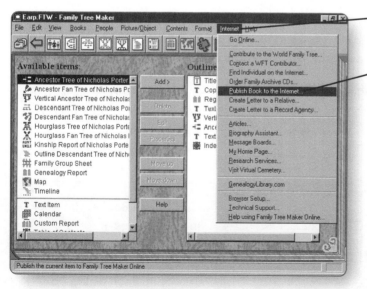

5. Click on **Internet**. The Internet menu will appear.

6. Click on **Publish Book to the Internet**. Family Tree Maker will upload the book, as it has already been designed, to your home page.

Removing Items from Your Home Page

Don't think that just because Family Tree Maker has uploaded these pages, you have no control over whether they remain on the home page. You determine what stays.

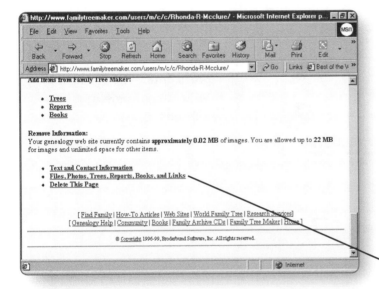

Removing a Family Tree Maker Report or Book

Removing a report or book that you have placed on your home page is not done through the Family Tree Maker program. This is done at the Family Tree Maker Web site, specifically at your home page.

1. Scroll to the **bottom** of your home page and **click** on the **link** for the information you want to remove. The Removing page will appear.

2. Click on the **check box** next to the item you wish to remove. A check mark will appear.

3. Click on the **Remove Selected Items button**. The item(s) will be removed.

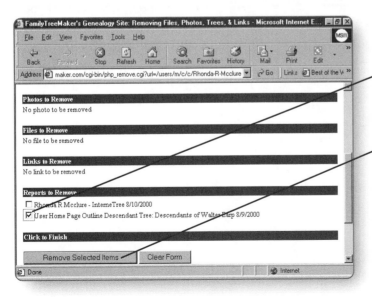

Deleting Your Home Page

You are not limited to removing specific items from your home page. You can also delete the entire home page if you need to—you can always recreate it at a later date.

1. Open your **browser.**

2. Type http://www.familytreemaker. com/ftm_uhp_home.html and **press Enter.** The Family Tree Maker User Home Pages site will appear.

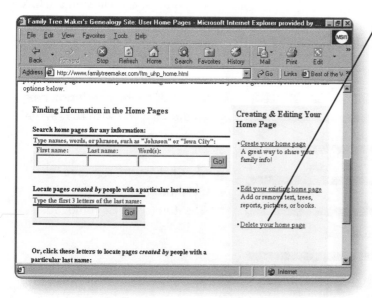

3. Scroll to the **bottom** of your home page and **click** on **Delete your home page.** The Delete Your Home Page page will appear.

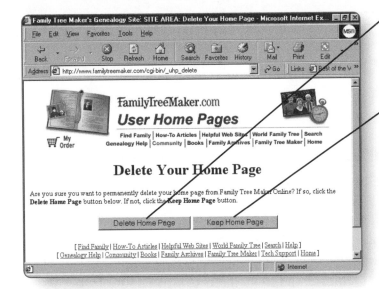

4a. **Click** on **Delete Home Page**. Your home page will be deleted.

OR

4b. **Click** on **Keep Home Page**. Your home page will not be deleted.

> **NOTE**
>
> If you elect to delete your home page, all the reports and trees that were attached to that home page will be deleted as well.

You have come from initial data entry to publishing your home page on the Internet. You will find that Family Tree Maker's features will make researching and sharing your genealogy much easier. Good luck.

Part V Review Questions

1. In Family Tree Maker, what is a scrapbook? *See "Using the Scrapbook" in Chapter 15*

2. What are the three different types of objects you can include in the scrapbook? *See "Inserting Scrapbook Images" in Chapter 15*

3. How can you rearrange the order of your scrapbook objects? *See "Rearranging Scrapbook Objects" in Chapter 15*

4. What reports can you include in a family history with Family Tree Maker? *See "Selecting Available Items" in Chapter 16*

5. How can you add a tree or report to your family history book? *See "Adding Trees and Reports" in Chapter 16*

6. How do you include pictures in your family history book? *See "Including Text with Pictures" in Chapter 16*

7. What are the ways you can customize the index to your family history book? *See "Creating a Customized Index" in Chapter 16*

8. What types of reports can you include on your family history home page? *See "Working with Your Home Page" in Chapter 17*

9. How can you add a family history book to your home page? *See "Adding a Book" in Chapter 17*

10. How can you remove a report or book from your home page? *See "Removing a Family Tree Maker Report or Book" in Chapter 17*

PART VI

Appendixes

Appendix A
   Installing Family Tree Maker 309

Appendix B
   Using Keyboard Shortcuts 315

A

Installing Family Tree Maker

Family Tree Maker has been designed to be easy to install. In this appendix, you'll learn how to:

- Install Family Tree Maker Version 8 on your computer
- Choose the options you want to install
- Uninstall Family Tree Maker from your computer

Installing Family Tree Maker Version 8

Most computers use an autorun feature when you put a new program CD into your CD-ROM drive—the CD begins to run without your having to do anything.

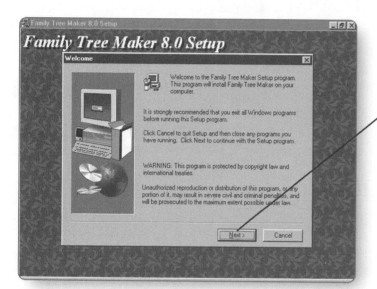

1. Insert the **Family Tree Maker 8 CD-ROM** into your computer's CD-ROM drive. The automatic installer will start.

2. Click on **Next** after you have closed all other programs. The Software License Agreement dialog box will open.

NOTE

Family Tree Maker's installer will encourage you to close any programs you have running at the time you begin to install Family Tree Maker 8. (This is a good idea whenever you are installing software.)

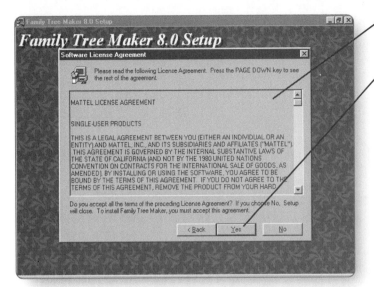

3. Read the **License Agreement**.

4. Click on **Yes**. The Choose Destination Location dialog box will open.

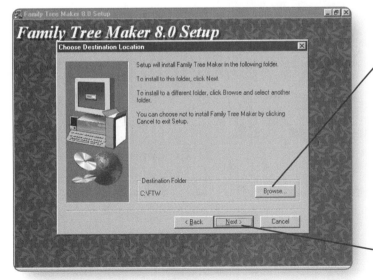

TIP

Usually the suggested Destination Folder is the most appropriate one. However, if you do not like where the installer is going to place Family Tree Maker, click on the Browse button and select another directory.

5. Click on **Next**. The Select Components dialog box will open.

Choosing Components

Family Tree Maker allows you to decide which of the available components you want to install.

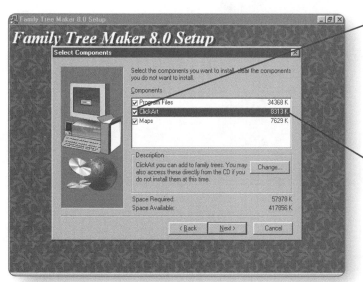

1. **Click** on the **check boxes** next to the components you wish to include. A check mark will appear next to each component you select.

NOTE

After you select a component, its size will be shown to the right, and the Space Required total will reflect the change.

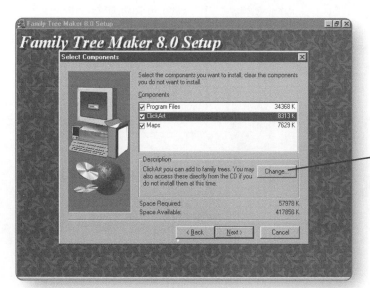

TIP

You can select all the ClickArt and maps or just some of them.

2. **Click** on **Change**. The Select Sub-components dialog box will open.

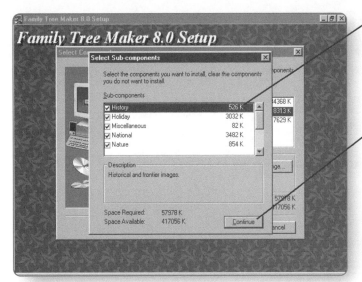

3. **Click** on the **sub-components** that you don't want to install. The check marks next to the sub-components you click on will be deleted.

4. **Click** on **Continue**. The Select Sub-components dialog box will close.

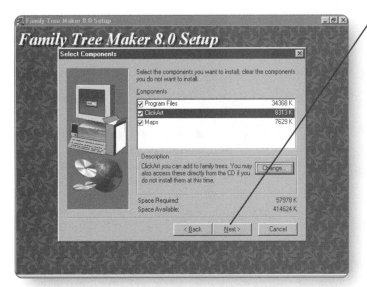

5. **Click** on **Next**. The Select Program Folder dialog box will open.

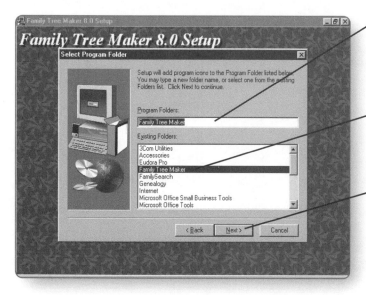

6a. Type a **program folder** if you do not want to use the one supplied by Family Tree Maker.

OR

6b. Select a **folder** from those already listed. The folder will be highlighted.

7. Click on **Next**. The program will be installed.

Uninstalling Family Tree Maker

There may come a time when you need to remove Family Tree Maker from your computer. Family Tree Maker has included an uninstall option.

1. Click on the **Start button**. The Start menu will appear.

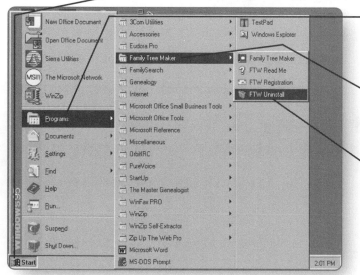

2. Move the **mouse pointer** to Programs. The Programs menu will appear.

3. Move the **mouse pointer** to Family Tree Maker. The Family Tree Maker menu will appear.

4. Click on **FTW Uninstall**. The UnInstallShield will remove the program.

B

Using Keyboard Shortcuts

Many people prefer not to have to reach for the mouse when they're entering information. Keyboard shortcuts allow you to accomplish many of the tasks for which you would normally need to use the mouse. Throughout the book your attention has been called to some of the keyboard shortcuts included in this appendix, but here you can see the information at a glance. In this appendix, you'll learn how to:

- Use the keyboard shortcuts found in Family Tree Maker
- Use keyboard combinations in text windows

Learning the Keyboard Shortcuts

While it may seem that you will never remember the shortcuts, you will find that the shortcut commands become second nature as you spend more time in Family Tree Maker.

Getting Help

Although you can always open the Help menu, you can use the keyboard shortcuts shown in the following table to get to the help you need more quickly.

To execute this command	Do this
Use Family Tree Maker Help	Press the F1 key
Use the What's This? Button	Press the Shift and F1 keys at the same time (Shift+F1)

Working in Family Tree Maker

The following table puts the keyboard shortcuts related to Family Tree Maker commands together for an easy reference.

To execute this command	Do this
Create a new family file	Press Ctrl+N
Open a different family file	Press Ctrl+O
Print a report	Press Ctrl+P
Create a new To Do Item	Press Ctrl+T
Access the Index of Individuals	Press F2
View a Source	Press Ctrl+S
Open the Other Spouses dialog box	Press F3
Access a More About Picture window	Press Ctrl+M
Get family file status	Press Alt+F1
Get system information	Press Ctrl+F1
Exit Family Tree Maker	Press Alt+F4

Working with Text

While most of the entries in Family Tree Maker are made in fields, there are a number of text windows for typing notes. The following tables contain some shortcuts you might find useful when working in the text windows.

Selecting Text

The first step in manipulating your text is to select it. The following table offers some keyboard combinations for selecting a letter, a word, a line, or more.

To execute this command	Do this
Highlight the character to the right of the insertion point	Press Shift+Right Arrow
Highlight the character to the left of the insertion point	Press Shift+Left Arrow
Highlight an entire word	Press Ctrl+Shift+Right Arrow
Highlight an entire line	Press Shift+End

Copying and Pasting Text

After you select the text you want to work with, you might want to remove it or copy it for placement elsewhere. The following table contains the keyboard combinations you need to manipulate selected text.

To execute this command	Do this
Copy text	Press Ctrl+C
Cut text	Press Ctrl+X
Paste text	Press Ctrl+V
Delete text	Press Del

Glossary

A

Ahnentafel. German for *ancestor table*. In addition to being a chart, it also refers to a genealogical numbering system.

Ancestor. A person from whom one descends.

Ancestor Tree. Also known as a pedigree chart, this chart begins with a specific individual and displays direct lineage of all of the individual's ancestors.

Annotation. Personal notes or comments that either explain or critique. Family Tree Maker employs annotations in the bibliography report.

B

Bibliography. A report that shows a list of sources used to compile the information included in the genealogy. The sources follow an accepted format, which Family Tree Maker has built into the program.

BMP. Bitmap. A file format for graphics.

Book. In Family Tree Maker, a compilation of reports generated for a family or individual, including family trees, miscellaneous reports, stories, photos, a table of contents, and an index.

Browser. See *Web Browser*.

C

Case sensitive. Differentiating between uppercase and lowercase characters.

Citation. The accepted notation of the source of information.

Cite. The act of making note of the proof that supports a conclusion or claimed fact in the genealogy.

Clipboard. A memory feature of the Windows environment that allows a person to copy or cut (but not delete) text or graphics from one document and paste them into another.

D

Descendant. A person who descends lineally from another.

Descendant Tree. A chart that lists an individual and his or her descendants.

E

Endnotes. Source citations and explanatory notes that appear at the end of a document, specifically a tree or report.

Export. To transfer data from one computer to another or from one computer program to another.

F

Family file. Family Tree Maker's name for the database that contains the information about your lineage.

Family group sheet. A form that displays information on a single, complete family unit.

FamilyFinder Index. A genealogical list containing over 170 million names that's included in Family Tree Maker's CDs.

Family Page. The main screen in Family Tree Maker, into which you will enter information about a particular individual and family.

Format. One of Family Tree Maker's options for developing the style and look of reports and trees.

G

Genealogy Report. A narrative style report that details a family through one or more generations and includes basic facts about each member in addition to biographical information that was entered through Family Tree Maker.

GEDCOM. GEnealogical Data COMmunication, a standard designed by the Family History Department of the Church of Jesus Christ of Latter-day Saints for transferring data between different genealogy software packages.

Generation. The period of time between the birth of one group of individuals and the next, usually about 25 to 33 years.

GIF. Graphic Interchange Format. A graphics file format that is widely used in Web page documents.

Given name. The first name (and middle name) given to a child at birth or at their baptism. Also known as a *Christian* name.

H

Home page. The main page of a Web site.

Hourglass Tree. A chart showing both the ancestors and the descendants of a selected individual. When printed, the tree resembles an hourglass because the ancestors spread out above the selected individual and the descendants spread out below.

HTML. Hypertext Markup Language. The standard language for creating and formatting Web pages.

I

Import. To bring into a program a file that was created using another program.

Inline notes. These are the sources that appear within the text as opposed to at the bottom or end of a page in Family Tree Maker's Genealogy Reports.

J

JPEG. Joint Photographic Expert Group. Graphics that use the .jpg extension include a compression technique that reduces the size of the graphics file.

K

Kinship. In genealogy, this refers to the relationship between one individual and any or all of his or her relatives. This can be displayed through the Kinship report in Family Tree Maker.

M

Maternal ancestor. An ancestor on the mother's side of the family.

N

NGSQ. *National Genealogical Society Quarterly*. A periodical published by that society. Also refers to the NGS Quarterly numbering system offered in descending genealogy reports.

O

OLE. Object Linking and Embedding. A technology that allows you to create items in one program and place them in another; including video clips, still images, pictures, word processing files, and spreadsheet files.

Outline Descendant Tree. A chart that shows in an indented outline format an individual's children, grandchildren, great-grandchildren, and so on through the generations.

P

Paternal ancestor. An ancestor on the father's side of the family.

Pedigree chart. A chart that shows the direct ancestors of an individual. Known in Family Tree Maker as an *Ancestor Tree*.

Preferred. A term Family Tree Maker uses in reference to parents, spouses, or duplicate events, meaning that you want to see that selection first or have it displayed in trees and reports.

Primary individual. The main individual in any of the Family Tree Maker charts or reports.

R

Research journal. A record used by genealogists to keep track of their research findings and tasks to be accomplished.

Reports. Any of a number of standard and custom displays in various formats that Family Tree Maker can create.

Register. Refers to the descending genealogy format used by the New England Historic Genealogical Society. This also refers to their periodical by the same name.

RTF. Rich Text Format. A cross-platform, cross-application text document format. It retains some of the formatting information that is supported by many word processors.

S

Scrapbooks. The term used by Family Tree Maker for the collections of photographs, images, video, sound, and OLE objects that can be stored for each individual and marriage in the family file.

Siblings. Children of the same parents.

Source. The record, such as a book, e-mail message, or interview, from which specific information was obtained.

Spouse. The person to whom another person is married.

Surname. Family name or last name.

T

Tree. The term Family Tree Maker uses to refer to its various charts. See *Ancestor Tree, Descendant Tree,* and *Outline Descendant Tree.*

U

URL. Uniform Resource Locator. The address used by a Web browser to locate a page on the Web.

W

WAV. Windows Audio Visual. The sound files that work with Media Player and Sound Recorder.

Web browser. The software that lets you access pages on the Web. The browser reads the HTML code and converts it to the pictures, colors, menu options, and overall design that you view on your monitor.

Web page. A document on the Internet that is written using HTML.

Web site. A location on the Internet maintained by a single individual, company, or entity that provides information, graphics, and other items.

World Family Tree (WFT) Project. A multivolume CD collection created by Genealogy.com from the genealogies submitted electronically by family history enthusiasts and indexed in the FamilyFinder Index.

World Wide Web. A graphical interface that is composed of Internet sites that provide researchers with access to documents and other files.

Index

A

Add Genealogy Report dialog box, 282
Add text item dialog box, 282
address reports, 221–222
Address window, 89–90
adoptions
    indicating relationships, 95–96
    parents, adding, 49–52
Ahnentafel format reports, 243–244, 319
AKA names
    adding, 94
    including in Index of Individuals, 135
aliases, adding, 94
All-in-One Trees, 204
    creating, 204–205
    display size, setting, 205
    pruning display, 206
Ancestor Trees, 20, 194, 319
    fan charts, 194–195
    pedigree charts, 195–197
    vertical, 197–199
ancestors, 319
Ancestors button, 215
annotated bibliographies, 252
annotations, 319
annulments, entering, 119–121
audio, inserting in scrapbooks, 261–262
AutoFix button, 165

B

background images, adding to trees, 209
Background Picture dialog box, 209
Beginning status drop-down list, 47
bibliography reports, 251–252, 319
birth order
    adjusting, 55–57
    sorting children in, 58
birthday reports, 222–223
Births screen, 7–8
BMP file format, 319
boldfacing text
    in notes, 111
    in reports, 230
book titles, italicizing, 66
books
    citing. *See* citing sources
    creating. *See* family books
Books menu, Open Book command, 301
box charts, 21
    Descendant Trees, 202–203
    Hourglass Trees, 201–202
    multiple-page, printing, 235
browsers (Web), 322
burial information, entering, 33

C

call numbers, 68
captions, adding to scrapbooks, 265
case sensitivity, 319
categorizing scrapbook objects, 265
chapters, creating (family books), 286–287
charts
    box, 21, 26
        Descendant Trees, 202–203
        Hourglass Trees, 201–202
    fan
        Ancestor Trees, 20, 194–195
        Descendant Trees, 14, 21
        Hourglass Trees, 22, 199–200
        selecting density, 195
        selecting shape, 195
    multiple-page, printing, 235
    pedigree, 195–197, 321
        connections, 196
        layout options, 196
checking spelling
    entry screens, 152–153
    notes windows, 154–155
children
    adding, 34, 48, 53–54
    associating with spouses, 35–36
    attaching to parents, 170–173
    detaching, 173–175
    moving, 55–57
    moving to primary individual, 39–40
    multiple parents, adding, 49–52
    sorting, 58
Christian names, 320
citing sources, 99, 319
    accepted fields, 64
    bibliography reports, 251–252
    call numbers, 68
    endnotes, 245–246
    entering citation text, 74

    master sources, 65
        creating, 65–69
        editing, 75–78
        searching for, 71–72
        switching between, 78
    publication information, 67
    Source Citation dialog box, 70–74
    Source location field, 68
    Source media field, 67
    Source quality field, 69
clipboard, 319. *See also* copying; cutting;
    pasting
closing Family Tree Maker, 24
color
    adding to relationship lines, 207–208
    applying to text, 232
    printing with, 237
columns, custom reports, 217
commands
    Books menu, Open Book, 301
    Edit menu
        Copy Picture/Object, 268
        Copy Text, 23, 101
        Cut Picture/Object, 267
        Cut Text, 23
        Edit Master Sources, 66
        Find, 105
        Find and Replace, 188
        Find Error, 163–166
        Find Picture/Object, 271
        Insert Page Break, 288
        Paste Picture/Object, 268
        Paste Text, 24, 105
        Spell Check Note, 155
    File menu
        Exit, 24
        Import Text File, 114
        Preferences, 29
        Print Tree, 237
    Format menu, Text Font, Style & Size, 109
    grayed-out, 10

Internet menu
  Go Online, 296
  Publish Book to the Internet, 302
  Publish Family Tree to the Internet, 300
  Publish Report to the Internet, 298
keyboard shortcuts, 11, 316
People menu
  Delete Individual, 158
  Delete Individuals in Ancestor Tree, 160
  Fix Relationship Mistakes, 157
  Insert Child, 54
  Merge Duplicate Individuals, 182
  Merge Specific Individuals, 186
  Move Child From, 55
  Move Child To, 55
  Other Parents, 49
  Sort Children, 58
Picture menu, Insert from Scrapbook, 283
Picture/Object menu
  Edit, 270
  Insert Object, 261, 263
  Insert Picture from File, 259
  Insert Picture from Scanner/Camera, 259
  Play Scrapbook, 273
  Tree Background Picture, 209
View menu
  Family Page, 19
  Source, 64, 70
comments, searching for, 144–145
conflicting facts
  searching for, 249–251
  selecting preferred, 122–124
Copy Picture/Object command (Edit menu), 268
Copy Text command (Edit menu), 23, 101
copying
  notes, 100–101
  scrapbook objects, 268–269

text, 23, 101
  keyboard shortcut, 105
  into notes, 111–113
Create New FamilyFinder Report dialog box, 146
Create New Parents dialog box, 50–51
cropping images, 271
cue cards, 12
custom reports, 212
  adding items, 213
  column widths, 217
  footnotes, 216
  including only preferred information, 213
  saving, 219
  selecting individuals, 214–215
  sorting, 218
  titles, 216
Cut Picture/Object command (Edit menu), 267
Cut Text command (Edit menu), 23
cutting
  pictures/objects, 267
  text, 23, 103, 105

D

data entry checking, 161–163
Data Errors report, 166–168
dates
  conflicting, 122–124
  double dating, 30
  entering, 27–29
  error checking
    automatically, 162–163
    Find Error command, 164–166
    Ignore Error feature, 165–166
  format, changing, 29–31
  searching for, 140–141
  standard genealogical, 27
Dates & Measures dialog box, 30
deaths, entering, 28
Deaths screen, 8

Delete Individual command (People menu), 158
Delete Individuals in Ancestor Tree command (People menu), 160
deleting people
    groups, 159–161
    individuals, 157–158
Descendant Trees, 14, 21, 202, 320
    box charts, 202–203
    fan charts, 14
    outline trees, 203–204
descendants, 320
Descendants button, 215
Destination Location dialog box, 311
dialog boxes, 13
    Add Genealogy Report, 282
    Add text item, 282
    Background Picture, 209
    Create New FamilyFinder Report, 146
    Create New Parents, 50–51
    Dates & Measures, 30
    Destination Location, 311
    Edit Picture, 260
    Error Checking, 162
    Find, 105–106
    Find Error, 164
    Find Individual, 138
        searching by comment, 144–145
        searching by date, 140–141
        searching by location, 142–143
        searching by name, 139–140
        searching by source, 143–144
    Find Master Source, 71
    Find Name, 132–133
    Find Picture/Object, 271
    Format for Ancestor Tree, 194–195
    Genealogy Report Format, 240
    Import Text File, 114–115
    Index of Individuals, 130
    Individuals to Include, 147, 214
    Individuals with Scrapbook Pictures, 283–284

Insert Object, 261, 263
Insert Picture, 259
Insert Scrapbook Picture, 284
Item Properties, 287
Items to Include in Report, 213
Master Source, 66
Maximum Width for each Column, 217
Merge Duplicate Individuals, 183
More About Picture/Object, 265
New Book, 278–279
New To-Do Item, 225
# of Generations to Show, 200, 206, 247–248
Open Book, 301–302
Options for All-in-One Tree, 204–205
Options for Book Index, 290–291
Options for Documented Events Report, 253
Options for Genealogy Report, 245
Other Spouses, 13
Parents of, 49–50
Print Scrapbook Print Preview, 274–275
Print Setup, 233–234
Print Tree, 237
Printer Properties, 235–236
Report Format, 212, 219–220
Select Components, 311–312
Select Program Folder, 313–314
Select Sub-components, 312–313
Select the Child, 171–172
Select the individual who..., 186–187
Select the spouse, 177
Sort Report, 218
Source Citation, 64, 70–74
Spouses of, 37
Styles, 207–208
Text Font, Style & Size, 109–110, 228
Title & Footnote, 246–247
Title & Footnote for Report, 216
Tree Format for Outline Descendant Tree, 204

divorces, entering, 119–121
documented events reports, 253
documenting sources. *See* citing sources
double dating, 30
double lines (on charts), 21
Down Arrow, changing fields with, 15
dragging scroll bars, 14
duplicate facts
    searching for, 249–251
    selecting preferred, 122–124
duplicate individuals, merging, 182–185

E

Edit command (Picture/Object menu), 270
Edit Master Source button, 76
Edit Master Sources command (Edit menu), 66
Edit menu commands
    Copy Picture/Object, 268
    Copy Text, 23, 101
    Cut Picture/Object, 267
    Cut Text, 23
    Edit Master Sources, 66
    Find, 105
    Find and Replace, 188
    Find Error, 163–166
    Find Picture/Object, 271
    Insert Page Break, 288
    Paste Picture/Object, 268
    Paste Text, 24, 105
    Spell Check Note, 155
Edit Picture dialog box, 260
endnotes, 245–246, 320. *See also* footnotes
Enter key, changing fields with, 15
error checking
    automatic, 161–163
    Data Errors report, 166–168
    Find Error command, 163–166
    Ignore Error feature, 165–166
Error Checking dialog box, 162

events. *See also* facts
    creating names for, 87–88
    entering, 27–29
excluding
    individuals from reports, 61
    relationships from reports, 96
Exit command (File menu), 24
exiting Family Tree Maker, 24
exporting notes, 116

F

facts. *See also* events
    adding, 83–84
    creating, 87–88
    selecting preferred, 84
family books
    author name, entering, 279
    available items, 278
    chapters, creating, 286–287
    front matter, 279–281
    genealogy reports, adding, 282
    headers/footers, 287
    home pages
        adding to, 301–302
        removing from, 303
    indexing, 289–291
    item properties, 286–287
    organizing items, 285–286
    page breaks, inserting, 288–289
    pictures, including text with, 282–285
    reports, adding, 281–282
    titles, entering, 279
    trees, adding, 281–282
Family File, 320
Family Group Sheet, 320
Family Home Page wizard, 294–295
Family Page, 17–19, 26, 32, 320
    navigating fields, 15–16
    opening, 17, 19
Family Page command (View menu), 19

Family Tree Maker
 exiting, 24
 installing, 310–311
  choosing components, 312–313
  choosing program folder, 314
 launching, 4
 uninstalling, 314
family tree, starting, 5–9
FamilyFinder Center
 opening, 145
 reports, 148–149
 searches, 146–147
FamilyFinder Index, 320
FamilyFinder Search screen, 8–9
fan charts
 Ancestor Trees, 20, 194–195
 Descendant Trees, 14, 21
 Hourglass Trees, 22, 199–200
 multiple-page, printing, 235
 selecting density, 195
 selecting shape, 195
females, maiden names, 47
fields
 citing sources in, 64
 moving between, 8, 15–16, 26–27
file formats
 BMP, 319
 GIF, 320
 JPEG, 321
 .txt, 116
 WAV, 322
File menu commands
 Exit, 24
 Import Text File, 114
 Preferences, 29
 Print Tree, 237
Find and Replace command (Edit menu), 188
Find and Replace feature, 188–189

Find command (Edit menu), 105
Find dialog box, 105–106
Find Error command, 163–166
Find Error dialog box, 164
Find Individual dialog box, 138
 searching by comment, 144–145
 searching by date, 140–141
 searching by location, 142–143
 searching by name, 139–140
 searching by source, 143–144
Find Master Source dialog box, 71
Find Name dialog box, 132–133
Find Picture/Object command (Edit menu), 271
Find Picture/Object dialog box, 271
finding. *See* searching
Fix Relationship Mistakes command (People menu), 157
fonts
 changing, 229
 selecting for notes, 110
footnotes. *See also* endnotes
 custom reports, 216
 genealogy reports, 246–247
Format button, 194
Format for Ancestor Tree dialog box, 194–195
Format menu, Text Font, Style & Size command, 109
formatting
 dates, 29–31
 notes, 109–111
front matter (family books), 279–281

G

GEDCOM, 320
gender button, 5
Genealogy How-To guide, 226
Genealogy Report Format dialog box, 240

genealogy reports, 320
   Ahnentafel format, 243–244
   changing number of generations, 247–248
   including notes in, 248–249
   NGSQ format, 242–243
   page numbering, 246–247
   Register format, 240–241
   titles, 246–247
generations, 320
GIF file format, 320
given names, 320
Go Online command (Internet menu), 296
Go to Family Page button, 133
grandparents, adding, 6–7
graphics. *See* images
Gregorian calendar, 30

H

headers/footers, 287
help
   Genealogy How-To guide, 226
   keyboard shortcuts, 316
Help Windows, 12, 59
highlighting relationships, 207–208
home pages, 320
   creating, 294–295
   deleting, 304–305
   family books, adding, 301–302
   InterneTrees, adding, 299–301
   links, adding, 299
   pictures, uploading, 299
   registering, 296–297
   removing items from, 303
   reports, adding, 297–298
   viewing, 298
Hourglass Trees, 22, 199, 320
   box charts, 201–202
   fan charts, 199–200
HTML (Hypertext Markup Language), 320

I

Ignore Error feature, 165–166
images
   adding to family books, 282–285
   background, adding to trees, 209
   cropping, 271
   inserting in scrapbooks, 259–260
   scanning into scrapbooks, 259
Import Text File command (File menu), 114
Import Text File dialog box, 114–115
importing notes text, 114–115
inclusion buttons, 215
Index of Individuals, 130
   family books, 290
   including AKA names, 135
   rearranging, 134–137
indexing family books, 289–291
Individual Scrapbook window, 18, 258
individuals
   deleting from files, 157–158
   selecting for custom reports, 214–215
Individuals to Include dialog box, 147, 214
Individuals with Scrapbook Pictures dialog box, 283–284
inline notes, 321
Insert Child command (People menu), 54
Insert from Scrapbook command (Picture menu), 283
Insert Object command (Picture/Object menu), 261, 263
Insert Object dialog box, 261, 263
Insert Page Break command (Edit menu), 288
Insert Picture dialog box, 259
Insert Picture from File command (Picture/Object menu), 259
Insert Picture from Scanner/Camera command (Picture/Object menu), 259
Insert Scrapbook Picture dialog box, 284
installing Family Tree Maker, 310–311
   choosing components, 312–313
   choosing program folder, 314

Internet menu commands
  Go Online, 296
  Publish Book to the Internet, 302
  Publish Family Tree to the Internet, 300
  Publish Report to the Internet, 298
InterneTrees, 299–301
italicizing
  book titles, 66
  notes, 111
  text, 230
Item Properties dialog box, 287
Items to Include in Report dialog box, 213

J

JPEG file format, 321
Julian calendar, 30

K

keyboard shortcuts, 11, 316–317
kids. *See* children
kinship, 321
kinship reports, 219–220

L

launching Family Tree Maker, 4
lineage. *See* More About Lineage window
Lineage More About button, 59
Location field
  Births screen, 7
  Deaths screen, 8
locations, searching for, 142–143

M

maiden names, 47
margins, adjusting, 234–235
marriages
  additional facts, adding, 119–121
  dates and locations, entering, 33

duplicate facts, selecting preferred, 122–124
maiden names, 47
notes, 124–125
reference numbers, adding, 119–120
spouses
  adding, 32–33
  associating children with, 35–36
  attaching, 175–181
  designating preferred, 37
  multiple, adding, 35–36
  switching between, 38–39
  undoing, 155–157
Master Source dialog box, 66
master sources, 65
  creating, 65–69
    call numbers, 68
    Comments field, 69
    publication information, 67
    source location field, 68
    Source media field, 67
    source quality field, 69
  editing, 75–78
  searching for, 71–72, 78–80
  switching between, 78
maternal ancestors, 321
Maximum Width for each Column dialog box, 217
medical information, adding, 91–92
menus, 10–11
  activating, 10
  arrows on, 10
  executing commands, 11
  grayed-out commands on, 10
Merge Duplicate Individuals command (People menu), 182
Merge Duplicate Individuals dialog box, 183
Merge Individuals report, 183
Merge Specific Individuals command (People menu), 186

merging
    duplicate individuals, 182–185
    specific individuals, 186–187
More About Address and Phone(s) window,
    89–90
More About Facts window, 82
    adding facts, 83–84
    creating facts, 87–88
    preferred facts, selecting, 84
More About Lineage window, 59–61, 93
    AKA names, adding, 94
    excluding relationships from reports, 96
    special relationships, 95–96
    titles, adding, 93
More About Marriage Facts window, 119
More About Marriage Notes window,
    124–125
More About Marriage window, 118
More About Medical window, 91–92
More About Notes. See notes
More About Picture/Object dialog box, 265
More About scrapbook objects, 265–266
Move Child From command (People menu), 55
Move Child To command (People menu), 55
moving
    children, 55–57
    notes, 101–105
    scrapbook objects, 267–268
    text, 23–24
multiple-page charts, printing, 235

N

names
    AKA
        adding, 94
        including in Index of Individuals, 135
    entering, 26
        maiden, 47
        unknown names, 47
        your grandparents, 6–7

        your immediate family, 5
        your own, 5
    preferred, selecting, 85–86
    searching for
        Find Individual dialog box, 139–140
        Find Name dialog box, 132–133
        quick search, 130–131
    variants, adding, 85
National Genealogical Society Quarterly, 240
navigating fields, 15–16
New Book dialog box, 278–279
New To-Do Item dialog box, 225
NGSQ format reports, 242–243, 321
nicknames
    adding, 85
    including in Index of Individuals, 135
notes
    copying, 100–101
    copying text into, 111–113
    entering, 98–99
    exporting, 116
    formatting, 109–111
    importing text, 114–115
    including in genealogy reports, 248–249
    marriages, 124–125
    moving, 101–105
    searching, 105–108
    source citation information, 99
Number of Generations button, 206
# of Generations to Show dialog box
    All-in-One Trees, 206
    genealogy reports, 247–248
    Hourglass Trees, 200

O

OLE objects (scrapbooks), 263–264, 321
online searches, FamilyFinder Center,
    146–147
Open Book command (Books menu), 301
Open Book dialog box, 301–302

Options for All-in-One Tree dialog box, 204–205
Options for Book Index dialog box, 290–291
Options for Documented Events Report dialog box, 253
Options for Genealogy Report dialog box, 245
orientation settings (printer), 233–234
Other Parents command (People menu), 49
Other Spouses dialog box, 13
Outline for list (family books), 285–286
outline trees, 203–204, 321
overlapping pages, 235

P

page breaks, inserting (family books), 288–289
page numbering, genealogy reports, 246–247
paper orientation (printing), 233–234
parents
    adding, 46
    attaching children to, 170–173
    detaching children from, 173–175
    multiple, adding, 49–52
Parents of dialog box, 49–50
Paste Picture/Object command (Edit menu), 268
Paste Text command (Edit menu), 24, 105
pasting
    pictures/objects, 268
    text, 105
paternal ancestors, 321
pedigree charts, 195–197, 321
    connections, 196
    layout options, 196
People menu commands
    Delete Individual, 158
    Delete Individuals in Ancestor Tree, 160
    Fix Relationship Mistakes, 157
    Insert Child, 54
    Merge Duplicate Individuals, 182

Merge Specific Individuals, 186
Move Child From, 55
Move Child To, 55
Other Parents, 49
Sort Children, 58
Picture menu, Insert from Scrapbook command, 283
Picture/Object menu commands
    Edit, 270
    Insert Object, 261, 263
    Insert Picture from File, 259
    Insert Picture from Scanner/Camera, 259
    Play Scrapbook, 273
    Tree Background Picture, 209
place names, entering, 28
place of birth, entering, 7
Play Scrapbook command (Picture/Object menu), 273
playing scrapbooks, 273
Preferences command (File menu), 29
preferred facts, selecting, 84, 122–124
preferred names, selecting, 85–86
primary individuals, 321
    moving children to, 39–40
    selecting, 220
Print Scrapbook Print Preview dialog box, 274–275
Print Setup dialog box, 233–234
Print Tree command (File menu), 237
Print Tree dialog box, 237
Printer Properties dialog box, 235–236
printer settings
    margins, 234–235
    Overlap pages option, 235
    paper orientation, 233–234
    Printer Properties dialog box, 235–236
printing
    notes, formatting text, 109–111
    scrapbooks, 274–275
    trees, 237–238
publication information, 67

Publish Book to the Internet command (Internet menu), 302
Publish Family Tree to the Internet command (Internet menu), 300
Publish Report to the Internet command (Internet menu), 298
Publishing Center, 278

Q

quoting from sources, 99

R

rearranging Index of Individuals, 134–137
reference numbers, adding to marriage events, 119–120
Register format reports, 240–241, 322
registering home pages, 296–297
Relationship with field, 51
relationships
    in box charts, 21
    emphasizing in tree views, 207–208
    excluding from reports, 96
    fixing mistakes
        attaching children, 170–173
        attaching spouses, 175–181
        detaching children, 173–175
        undoing marriages, 155–157
    selecting, 51, 60, 95–96
removing people from files
    groups, 159–161
    individuals, 157–158
replacing text (Find and Replace feature), 188–189
Report Format dialog box, 212, 219–220
reports, 322. See also trees
    address, 221–222
    bibliography, 251–252, 319
    birthday, 222–223
    conflicting facts, 249–251
    custom, 212
        adding items, 213

        columns, 217
        footnotes, 216
        including only preferred information, 213
        saving, 219
        selecting individuals, 214–215
        titles, 216
    Data Errors, 166–168
    documented events, 253
    excluding individuals from, 61
    excluding relationships from, 96
    family books, adding to, 281–282
    FamilyFinder Center, 148–149
    genealogy
        Ahnentafel format, 243–244
        changing number of generations, 247–248
        including notes in, 248–249
        NGSQ format, 242–243
        page numbering, 246–247
        Register format, 240–241
        titles, 246–247
    home pages, adding to, 297–298
    home pages, removing from, 303
    kinship, 219–220
    Merge Individuals, 183
    printer settings
        margins, 234–235
        Overlap pages option, 235
        paper orientation, 233–234
        Printer Properties dialog box, 235–236
    printing, 237–238
    Research Journal, 224–225
    sorting, 218
    text
        applying color, 232
        changing font, 229
        changing size, 231
        changing style, 230
Research Journal, 224–225, 321

right-clicking selected text, 103
RTF (rich text format), 322
running footers, 216

S

saving custom reports, 219
scanning images into scrapbook, 259
Scrapbook button, 18
Scrapbook Print Preview window, 274
scrapbooks, 258, 322
    captions, 265
    including items when playing, 266
    including items when printing, 266
    inserting images, 259–260
    inserting sound clips, 261–262
    objects
        categorizing, 265
        copying between books, 268–269
        cutting, 267
        descriptions, 266
        editing, 270–271
        moving, 267–268
        OLE, inserting, 263–264
        pasting, 268
        searching for, 271–272
    playing, 273
    preferred items, selecting, 266
    printing, 274–275
    scanning images into, 259
scroll bars, 13–14
    clicking inside, 14
    dragging, 14
searching
    by comment, 144–145
    by date, 140–141
    for duplicate facts, 249–251
    FamilyFinder Center, 146–147
    FamilyFinder Search screen, 8–9
    Find and Replace feature, 188–189
    by location, 142–143

    for master sources, 71–72, 78–80
    by name
        Find Individual dialog box, 139–140
        Find Name dialog box, 132–133
        quick search, 130–131
    notes text, 105–108
    for objects, 271–272
    by source, 143–144
second marriages
    adding additional spouses, 35–36
    designating preferred spouse, 37
    switching between spouses, 38–39
Select Components dialog box, 311–312
Select Program Folder dialog box, 313–314
Select Sub-components dialog box, 312–313
Select the Child dialog box, 171–172
Select the individual who... dialog box,
    186–187
Select the spouse dialog box, 177
selecting
    relationships, 51, 60
    text, 23
siblings, 322. *See also* children
    adding, 48
    associating with parents, 173
    detaching from parents, 175
single lines (in charts), 21
Sort Children command (People menu), 58
Sort Report dialog box, 218
sorting
    children, 58
    reports, 218
sound clips, inserting in scrapbooks, 261–262
Source Citation dialog box, 64, 70–74
Source command (View menu), 64, 70
Source media field, 67
sources, 322
    citing, 99
        accepted fields, 64
        bibliography reports, 251–252

call numbers, 68
endnotes, 245–246
entering citation text, 74
publication information, 67
Source Citation dialog box, 70–74
Source location field, 68
Source media field, 67
Source quality field, 69
master, 65
creating, 65–69
editing, 75–78
searching for, 71–72, 78–80
switching between, 78
searching for, 143–144
Spell Check Note command (Edit menu), 155
spell checker
entry screens, 152–153
notes windows, 154–155
spouses, 322
adding, 32–33
associating children with, 35–36
attaching, 175–181
detaching, 155–157
multiple
adding, 35–36
designating preferred, 37
switching between, 38–39
Spouses button, 19
Spouses of dialog box, 37
starting Family Tree Maker, 4
stepparents
adding, 49–52
indicating relationships, 95–96
stories. See notes
Styles dialog box, 207–208
surnames, 47, 322

T

Tab key, changing fields with, 8, 15, 26–27
tabs, 10

text
boldfacing
notes, 111
in reports, 230
color, changing, 232
copying, 23, 101
keyboard shortcut, 105
into notes, 111–113
cutting, 23, 103, 105
finding and replacing, 188–189
fonts, changing, 229
including with pictures (family books), 282–285
italicizing, 230
book titles, 66
notes, 66
moving, 23–24
pasting, 105
searching for in notes, 105–108
selecting, 23, 317
size, changing, 231
Text Font, Style & Size command (Format menu), 109
Text Font, Style, & Size dialog box, 109–110, 228
Text Item window, 285
The New England Historic Genealogical Register, 240
Title & Footnote dialog box, 246–247
Title & Footnote for Report dialog box, 216
titles
book, italicizing, 66
family books, 279
genealogy reports, 246–247
of people, adding, 93
reports, 216
To-Do items, adding to Research Journal, 225
toolbar, 12
tooltips, 12
Tree Background Picture command (Picture/Object menu), 209

Tree Format for Outline Descendant Tree
    dialog box, 204
trees, 322. *See also* reports
    adding to family books, 281–282
    All-in-One, 204
        creating, 204–205
        display size, setting, 205
        pruning display, 206
    Ancestor, 20, 194
        fan charts, 194–195
        pedigree charts, 195–197
        vertical, 20, 197–199
    Descendant, 14, 21, 202, 320
        box charts, 202–203
        fan charts, 14
        outline trees, 203–204
    enhancing
        adding background images, 209
        emphasizing relationships, 207–208
    Hourglass, 22, 199, 321
        box charts, 201–202
        fan charts, 199–200
    outline, 321
    printer settings
        margins, 234–235
        Overlap pages option, 235
        paper orientation, 233–234
        Printer Properties dialog box,
            235–236
    printing, 237–238
    text
        applying color, 232
        changing font, 229
        changing size, 231
        changing style, 230
    viewing, 228
.txt file format, 116
type size, selecting (notes), 110

U

Uniform Resource Locators (URLs), 322
uninstalling Family Tree Maker, 314
unknown names, entering, 47
Up Arrow, changing fields with, 15
URLs (Uniform Resource Locators), 322

V

variant names, adding, 85
Vertical Ancestor Trees, 20, 197–199
View menu commands
    Family Page, 19
    Source, 64, 70
viewing trees, 228

W

WAV file format, 322
Web browsers, 322
Web sites. *See* home pages
women, maiden names, 47
World Family Tree (WFT) Project, 322
World Wide Web, 322

Z

zooming, 197

Genealogy.com

—— The leading resource for family history ——

Genealogical data still comes from the same places it did 50 years ago — government records, published research from historical and present-day genealogists, and societies. The difference these days is that you can have instant access a to far greater quantity of data than ever before — and you don't have to leave the comfort of your own home!

Genealogy.com is committed to helping you find your ancestors and build your family tree. In addition to our popular Family Tree Maker® software program, we are constantly enhancing the valuable computerized data resources available to you. We offer many different types of resources to help you find your ancestors guaranteed — or your money back!

Family Tree Maker® Software

The #1-Selling and Rated Family History Program for over a decade! For beginners and experts alike, Family Tree Maker is the easiest and most complete resource for building your family tree.

World Family Tree

The Web's largest collection of compiled family trees where you can reach others who are researching the same names as you. Add whole branches to your family tree with just one match!

Family Archives & New Internet Family Archives

Over 300 Million names on 280 CDs archived within a rapidly growing collection! Buy the Family Archive CD ROM or get instant access over the Internet wth an Inernet Family Archive !

GenealogyLibrary.com

GenealogyLibrary.com puts over a 100 million names at your fingertips, 24 hours a day. This powerful Web site holds a rapidly growing collection of online books, databases, and family-finding resources, including handwritten images of the 1850 U.S. Census.

Read on for more details…

World Family Tree

The Web's largest collection of compiled family trees!

What is the World Family Tree?

▶ A growing collection of family trees contributed by genealogists like you, currently containing more than 114 million names on over 160,000 family trees.

▶ A collaborative community, where you can reach others who are researching the same names as you.

▶ Much more than linked relations and vital dates; many trees contain notes, sources, and images.

Incredible discoveries are waiting for you!

▶ You are guaranteed* to find compelling information on your ancestors!

▶ An average tree contains over 600 individuals — find just one ancestor in the World Family Tree and your tree could grow by branches!

How do you use it?

Easy! Just go to our Web site at:

www.FamilyTreeMaker.com/wftonline

And for only $19.99 a month, you can have unlimited online access to the World Family Tree!

* 90 day money back guarantee

Once you find a particular tree and purchase a subscription, simply click "Transfer"...

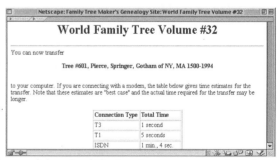

...and download the tree to your own computer!

Family Archives:
Genealogy Data Online & on CD!

What are Family Archives?

▶ Information-rich, indexed records that may be helpful to your family research. The collection includes marriage and census information, actual family trees, and much, much more. You'll find records on 300 million names.

▶ A convenient, time-saving way to research your family. The records are on CD and many are also online, so you can skip that trip to the library!

▶ And, they're guaranteed. You have 90 days to decide if a Family Archive is helpful and convenient. If you aren't satisfied, we'll refund the purchase price, no questions asked.

How are CD-ROM and Internet Family Archives Different?

CD-ROM and Internet Family Archives contain the same data. The difference is that with Internet Family Archives, you access the data online.
This means that right after you make your purchase online, you can start exploring the records — no waiting for the CD-ROM to arrive in the mail!

1900 U.S. Census Microfilm Images now available!

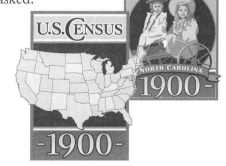

www.FamilyTreeMaker.com/cdhome.html

Genealogy.com